Ange and Ed Forhan, in 1965,
with their middle children: Kevin, Dana, and Chris

MY FATHER BEFORE ME

– *A Memoir* –

CHRIS FORHAN

SCRIBNER

New York   London   Toronto   Sydney   New Delhi

for Milo and Oliver

I cannot read that wretched mind,
so strong & so undone.

—JOHN BERRYMAN, "DREAM SONG 145"

Part I

A Father's Son

1

I'm clinging to my father while he holds me loosely. I'm two, my head against his chest, his right arm around me; his other arm hangs at his side. He has carried me to the edge of an observation deck, to a metal railing only as high as his waist. He leans forward, gazing away from me. I grip his shirt. Thick orange steel girders jut out beneath us, unbudging sunrays. He lifts his free hand and waves at the world before us: a sprawl of tall buildings, exuberantly green and distant hills, the glittering silver blue of Puget Sound. My body slips a little; his hip and the crook of his arm support me, barely. Five hundred feet below, a sleek white train slides by in silence. I understand that my father means to drop me, to let me go, to watch my body tumble from the top of the Space Needle and shrink quickly from his view.

This is my earliest memory—and a false one, of course. Of course. How could it not be? My young, stumbling mind, developing slowly, must have conflated several disconnected events and impressions and arrived at this fiction.

Forty years later, I mention it to my mother.

"Oh, that was true," she says. "I remember. He made me very nervous, holding you close to the edge like that."

*   *   *

1965. In the white Chevy station wagon, the family is driving south to California—days of spontaneous roadside picnics, the tailgate down, a makeshift table for little boxes of Sugar Pops and Frosted Flakes that you can open and pour the milk straight into. "I'm Henry VIII I Am" and "I Got You Babe" are the only songs on the radio. At Lake Tahoe, photos are taken; they will intensify my memory of this trip—or mis-shape it. In one, my little sister Dana and I stand side by side. She smiles beneath a white rubber bathing cap; surrounded by the pointed petal shapes at the cap's border, her face appears to be rising from the center of a flower. I wear blue plaid bathing trunks and a white terry-cloth shirt opened wide, hanging loose on my shoulders. I am five, but I look like a beach-town retiree.

And I can't swim: not in any photograph is the moment when I wade at the lake's lip, waves lapping at my ankles, then at my shins and knees. My balance shifts, I stumble, and I'm under—all around me, bright, churning, sunlit froth. I flail—which way is up?—and try not to swallow, then I'm coughing, lying on the sand.

Who has pulled me up and out of the water? Maybe my father, but all I remember of him on this trip is what remains, fixed and still and silent, in the photos: in black swim trunks, on a picnic bench, he sits alone in the sun, pale and narrow-shouldered but handsome, even strikingly so, his thick black hair brushed high off his forehead, his smile easy and open. Then, one leg crossed before the other, he leans, coolly, against our car, hand on one hip, cigarette dangling from his lip. Then, on a rock amid the shade of tall pines, he sits by himself again, staring off at something the camera can't show.

1968. It's a Saturday. My father needs to visit his downtown office for a few minutes. In a good mood, he agrees to take three of us kids—my older brother, Kevin; Dana; and me—to this other world of his, the world he lives in when he's not with us, a world therefore glamorous and inscrutable.

The building is empty of people, the hallway dim. His office is closed, but he rattles the door open with his key, then clicks on the fluorescent lights. The room is huge, lined with filing cabinets and crowded with heavy desks, on top of which are typewriters and telephones and calculators and piles of paper and pen sets and small, upright framed photos—other people's families. He'll be just a minute. In the meantime, okay, yes, we can play with the Xerox machine, but carefully.

Hesitantly, one of us pushes the start button. The machine jerks awake; on its top, a bar of green light glides beneath glass. With borrowed office pens, we draw pictures of animals, set them upside down on the glass, and photocopy them. We copy a pile of paper clips. We copy the bottom of a saucer—the imprint of its origins—hard to make out in the resulting shadow. Then we copy ourselves, or parts of us: our palms and outstretched fingers, the backs of our hands, our faces, eyes squinched shut against the light.

1971. Our bikes have been stolen—three of them: new ten-speeds, chrome spokes and fenders still shimmering. While we were away from home, some brazen bandits entered our breezeway, a shadowy space hidden from street view, and rode off with them.

Our father, who has been taught that if you want something, you work for it, has a solution: he will not pay for replacement bikes. Instead, he will hire Kevin, Dana, and me to do odd jobs around the house, and we will earn the money ourselves. All summer, I keep a chart recording my labors and the time I have devoted to completing them, handing it to my father in the evening so he can initial each entry and signify his approval. During one two-day stretch, desperate for that bicycle, I weed the sandbox and garden, mow the lawn, sweep the playhouse, clean and arrange the storage shed, burn a heap of branches, and babysit my two little sisters. All of this takes me seven hours and forty minutes. I dutifully—and proudly—record the figure on my chart and bring it to my father. He holds the chart before him, examining it, then says, "Hmmm." He slips a pen from his shirt pocket, draws a neat line through my figure, and jots a revised one beside it. "I'll give you six hours."

My shoulders slump. "But it took me almost two hours more than that," I complain. "It did, really."

"Six hours. A boy can do this work in six hours."

My plan for the summer has been to accumulate one hundred hours of work. As the weeks disappear behind me and the days shorten, my goal begins to seem Sisyphean. How long must I continue to work? When will my reward come?

1973. Our father has been fired from his job, the one that has consumed and frazzled him for fifteen years, the one that, for months, he has been too distracted, too depressed, too sick, too *something* to perform adequately. The company, drained of patience, has let him go. It's a relief. His severance package is generous; he has months, if necessary, to persuade another firm to take him on, and, until then, we will have our dad back, and our mom will have her husband. One of the first things he does with his sudden free time is take a few of us kids to the most popular movie of the year, the one we've been longing to see: *The Poseidon Adventure*. We sit side by side in our plush seats, munching popcorn, slurping 7-Up and Orange Crush, while a massive wave washes over an ocean liner, capsizing it, transforming the ceiling of the ship's vast ballroom into a floor, dozens of New Year's revelers crashing to it, then lying dead or injured. We watch a small crew of plucky survivors decide to try to escape the ship by climbing up to the hull, which is floating atop the water. We munch and slurp as they raise a giant Christmas tree and employ it as a ladder, climbing high above the floor, which is beginning to fill with water. Other survivors beneath them, oblivious to the severity of the crisis, have jeered at the escape plan; they are extras, minor characters paid to die early. Suddenly desperate, a flood rising around them, they leap at the tree, dragging it down, and themselves down, into the deepening water.

2

Six months later: my father is dead. He has ended his own life, doing it while sitting behind the wheel, going nowhere.

Three days before Christmas, in the middle of the night, while his wife and children slept, Edward Forhan drove home from who knows where—we rarely knew where he went—parked his white Dodge Dart in the carport, ran a garden hose from the exhaust pipe to the driver's-side window, slipped inside, breathed, then breathed, then breathed, then stopped breathing. He was forty-four. He left no note.

I was fourteen. What did I know of him? He was a dad. He did what dads do: put on a suit and tie, say goodbye, walk out the front door carrying his briefcase, and drive downtown to the office. "Awr-fuss," he'd say. "Where're you going, Dad?" "Awr-fuss"—maybe mocking the way one of his kids pronounced it, maybe mocking the office itself. At the end of the day, he would come home for dinner. Or maybe he wouldn't, in which case his unused plate, fork to the left of it, knife and spoon to the right, gleamed meaningfully on the table at his place across from our mother's, while we children ate. We waited for the click and creak of the downstairs door opening, hoping not to hear it—hoping not to hear whatever argument or seething silence and slammed doors might follow—before we finished our meal and escaped to the refuge of our separate bedrooms. On weekends he made pancakes for the family—

sometimes, in his better moods, pouring the batter onto the griddle in funny shapes: a rabbit, a dog. At ease, he would grin, eyes twinkling, and deliver a goofy wisecrack or slip into a punny riff, riding an agreeable wave of Irish humor. His laugh was a guffaw, bursting from him, loud, free, a crescendo that ended on a high, held note: *Ah-HAAA!* Every morning he sat on the toilet seat in his underwear and stabbed his thigh with a hypodermic needle filled with insulin. Occasionally, unexpectedly, while planing a piece of wood on the patio or painting a deck railing or, worse, driving, he would begin to speak oddly, as if to himself, then more loudly, rapidly, manically. His movements would become fast and agitated, and when we spoke calmly and with concern to him, he ignored us or reacted with a dismissive laugh. He was the other dad then, having a diabetic reaction; someone would have to inveigle him to down a glass of orange juice or eat a chocolate bar. Downstairs, he kept a workbench with a vise and drill and hammers and tidy rows of jars filled with screws and rivets. He procured some old railroad ties, heavy and splintery, and built a sandbox out of them in the backyard. When we outgrew our swing set, he transformed it into a playhouse, using the metal posts as a triangular frame, laying sheets of wood on them for walls and fashioning a small door out of plywood that he attached with hinges and painted blue. He drove his children to professional baseball games and basketball games and sat quietly in the stands, sipping a beer from a big waxed paper cup and methodically shelling peanuts he lifted one by one from a plastic sack. He smoked Tareytons. He broke briefly into song: "Oh, look-a there, ain't she pretty. She looks like a beautiful wax doll. . . ." Feeling put upon, he muttered, "For cryin' in the beer" or "For the love of Mike." Feeling cheated, he complained, "That's dirty pool." "He's got running off at the mouth," he'd say of some indiscreet gossip. He taught us once, because we asked, about the solar system, all that distant, intricate orbiting. He looked a little like Gregory Peck: the strong brow, the rich dark hair, the lean frame—less the composed and bookish Peck of *To Kill a Mockingbird* than the distracted, disquieted one of *Spellbound*. When he died, he had been married twenty-four years. He had fathered eight children.

And who had fathered him? He didn't speak of his parents, whom we never met. I knew his grandmother—his mother's mother. We called her Grandma; she was the only person from his side of the family whom I knew, and I never wondered much about the others. I was a child; what mattered was the present that I was part of, the world of people that I'd been plopped into. Anything that happened to my parents before I was born might as well have occurred when toga-clad men ambled among marble fountains, nibbling figs. We did hear of a brother my father once had who died young; there was another brother who lived far away, whose wife sometimes sent us Christmas cards. But what had become of my dad's mother and father? Who were these absent grandparents of mine? When I was eight, I carried my Bear Scout handbook to the dining room table and showed it to my mother, opening it to the page that contained the diagram of a family tree, with blank spaces for names. I was working on a genealogy merit badge; I preferred any badge I could earn without doing squat thrusts or hiking through woods with a pocketknife and a length of rope. In the handbook, I had printed my name and those of my parents, but after that I was stuck. My mother told me that my father's parents' names were Nathaniel and Bernadine and that Nathaniel's mother's name was Marie and his father's name—well, she didn't know for sure. Forty years later, as I tried a second time to fill in those blanks, I discovered that my father's grandmother's name was not Marie but Ellen—my mother hadn't even been close—and my great-grandfather's name was Thomas. My father clearly didn't talk much to his wife about his family, and it says something that, in trying to earn that badge, I didn't ask him to talk to me, either.

Around the time I turned the age my father was when he died, I began to wonder more seriously about him—or, more accurately, feelings associated with him began erupting, in dreams, in poems. I wrote a book of poems that centered on my childhood and the loss of my father, but he remained, in that book, the dad whom an eight-year-old or twelve-year-old might know: the briefcase-carrying breadwinner, the mute figure in the easy chair thumbing through the evening paper, a mannequin, a phantom, half absent already, and silent.

But he was here once and was real, my father in the flesh, a man holding his son in his arms. I try to recall him exactly—the timbre of his voice, some precise gesture with his hands as he spoke, the smell of cigarette smoke on his sweater. But he's a scattering of fragments, shreds of memory I have lived with so long that, no matter how I gather and shape them, they constitute less my father than some idea that, long after his death, he has come to represent—about absence, about solitude, about secrecy, about time, about memory itself.

I begin to ask questions—of my mother, of my siblings, of any acquaintances of my father or relatives previously unknown to me whom I might track down. In my fifties, I, too, have become a father, of two small boys. I would not willingly abandon them ever, let alone abandon them without a word, and permanently. How did my father become a man who, halfway through his life, could decide he'd had enough of that life and leave it—and his wife and eight children, the youngest of them only five years old—without explanation?

And who am I, so restless for those answers, so restless to write them down?

3

Suicide is a paradox: self-expression through self-annihilation. It's the last word: perfect, unanswerable. The content of the message is ambiguous, and the ambiguity can never be fully resolved; a suicide leaves behind it a wake of silence. I have wanted to fill that silence. I have filled it with *Daddy, come back*. I have filled it with *What kind of man could do that to his family?* Or *Life is essentially absurd; he who mocks it most relentlessly is most relentlessly alive and honest*. Or *Poor man, sad man, deeply troubled for years—he's to be admired for lasting as long as he did*. I have filled it with *I must try not to live as he did—silently, suffering silently, out of shame or pride or fear or some intractable habit of obscure origin*.

And I have filled it with poetry. Or, no: poetry has risen from that silence and contains it. Of that which is most unsayable and wreathed in uncertainty, I have found, to my relief and comfort, poetry speaks.

In the private act of reading or writing a poem, in the solitary immersion in language, in its exquisite balancing of meanings and its nuanced music, I have felt most deeply myself, most intimately aligned with my sense of the mystery of existing, with my sense of being small and temporary compared to whatever it is that is operating beyond me, maybe through me. A poem can feel like an intermediary, a minister, between me and the bewildering universe. It completes an electrical circuit between the known and the unknown, between my own individual experience and the shadowy operations of the reality of which that experience is a part. That might be why, reading a good poem, I feel a jolt.

Such pleasures, I nonetheless remind myself, occur in solitude, in the safe cave of the mind. I am, finally, my father's son—and my mother's. I crave my privacy, including privacy of thought.

Picturing my mother and father as children, I imagine them, even among their siblings and parents and grandparents, as being essentially alone, within a spotlight and surrounded by shadows. They were products of the Depression and were not long removed from their ragged ancestors who first came to this continent: hungry, hard-drinking Irish immigrants, illiterate but skilled at farm and railroad work; and sturdy, stoic Norwegians and Swedes who helped people the hardscrabble landscape of the upper Midwest. From family habits passed down to them and from their own uncertain circumstances, my father was trained to rely on himself and my mother on herself. If the story of their lives together is a tragedy, maybe it is the tragedy of two people who never learned fully to rely on each other. My father was expert at the wry aside and explanations of the intricate workings of a home's electrical wiring, but he kept the intricate workings of himself to himself—the feelings and thoughts that would have helped his wife and his children know him better, maybe love him better. And he passed that inwardness on to his children.

In the household created by my parents, I learned to speak carefully, with forethought, or not speak at all. I am not gregarious. In a group of people, I sometimes find myself watching myself being among them; I watch myself watching myself. "What are you thinking?" someone asks, and I can't say. How could I begin to? I tend to be reticent, slow to articulate my thoughts to myself, measured and deliberate in my articulation of them to others. As a child, I had a word for what I was: shy. As an adult, I forgive myself sometimes for my reserve, telling myself that I merely desire to express my thoughts as accurately, as precisely, as possible. At other times, I tell myself I am lazy or scared, unwilling to say aloud the wrong thing for fear of making myself vulnerable: to some hazy, undefined reprisal from my listener or, worse, to some discomforting knowledge about myself.

Silence, truly listened to, can begin to whisper and reward us with inklings of understanding. It can remind us of the unfathomable mysteries into which, and out of which, we are born; it can reward us with the consoling news that we are necessarily small and imperfect and therefore deserve to forgive ourselves; it can reward us with poetry. Silence, retreated to long enough, and used by a man as a hiding place, even as he projects to the world one identity after another—soldier, husband, father, career man—can make that man a stranger, to his family and to himself.

– Part II –

Asleep at the Post

4

Girls are lined up on one side of the gym, boys on the other. It's a high school mixer, 1946: the big-band records are playing. Eddie Forhan, sixteen, a junior, is there; he doesn't miss many dances. A few teachers—chaperones—stand discreetly in the corners, responsible looks on their faces. Most of the boys and girls linger shyly on their side of the room. Only a few brave souls have met in the middle. Among them is someone Eddie hasn't noticed before: a slim, pretty girl with wavy dark brown hair who has been twirling dance after dance in and out of the arms of a boy named Brodie. The two of them seem to know each other well, but Eddie is interested and bold. In a pause between songs, he approaches Brodie and asks if he can take his place for a dance, and Brodie replies, "Be my guest."

The girl is a sophomore but only fourteen: round-faced, with a smattering of freckles across her high cheekbones and a cute swoop of a nose. She tells Eddie her name is Ange—it sounds like *Angie* but has no *i* in it. Her last name is Peterson. She will one day become my mother.

But now they're just dancing, first to one song, then another. Brodie, poor, courteous, understanding Brodie, who has recently begun dating Ange, doesn't stand a chance. "Your father asked me to dance," as my mother explains, "and we were together ever after."

On the gym floor, Eddie is smooth, and he knows it—a jocu-
lar talker and slick dancer, though not as slick as he thinks. He and
Ange are doing the slide, and Eddie can't help himself: he's sliding
this way, sliding that way, sliding in exaggerated fashion, goofing off,
showing off. To Ange, he's adorable. And nice. Handsome. Charming
as all get-out—and she's a sucker for charm. As a child of divorced
parents—a mother glum and inward, a father far off, with little affection to spare her—she hasn't had much of that in her life.

They begin acting as smitten teenagers do. At basketball games,
they sit in the bleachers side by side, hand in hand. When other dances
are held, they attend them together. When Eddie learns to drive, he
escorts his sweetheart to a movie or to the Triple XXX drive-in. He
cracks silly jokes—real groaners—and nudges her, telling her she ought
to lighten up, abandon some of that Scandinavian reserve. Sometimes
he visits Ange's house; less often, she visits his, where he lives with his
grandparents. They are not keen on the idea of him being so involved
with a girl, and such a young one. The welcome in that home is chilly.

But what, think Eddie and Ange, can be wrong with their devoting so much time to each other? For their ages, they are quite grown
up, they think. And they understand each other well, they think. Still,
there are parts of Eddie's life—some invisible, tangled shadow he trails
behind him—of which he will not speak. When Ange asks about his
father, Eddie clams up. The man is gone. Why mention him? And his
mother, yes, is dead. Forget it. There's nothing to say, nothing to figure
out about that.

Why talk about the past when one can sing? "To each his own, and
my own is you," Eddie croons. This is their song, he informs her. The
first months of their romance, they can hardly listen to the radio for
an hour without hearing "To Each His Own." "I need you, I know, I
can't let you go." They might be, they probably are, in love, whatever
that might mean. They have a chance to prove that to the camera one

spring day—Roosevelt High's White Clothes Day. From the school, they amble down to a nearby lake, Eddie in a white button-down shirt, white sailor pants, white socks, and white shoes; Ange in a plain white knee-length dress, white ankle socks, and dark penny loafers. For one photo, they stand near the water, on a wooden dock, arms around each other, gazing into each other's eyes; they look gorgeous and jubilant. For another, they sit on a low wall at the edge of the dock; their knees point in opposite directions, but Ange falls backward into Eddie's arms, her arms wrapping fully, decisively, around his neck, and he leans down and kisses her on the mouth. It is their version of the famous Times Square VJ Day sailor's kiss, but they seem to mean it more.

In this brief moment, existing only in each other's arms, they are citizens of a kingdom of innocence and bliss; they wear its white uniform. If only they could stay here, stay in this moment—alive in it, alive to it—in the way the image of their kiss will remain, unchanging, in the photographs. If only they could remain as they are: impossibly young, impossibly happy, possibly wrong for each other, but with no clue of that yet. If only they could cling to each other on this dock forever: marriageless, childless, deathless, eyes half closed, each wave of lake water stilled, the camera in mid-click.

5

They were thinking about the future; they were getting serious. College—that would come next. They would go together. But Eddie's grandparents, who had been raising him for the past five years, didn't see much point in college, and it wasn't likely they would have money to help him, anyway. There was this, though: the war was over at last—not a bad time to join the military. If Eddie could find a way to leave high school early, skip out on his senior year, and enlist, he could take advantage of the original GI Bill, which might expire soon, and get government help with tuition. As many soldiers and sailors were doing, he could try to earn his high school diploma by passing the GED tests.

He picked the marines—maybe they were the only branch that would take a recruit so young. One of Eddie's first orders: return to the orthodontist. "If you're old enough for the marines, son," he was told, "you're old enough to get those braces off." His grandparents, my mother imagines, must have been livid; living on little, they had nonetheless scraped together enough to fix their grandson's teeth. The braces came off. Until his death, my father's teeth stayed crooked. Semper fidelis.

He might have had a steady girlfriend, his best pals might have been tossing spit wads at each other in chemistry and trigonometry, and he might have just celebrated only his seventeenth birthday, but

Eddie was suddenly in San Diego, at boot camp, all 140 scrawny pounds of him, crawling across the dirt on his belly, rushing up steep hills, breathless, suffering rope burns on his palms and thighs, being deprived of food and sleep, being jawed at by a pit bull of a drill instructor until he was mentally broken, until he thought of himself as nothing, until he did not think of himself at all.

In a boot camp photograph, wearing his khaki service uniform, utility belt, and garrison cap, holding his upright rifle at his side, Eddie is gaunt; the brilliant southern California sun bleaches his pale Irish skin. He looks done in, ready to come home.

He did come home, in time for Christmas, but within weeks he was off again, this time for his twenty-month assignment to a military base where, six years before, he would have had a target on his back. Now the most meaningful thing on his back would be tanning oil. He was going to Pearl Harbor.

For the two-thousand-mile journey from Seattle to Hawaii, he boarded the USS *General William Mitchell*, a troop transport that, during the war, had carried soldiers to England, North Africa, and the Pacific; on return trips, it had brought home veterans of battle: the weary, the wounded, the dead. The hulking ship must have felt thick with ghosts. It was enormous: two football fields long, its sides lined with gun mounts, two mammoth smokestacks looming above. I can picture, some late evening, Eddie on the ship's deck, leaning on the rail, peering at the ragged spumes of the Pacific, wind whisking through his crew cut and billowing through his jacket sleeves. A century earlier, his father's father's father had sailed west across another ocean, improvising a future he would have to struggle into, as into an ill-fitting suit. That ancestor was young—about the age Eddie was now—Catholic, and barely educated; he brought little with him, I imagine, but his youth, muscle, faith, and desperation. And how much more than that did Eddie possess? He had a rank: private. A modest monthly salary that was sent to his grandparents. A girlfriend who, though only fifteen, was intent on waiting for him until his return. And, like that Forhan of a hundred years before, a vaguely formulated notion of what the future had in store for him. He was a skinny American kid, absurdly small on that colossal ship, on that broad ocean, beneath that star-strewn sky, in that trim uniform that signified his sworn allegiance to a set of immutable values: the necessity of acting with honor and courage, of doing his duty, and, no matter the duress he was under, of always making the right decision.

Upon his arrival in Honolulu, Eddie went with a couple of buddies to a portrait studio and posed in front of a painted backdrop that made them appear to be, in fact, in Honolulu: wind-tossed palm trees, an ocean beach receding into a mountainous background. The three of them stood before this simulated scene in their pressed khaki service uniforms, caps at a requisite jaunty angle. Eddie threw his arm over the shoulder of his pal in the middle, and the third marine, from the other side, did the same. Each of them, wearing a look of exaggerated self-assurance, held a full bottle of whiskey, supporting the bottom of the bottle with his hand as if advertising it, as if making certain it was understood that the seemingly fresh-faced teenager holding the bottle was no boy but a man, a real man, a marine, no less, and by God, this marine drank—oh, how he drank.

The result is that it looks as though none of them has tasted a drop of liquor in his life.

Ange wasn't impressed with the picture, which she found slipped into one of the regular letters Eddie mailed to her. She liked better the other one he sent: the formal photograph taken a year into his stint at Pearl Harbor, the one in which he flashes a wide, genuine grin, the one in which his hair is exquisitely combed and long enough on top to be swept up neatly over his forehead, Errol Flynn–style—the one he signed, *With All My Love, Eddie*.

A third photo from his time in Hawaii shows a different Eddie. This is a military document, a mug shot, meant simply to depict a soldier; there is nothing theatrical about it. By this time, my father has been at Pearl Harbor for a year and a half; he is only three months away from the end of his assignment. He stares straight ahead, expressionless. His eyes are slightly narrowed, as if he's sleepy. His stiff uniform collar looks on the verge of choking him.

Two months later, Monday, August 9, 1948: the day dawns bright and balmy on Oahu. The sky is cloudless. A light breeze rustles the palms. Three years before to the day, the second atomic bomb was dropped on Nagasaki. Less than seven years before, soldiers and sailors at Pearl Harbor looked quizzically toward the sky, hearing the drone of Japanese fighter planes approaching. This morning, on the same base, Marine Private 1st Class Edward Forhan is on guard duty. And he is fast asleep.

It is ten A.M. when he is caught. How long has he been snoozing? And why? What could have caused him to slip into sleep so early in the day, especially when his duty is to be alert, eyes fixed on the area assigned to him, hand ready to reach for his pen and inscribe in his log any suspicious activity or to salute smartly any passing officer? Has he been out on the town, carousing late with his buddies?

Whatever the reason, the infraction is serious. It could mean a court-martial, even a dishonorable discharge. Eddie has no explanation. "I just fell asleep," he writes to Ange. "Big trouble."

Luckily, the trouble is smaller than he feared. He pleads guilty and is sentenced to a hefty fine: thirty dollars a month for the next three months—more than half his pay. In September, he leaves active duty with an honorable discharge and returns to the U.S., where he enrolls in the marine reserve—and where Ange awaits. During his two years away at boot camp and Pearl Harbor, she hasn't been merely lying on her bed mooning over his weekly letters. She is a teenage girl—she recently celebrated her seventeenth birthday—and she hasn't considered the fact of her boyfriend being out of town a reason to miss two years of dances and parties. Ange has been dating a very nice fellow named, go figure, Eddie, who, as is often the case in these situations, has fallen hard for her, while she, on the other hand, finds him to be a very nice fellow. The day my father is scheduled to arrive home, the other Eddie, the stopgap one, has arranged a date with her. As my mother explains it, "I had to tell Eddie, 'Well, the real guy showed up. I can't go out with you tonight. Sorry.' It must have been hard for him, but he was a peach."

My father's unexpected and expensive morning nap is soon forgotten. It was an accident, after all. It might have happened to anyone.

6

Ange had swiftly completed her required high school courses and, when she reunited with Eddie, was already taking classes at the University of Washington. She and my father picked up where they had left off, seeing each other regularly throughout the autumn and winter. In February, they attended a university dance; afterward, Eddie, nineteen, and two years a marine, was ready to do something other than stop by Triple XXX or drive his virgin girlfriend back to her home and give her a good-night peck at the door.

"I remember the night," my mother says over sixty years later. "I didn't want to do it. I just didn't think it was right." She looks at me directly, with the hint of a shrug. "But he was young and randy.

"I remember the dress I was wearing."

In her eighties, my mother is a proud and dignified woman; people speak admiringly of her regal bearing. In response to my desire to learn more about my father, she has been kind and candid. After she tells me about the first time she had sex, I report the conversation to my wife, a poet, a woman of great psychological insight and sensitivity. She says, "Did you ask about the dress?"

No, I did not ask. Sitting beside my mother, listening to her speak thoughtfully, deliberately, of a night whose details remain vivid to her, I felt myself deciding I would not ask about the dress. And I would not ask about the location—the back of a car parked discreetly at the lakeside? A friend's vacant basement? I am, finally, my parents' child. Out of politeness, or fear, or a sense of how easily interest becomes intrusiveness and a thirst for the truth becomes a hunger for the sensational, I will not ask everything.

By the end of March, as my mother was preparing for the third quarter of her freshman year, she could not ignore the obvious: she was pregnant. "I know that every pregnant woman says this," she tells me, "but we did it only once!"

Abruptly, her fate was altered. She would not spend the next years strolling the university quad, books cradled in her arm. Her fate was now the common one for girls of her generation: to be a mother—which, in 1949, meant to be a wife, even if she was not fully conscious of who she was, of who she might become, or of how she might find a way to exist in this world as that person.

She dropped out of school. She would have this baby. She did not doubt that. She would not be the type to leave town unnoticed and then return months later, alone, sad, and silently knowing.

Ed—old enough not to be referred to by the boyish name Eddie anymore—and Ange could see their future distinctly. They would be husband and wife. Ed would finish college and start a career. Ange would tend to their home and to the baby—or babies. First, though, they had to break the news to their families.

"We want to get married," they told Ange's mother, Esther, and her stepfather, Lee.

"But why?" asked Esther.

"Well, because—" Ange answered.

"Oh my God!" her mother said.

Lee leaped up, grinning, pumped Ed's hand, and said, "Congratulations!"

Then they went to Ed's house to sit down with his grandparents and repeat the conversation.

His grandfather, nearly seventy, bald, compact, and craggy, leaned back and said, "Uh-huh. And what are you going to live on—love?"

Like generations of Forhans before him, Ed was Catholic; he would be married in the church. Ange, however, was not Catholic; if a priest were to perform the ceremony, she would need first to receive instruction about the faith and about what it meant to be married to a Catholic. This would have to happen quickly—all of the wedding arrangements would need to be made in a flurry, before Ange began to show. A date for the ceremony, only a couple of weeks away, was chosen. In advance of the big day, Ange met with a priest. In an office in the church's priory, she listened carefully as she was told of the tenets of the faith, its sacraments and rituals, and its implications for the life of a husband and wife. Marriage, she was instructed, was a life-long union of a man and a woman who vowed before God to remain absolutely faithful to each other; as for sex, its sole purpose was the begetting of children, and those children were to be educated in the faith of their parents. I imagine my mother, that surprise of a new life stirring within her, nodding as she listened, glancing occasionally over the priest's shoulder at the crucifix on the wall. I imagine her telling herself that she had no choice but to be ready.

They would be married on a Friday night—an odd time for the pastor to choose, as the church didn't typically hold weddings at night—but my parents didn't question it. They invited more than a hundred people. Though few of the guests would have been unaware of the reason for the abrupt wedding, my parents wanted to celebrate their marriage openly, in front of family and friends. They were not ashamed. Not much.

When they arrived in the afternoon for the rehearsal, they found the church dim and empty. They were summoned to the priory, the small redbrick building in the church's shadow. It was there, they were told, that the ceremony would take place: it would be unlawful to cel-ebrate the wedding in the church, since the bride was not a Catholic.

Ange was crestfallen. Furious. But what could she do? And what could her mother do? Nothing—except allow her indignation to turn her against the Catholic Church forever. Ed's grandparents said nothing, and Ed said nothing, although it must have begun to dawn on everyone that the pastor, in planning a night wedding in a small building without altar or spire, was intent on marrying these two children only technically: surreptitiously, without immodest pomp.

The sky darkened, a light rain fell, and the arriving guests were directed away from the huge church entry doors and toward the narrow walkway to the priory. A couple dozen people were allowed inside the building, but no more than that would fit. The rest of the guests, with little to look at but one another's bewildered faces, gathered in the drizzle on the walkway and on the priory's concrete steps. Those nearest the door might have strained to catch a few words of what was happening inside.

And then it was over. The teenage newlyweds emerged. The guests stepped aside to let them pass.

7

The honeymoon, at least, would go well. True, the vacation would be short—just the weekend—because Ed had to be back to work on Monday; he was planning to enroll in the university in the fall, but, in the meantime, like many other Seattleites, he had signed on at Boeing, the airplane manufacturer that was the city's biggest employer. Still, for the next two days, Ed and Ange would be on their own, accountable only to themselves, free to breathe easily, to follow their whims, and to begin to grow accustomed to each other as what they now were: Mr. and Mrs. Forhan.

They would spend the weekend in Victoria, British Columbia, a harbor town named after the great queen, a place of genteel manners, handsome Victorian- and Edwardian-era architecture, and luxuriant, well-tended flower gardens. Victoria would supply the splendor and pageantry that had been missing from the wedding.

Around midnight, after the reception, the newlyweds boarded the grand steamship *Princess Kathleen,* which would travel unhurriedly through the night to the southern tip of Vancouver Island. In the morning, they would awake, disembark, and check in to their hotel; they would devote the long day to seeing the sights—and each other.

They would stay in the opulent Empress Hotel, an imposing château-style building surrounded by gardens and courtyards, abun-

dant ivy climbing its outside walls. The hotel had played host to Rud-
yard Kipling and kings and queens. Edward, prince of Wales, had
waltzed in its ballroom till dawn. Now Ed and Ange could waltz in
that room. In the afternoon, they would dress in their best duds and
partake in the hotel's famously posh English tea service. The tea was
dauntingly pricey, but this was special, said Ed: this was their honeymoon. As soon as they arrived at the Empress, he made sure to secure
two tickets for tea, as well as for an evening dinner dance. Beyond
those events, there would be gardens to meander through and carriage
rides to take. The day was set—and afterward, after dining, after dancing, they would wander, blissfully weary, down wide carpeted halls,
beneath extravagant chandeliers, back to their room. They would do
what honeymooners do in private.

First, though, Ed said, he felt a little tired. He wouldn't mind rest-
ing for a bit before they started their day. He lay down, pulled the
covers up, and fell swiftly asleep.

An hour passed. Then another. He showed no sign of rising. Ange
nudged him. No response.

Later, she nudged him again. Teatime was approaching. "Yes, okay,"
Ed mumbled. "Just a little longer. I'll be up."

But he wasn't. He slept through the tea, and Ange decided not to
go to it alone—she dropped the tickets into the trash.

Through the afternoon, through the evening, as the dinner dance
came and went, he dozed. PFC Forhan had fallen asleep at his post.

Ange was baffled, exasperated. How could this make sense? Was
he weary from work, from the frenzied preparations for the wedding?
Maybe. But a person doesn't sleep through his honeymoon.

Ange was starving. She sat on the bed. She told Ed it was time;
he needed to wake up, really. They both should eat something. He lay
still, eyes closed, breathing deeply. Ange rose, found his wallet, slipped
a few bills out of it, and left the room to buy herself a hamburger.

When she returned, Ed was sleeping.

Finally, Ange, too, lay down in the dark and closed her eyes. In the morning, she woke, but he did not. She waited. She dressed. She left the room and wandered around, then returned. Just in time for them to leave and catch the afternoon boat back to Seattle, Ed woke. He rose slowly. "I'm sorry," he said. "I'm sorry. I didn't mean to sleep so long."

They hardly said a word about it; they certainly did not argue. Ange was despondent, but she would not confront her husband. She was dumbfounded and too unknowing about people, especially this person she had married. Decades later, she wondered whether Ed wasn't depressed, but, at seventeen, she didn't think about such things. Nor did she yet understand how sleep can be a means of avoidance. If you're still in bed, there's no telling what you might not have to do.

On Sunday afternoon, they steamed south to Seattle on the long, luxurious *Princess Kathleen,* the gleaming ship that, three years later, in the fog of night, would run aground in Alaska, jarring its passengers awake, and then, as the tide rose—everyone having scurried off safely—slide gradually, serenely, permanently into the deep.

8

On their return from Victoria, the newlyweds settled into their first home: the top floor of a house lived in by a woman whose husband had died; she had space and could use the rent money. She cleared a shelf in her refrigerator for them. Eddie and Ange examined the gifts they'd received: a set of silver, a singing teakettle, an electric kitchen clock, a lace tablecloth, a set of Revere ware, a crystal relish dish, a Toastmaster toaster, a gravy ladle, a *Better Homes & Gardens* cookbook. They were set.

On the Monday after the honeymoon, Ange surprised herself by cooking, on a two-burner hot plate, a complete meal—pork chops and gravy, mashed potatoes, peas, and applesauce—and doing a serviceable job of it. She'd had no idea she could pass herself off so quickly and easily as a homemaker, but, in the widow's home, as if fated to it, she did.

Pork chops. Pot roast. Chicken potpie. Ange and Ed were young, deeply intelligent, and willing to work hard; in a later era, they might have been anything—or tried to be. But it was 1949, boom time in America, boom time for the family, boom time for young husbands in flannel suits snapping shut the golden clasps of their briefcases, boom time for young wives in the bathroom, scouring clean that bowl, that sink, that floor, boom time in the kitchen. Spaghetti and meatballs. Swedish meatballs. Meat loaf with bread crumbs. A gravy ladle, a relish dish. Ed and Ange had both come from brokenness and patched-together families. Now they would be making a family together, although only two months before they had not planned to do so, at least not so quickly, not now. They each must have needed mending, in essential ways. They must have had secrets, even to themselves. But did they sense that this was so? People did not talk about the self much then. Melon balls. Deviled eggs. Tuna noodle casserole. My parents believed in what they had been taught by example: reticence, discipline, duty, pleasantness, courtesy, self-denial, and elbow grease, elbow grease. The newest cleanser for unsightly stains. And disinfectant. Tide, so he can wear the cleanest shirts in town. Lux soap to prevent runs in stockings because "husbands admire wives who keep their stockings perfect." For the kids, to improve their marks in school, a Motorola television.

They were a team now, Ed and Ange, a team of two, relying solely on themselves to make a life of purposefulness and joy. But how much did they know about what might give them joy and whether such joy was possible in the world in which they lived, a world that offered a few narrowly defined, cramped structures to inhabit: marriage, family, church? Or maybe joy wasn't the objective; maybe success was—or mere contentedness—which, for Ed, would mean a professional career with potential for advancement and, for Ange, an orderly household, a cozy home.

Turning that smile upside down, that's what it would take, and, if the advertisements were right, a Hoover vacuum and a Kelvinator refrigerator and heels and earrings and a pinched-waist dress and a dainty apron to waltz through rooms in and giddiness about that spick-and-span frying pan. Mop, wax, and buff. Mop, wax, and buff. And to make yourself pretty for him and keep that zip in your step, a trip to the beauty parlor to sit with your head in a metal cone. And he? He needs a close shave and cuff links and a stiff-bristled brush to maintain that mirror shine in his shoes and someone to happily hand him a highball when he comes home. He needs to loosen his tie, ease his slippers on, light a pipe, bury his nose in the newspaper. Daddy's home—*shhh*. Weekends he keeps the lawn trim and the whitewalls white. He writes checks for the mortgage and utilities and writes one to his wife—her allowance to run the household: to pay for the groceries, the children's clothes and shoes, the schoolbooks and fees, the birthday parties, the Christmas presents. What might she want for Christmas? Wow her with Pyrex ovenware or a Rid-Jid ironing table—she'll want to marry you all over again. In the meantime, Pep vitamins to keep her going, because "the harder a wife works, the cuter she looks."

His nose in the newspaper. Her head in a metal cone.

9

How hard it is even to know what is true, let alone to speak of it. And who says you should speak of it? What good would it do?

My father did not talk with his young wife about his past, about his parents. When she asked, he went silent—or responded brusquely, with tepid, near-meaningless words. Maybe he was too profoundly sad about his early years to be able to speak of them. Maybe he couldn't admit to himself how sad he was.

The young couple must have recognized themselves in each other. Even in their first days together, they might have sensed that they shared something deep and broken, something each desired to repair. Or to forget. In some ways, they had been living the same life already. Like her husband, with generations of Irish laborers behind him, Ange came from a family steeped in the ways of hardworking immigrants—in her case, Norwegians and Swedes. They were stolid and taciturn; when compelled to speak, they were often, like Ed, self-disparagingly wry. Like Ed, Ange had been raised among people who kept to themselves, who kept their secrets. And, like him, she didn't have much of a father.

Her mother, Esther, was raised by Norwegian immigrants in the rugged wintry flatlands of northwest Minnesota, in Lake Bronson, a village of only a hundred people. A photo taken when Esther was seventeen shows her wearing a mop of thick black hair that threatens to cover her eyes completely. She has unsubtle features: a strong nose, big dark eyes, high cheekbones, and a large jaw with a wide mouth. She is pretty but awkward, stoop-shouldered, as if dropped onto the earth and still in a daze about it. This is the year she fell for the handsome Ed Peterson. In rural Minnesota, where there couldn't have been many possibilities for romance, Esther might very well have taken him for dashing. Ed, four years older than she, son of Swedish immigrants, had the looks of a silent-movie star: he was square-jawed, like a young Gerald Ford, with a broad, big-dimpled grin and wavy blond hair parted down the middle.

Don't marry him, Ed's older brother warned Esther. He can't be trusted. Stay away, her friends said. He's a lady-killer.

She thanked them for the advice, then married him.

We live two lives; we have two selves—at least. There is the self within us that is always mute but never deserts us: the self we think we are, the one we yearn for others to understand, the one we struggle to protect. The other is the self defined by and exhibited in the roles we take on in the world: son, daughter, parent, student, pilot, accountant, actress, wife. The two selves, happily, occasionally overlap and sustain each other. Often they do not, and that is the world's fault, a dark joke at the root of human existence about which we can do nothing. Or the fault is ours: we make a choice out of fear or unwarranted hope or blind faith in the rightness of the customs of our tribe. We turn away then from the self within, which turns away, too, cringing.

Like my own mother after she met an Ed of her own, Esther had suddenly become a housewife. Her husband got work as a customs agent. That's why my mother was born, in 1931, not far from the Canadian border, in Noonan, North Dakota, a town of about four hundred whose primary claim to fame was its aversion to color: an ordinance required that all buildings be painted white.

If life in Noonan was monotonous, at least Esther had the movies. She was nuts for Janet Gaynor. While pregnant, Esther sat enthralled in the dark, watching Gaynor play a wronged woman who descends into addiction and degradation in a Shanghai opium den. If Esther's baby turned out to be a girl, she knew what she would call her: Angie, after this dissipated junkie.

The world my mother entered would offer little in the way of comfort or merriment. The Depression was on; she would spend her first five years in a series of tiny towns with few pleasant diversions; and her mother's mood was often grim and sad. Nonetheless, she was sprinkled at the start with fairy dust: with a name, accidentally mis-spelled though it might have been, pilfered from the silver screen—a reminder to Esther of a world of glamour and enchantment that she might yearn for but could never enter, not least because it wasn't real.

Esther couldn't help herself: she wrote a fan letter to her favorite actress, informing her of the tribute. My mother still has the photo Gaynor mailed in return inscribed to "Baby Ange."

Within two years, Esther gave birth to twin girls, Janet (naturally) and Janice. Eventually, the family moved back to Lake Bronson. In photos from her infancy and childhood, my mother poses alone or with others in a landscape invariably bleak and forbidding. The twins appear like cute ghosts—blond, unsmiling, in identical outfits: cotton dresses that fall to mid-thigh; overalls over striped short-sleeved shirts.

Then their father got lucky: a better customs job opened up in the port of Seattle, at the airport. If he was willing to move fifteen hundred miles west, the position was his. Esther wasn't keen on the idea. She had never traveled so far from home, and her mother was ill; she couldn't imagine packing up their three little girls and moving to a new, strange city without even a place to live. She would prefer to stay, for a time, in Lake Bronson with the girls and tend to her mother. They would join Ed in Seattle later.

After a few months, Esther and the girls boarded a train west. When they pulled in to the Seattle station, Ed was there, standing on the platform, ready to greet them as they descended from the car.

Standing a little farther off, at a discreet distance, was his new girl-friend.

Betty was only twenty, nine years younger than Ed. "I'd like you to meet my friend," he said to his wife and daughters. The next part of the story, my mother believes, may be apocryphal, but it's part of the tale as Esther remembered it: standing at the station, only moments after greeting her, he handed her divorce papers. "How could you do this?" she demanded. "What am I going to do?"

What, indeed, could Esther do—a woman with a high school diploma but no particular marketable skills? It was 1936. Seventeen percent of Americans were out of work. Even finding a home could be difficult, since divorce was frowned upon, and some landlords weren't interested in renting to a single mother.

She and her daughters spent the rest of the decade, nearly penniless, moving from home to home, in Seattle, Lake Bronson, Minneapolis, and Chicago, usually rooming with relatives or friends. Sometimes quarters were so cramped that the whole family shared one double bed, the three girls sleeping side by side, their mother wedged in horizontally at their feet.

At least Ed was sending her fifty dollars a month. The gallant Ed. It was his money, mainly, that the family lived on. Intent on divorcing Esther, he chose the grounds of cruelty. Later, Esther told her children that the grounds were desertion: Ed had gone west without her and their daughters and, when they followed him there, turned his back on them. His grounds, her grounds, and the truth somewhere in between, or nowhere to be found.

Ed married Betty, the young woman who had accompanied him to the train station. Two years later, Esther had a mystifying surprise for her daughters: she decided it would be best for the three of them to live for an entire school year with their father and his new wife. Ange was almost ten and her twin sisters eight when, at the end of August 1941, Esther packed a few suitcases, telling her girls that there was just no place for all four of them to live together. With war having broken out in Europe, shipyards and airplane factories in Seattle were in a frenzy of activity, and workers were streaming into the city. Every room in town, it seems—every bed—was filled. Esther would come for her girls when she found a place where they could all be together. I know, I know, she said, I'll miss you, too, horribly. But there's no choice, as you can see. No choice. Really.

10

September passed, then October, then Thanksgiving. Esther stayed away. Even on Ange's birthday, even at Christmas, she did not appear. Betty was kind to the girls, but their father was distant and dictatorial, ordering Ange to shine his shoes and roll his cigarettes.

From her weekly allowance of ten cents, Ange would use a nickel to call her mother. "Mom, why can't we see you?" she'd say. "We miss you. Let us visit." The situation didn't make sense; they lived in the same city, after all. She understood that Esther was busy, working long hours at the dime store and spending any extra time searching for an apartment big enough for the four of them. Still, couldn't she visit with her daughters for an hour or two?

"I know, sweetheart. I miss you, too," Esther would say. "But it's impossible—I've explained that. Keep being a good girl, now."

Finally, a reunion was arranged for Mother's Day. The girls saw their mother for the first time in nine months at the home of Esther's brother and his wife, across Lake Washington from Seattle. Ange, Janet, and Janice were thrilled to see their mom again and thrilled as well to be free of their steely, autocratic father. The reunion was permanent. Esther had found, at last, a place for them to live together, although the new quarters would be like most places they had stayed in: tiny and temporary. They would move to Bremerton, across the waters of Puget Sound, and stay in the small apartment of Esther's oldest sister and her husband.

This story has a long-delayed coda. Six decades after that reunion of the Peterson girls with their mother, Esther had been in a long second marriage—over fifty years—and given birth to two more children, another daughter and a son. Now she lay dying in a Seattle hospital bed, and she was in distress, in despair. She would not, she lamented, be able to see her twin boys. "Twin girls," someone corrected her. She'd had twin daughters. Weeks earlier, probably sensing that she would not be alive much longer, Esther had stammered to my mother, "I have a terrible secret, and I'm taking it to my grave."

And so she did.

Not long after Esther's death, her son received a phone call from a man he had never heard of: his older brother. That brother revealed to him that he had yet another brother: his twin. In 1941, when Esther had dropped her little daughters off at their father's home to live, she was three months pregnant. During all of those months when her children begged to see her, she couldn't bear the thought of exactly that: their seeing her, seeing her swelling belly. She hid it from Ed and Betty, too. The man who had impregnated her was someone Esther had known in high school in Minnesota. Tommy. My mother remembers him. Yes, Tommy came to visit once. During her pregnancy, Esther lived in a small apartment with a girlfriend and often visited one of her brothers and his wife. These three people, apparently, were the only ones in whom she confided her condition. Maybe she didn't even tell Tommy. In March, two months before she reunited with her daughters, she did what Ange, years later, surprised by her own pregnancy, would not do: she took an eastbound bus over the Cascade Mountains to Yakima, gave birth, offered the baby boys up for adoption, took a bus back, then kept her mouth shut about it. She was thirty years old.

Until her death at eighty-eight, she kept her silence—she did, indeed, take a terrible secret into the earth with her. But what secret, exactly, is the one that haunted her? What made her feel the deepest shame and remorse? The secret that she had gotten pregnant out of wedlock? The secret that she had given up her babies? Or the secret that for months, then years, then decades—her whole life—she had lived alone with those original secrets? She had told no one, not even her second husband. A few years before she died, Esther received a phone call from an agency that reunited adopted children with their birth parents. Her twin boys were searching for her. They didn't know her identity, and the agency wouldn't tell them her name if Esther preferred that it not. Would she be interested in meeting her two middle-aged sons? No, she said. No. Never. Her husband didn't know about them. No one knew about them. "Please," she pleaded, "don't call me again."

11

Only weeks after reuniting with her daughters, Esther found a job with Boeing, which had become central to the war effort, already rolling out sixty B-17 Flying Fortresses a month. Almost immediately, among the tens of thousands of workers in the massive plant, a lean, genial bachelor a year younger than she, a machinist named Lee, caught her eye, or she—with her big eyes, high cheekbones, and dark wavy hair—caught his. She brought Lee to Bremerton to see what her daughters thought of him.

They loved him. Unlike most of the adults they had known, Lee had a relaxed way about him; he laughed easily and was open and unstinting in his affections. Lee was not sour on life or distrustful of it; he was an enthusiast of it, especially of the simple things that gave him pleasure: an easy-handling car, polished to a gleam; a smooth Scotch; a brisk autumn afternoon in the bleachers at a college football game; and jazz. He would spend his pocket money on evening trips downtown to the opulent Trianon Ballroom, with its vast polished floor that could hold five thousand dancers, swinging to a big band. He would stand toward the side and tap his wing tips, take a spin or three, or edge as close as he could to the bandstand, where, between numbers, he might shout out some words of admiration to the clarinetist. Lee loved the music that had first made his teenage heart leap: snappy syncopated beats, a band in the groove, and virtuoso solos that rose organically out of that sound, set your mind swirling, then settled back naturally into the arrangement. He was devoted to Louis Armstrong, Bix Beiderbecke, Jack Teagarden, and Pee Wee Russell. Decades later, not long before he died, he bequeathed to me one of his treasured possessions: a well-thumbed, massive encyclopedia of big bands, page after page marked with his hand-scribbled annotations. With little arrows, he had drawn attention to blurred figures in back rows of posed portraits of bands, important players he remembered—Bennie Bonacio, Doc Ryker, Miff Mole.

One day not long after meeting Lee, Ange took a walk with a friend of hers and burst out, "I hope they get married! I hope they get married!" Marriage would mean that, overnight, everything might be fixed: Esther, no longer struggling by herself to raise three young girls, would be happier; her daughters would have a new father, a loving and kind one this time; and they all might finally have a house of their own.

Esther and Lee did get married, and quickly: within two months of meeting each other. Esther was by natural inclination intractable, undemonstrative, and befuddled by the unfamiliar; Lee's unforced good cheer was a tonic for her—although eventually it began to grate, if it didn't from the start. In retrospect, my mother understands that the marriage was mainly one of convenience. What better choice did Esther have? Marriage would mean stability and security. She could stop working and devote herself to raising her children. She could stop moving from place to place, relying on the generosity of friends and family members for a bed to sleep in.

And, for Lee, what did this marriage mean? Joy, maybe.

In a wedding photo, he turns sideways to the camera and gazes at his new bride, embracing her waist with one arm and her shoulders with the other. He wears a barely suppressed, big-chinned grin.

Esther's smile is directed not at Lee but at the camera. She does not hug him back; her hands, lowered before her, are gripping her white dress gloves and small black purse.

Ange was right about the house. The wedding was in August, and only weeks later Lee moved his new family into a recently built two-bedroom home, with polished wood floors, a fireplace, a driveway, and a trim front lawn, in northeast Seattle—in Wedgwood, a neighborhood that three years before had consisted only of trees and that had been christened (why not?) after the British makers of elegant bone china. For Ange, for a moment, anything might have seemed possible. You just had to name it.

12

True love. Romance. A happy future with a loving, devoted husband and child—or a passel of children, who knows? At seventeen, Ange dared to believe these things would happen with her new husband, who, though he shared the name of her untrustworthy father, was not like him—this Ed was attentive and responsible. And funny: with his wry Irish wit, he could ease a tense moment, alluding to and defusing what was difficult and painful by making light of it.

He had been born in late summer 1929: just in time, he was fond of cracking later, for the Great Depression. Accompanying the small news of his birth, the big national news was that at midnight on the night before he entered this world, seventy-three people had died off the California coast when the steamer *San Juan* collided with an oil tanker. The *San Juan* had left San Francisco and, for five hours, groped her way southward through thick fog; the captain, who went down with his ship, seems to have steered his craft into the tanker's path willfully and blindly.

That might have been how my father's parents fell in love—or fell in—with each other. Their union did not last long. I know Bernadine Carey, his mother, only from childhood pictures that, until decades after my father's death, I did not know existed. In the photos, she is round-faced and black-haired, with an upturned nose, an unassuming, boxy Prince Valiant haircut, and the fidgety, intrepid look of a tomboy. Bernadine was Irish through and through, her family tree blossoming with Dwyers, McLaughlins, and Murphys, mainly poor Catholic farmers.

Her family moved from rural Missouri to Seattle when she was a toddler. When she was seventeen, Bernadine married Nat Forhan, who was three years older and, like her, pure Irish. Nat gave my father little more than a name. He is the trickster in this tale, the mysterious father of my own mysterious father, the cryptic, slippery figure who turned his back on his wife, who abandoned his three sons when two of them could barely walk and the third was in the womb. He would change his name and move out of state, return suddenly, briefly, decades later, then leave again and vanish so thoroughly that even his sisters and brothers wondered what had become of him. When at last he died, Nat had lived so long under an assumed name, and he had been so long a stranger to his family, that he might as well not have been himself at all. He is the mythic father—or, for me, grandfather: the object of the unending quest. And he was a cad and a bum.

He grew up on the lakeside in the shadow of the gasworks, near the giant pump house and boiler house and coal storage bunker and the trestles that coal cars rumbled up to deliver their load. His father, as foreman of the plant, was given a modest house on the site, so Nat and his siblings grew up amid a continual stink. The air was smoke-filled, the outside walls and windows of every house in the neighborhood grimed with soot. It wasn't just the gasworks that were to blame; it was the nearby tar plant and asphalt company and garbage incinerator and Pacific Ammonia Chemical Company.

By the time he married Bernadine, Nat—known now sometimes as Fred, from his middle name—had a job at the gas plant. He was young and suddenly married, suddenly a father, suddenly a husband not just to a fun, cute girl but to a chronically sick one: Bernadine had contracted diabetes and would suffer from it, just as my father would after her. Nat was blue-collar, black Irish, probably not ready for what marriage would mean, probably overly fond of the bottle. Maybe liquor was involved when he lost control of the wheel and smashed into another car, injuring its passengers. That was in April 1929; Bernadine was four months pregnant with her second child, my father.

A year after my father was born, Bernadine became pregnant again, but her husband soon was gone, back to living with his parents near the gasworks. I can imagine his mother, Ellen, scolding him mildly, then smiling and hugging him tightly. She was a woman simultaneously exacting and generous and extravagantly protective. She refused to spank her children. She raised them to pray: each evening, as she sat in her rocking chair, the smallest of her boys and girls knelt before her and declaimed, "God bless Mama and Papa, God bless my brothers and sisters, and God bless me and make me a good child." When they were tucked in their beds, she sprinkled each of them with holy water. They would be model Christians, all of them, she hoped—humble and charitable. She and her husband were firm, assured, and forgiving—the kind of parents, perhaps, who could raise a half-dozen reckless, irresponsible sons, send them into the world, and then, when things went badly, smile wearily and take them back in.

Bernadine's parents took her in, too, along with her two little sons, and, in the summer of 1931, she gave birth to her third, John Francis Forhan. Even after Nat's departure, she remained true to their habit of naming their children after Nat's own brothers. Their boys, as were Nat's older siblings, were named James, Edward, and John. The baby, however, was soon given the nickname Skippy, as my father was given the nickname Buddy—or Bud. Decades later, in the 1960s, I often heard my great-grandmother refer to him by this name.

Skippy and Buddy: the names of lovable scamps, little rascals. The only Forhan child who didn't earn an adorably boyish nickname was the oldest, Jim. Through the years, the Careys made Jim pay for his face, for his rakish and slightly cartoonish look, as if gravity were pulling all of his features downward. "He looks just like his father" was an insult, and not a veiled one. Eddie was lucky: he inherited his mother's looks, one childhood photo showing him with a rounded face, a bit elfin, his expression hinting paradoxically of both ingenuousness and mischievousness. His grandparents regarded him with ungrudging love. My father was Bud: the chum, the pal, the dependable one. His grandparents told him continually that he was the good and faithful one. Or he would prove to be so. He would be the one who would make them proud.

13

Within a year of Skippy's birth, Nat had moved out of state and was neglecting to pay child support. Bernadine, only twenty-two years old, minimally educated and untrained for employment, was left, in the midst of the Depression, to do what my mother's mother, Esther, was being forced to do at the same time: raise three children by herself. Throughout the next few years, Bernadine earned some income doing housework, but she was often in the hospital for illnesses related to her diabetes, and her parents cared for the children then.

In the first decade of his life, my father—as my mother was doing simultaneously—lived in one home after another, barely long enough each time to memorize the address; he moved at least ten times, sometimes from a small, cheap apartment back to his grandparents' house and then out again, sometimes into the home of his mother's latest boyfriend. She seems to have had quite a few. Maybe she wasn't picky; maybe she couldn't afford to be. Or maybe, as her choice of husband suggests, she just had crummy taste in men.

And where was that husband? His parents and siblings might have known, but they weren't telling. Not long after Nat left, a formal photograph was taken of that family, and it includes him. Was he living in Seattle then, skulking around, keeping clear of the streets where he might meet his wife and sons? Or had he slipped into town for some party, for the picture, before sauntering off again? In the photograph, all of the Forhans are gussied up, the men in suits and ties, the women in fancy dresses adorned with elaborate collars and flowers—except for three of the daughters, who, pious Catholics that they are, have become nuns; they sit fully habited in the front row, on either side of their parents. Five of the six sons, black hair slicked back, stand behind them, eyes fixed in straight stares, shoulders square to the camera. Only Nat gives a slightly sideways look—wide-eyed, as if stunned. He is twenty-four.

Not long afterward, he is not Nat. The person who began life as Nathaniel Frederick Forhan, who then became Nat Forhan, then Fred Forhan, has become Fred Grant. He is that intent on stepping offstage, or onto another one, vanishing into some imagined life. His father's obituary, a year later, states that Fred has moved to San Francisco. But to the law, and to his wife and children, he is in hiding, his new name nearly perfect, in its aggressive banality, for the purpose of anonymity. Shrewdly, he has not chosen the last name of Smith—too evidently counterfeit. But Grant is good: Grant is common but not overly so. Coincidentally, while Nat Forhan is melting away, farther south, in Hollywood, Archibald Leach is becoming a Grant, too: Cary. An odd and elegant touch, that: a first name that sounds like a last one—that sounds like Carey, the last name of my father's mother and, ultimately, my own middle name, which I cringe at throughout my childhood, since it is a girl's name, isn't it? Or so I am reminded by my taunting school chums. With little to cling to, I defend myself with the fact that Carey is the name of a movie star, although, okay, he spells his name differently. And, yes, it is not his real name. But it's not my name, either; it's only a middle name that my parents burdened me with before I could fight back.

Cary Grant has chosen his name: a name suggestive of an everyman except for that hint of the aristocratic in "Cary." There may be something aristocratic about Frederick, but not Fred. Not Fred Grant: the name of an accountant, a tax lawyer, a best buddy in a middling mid-century American play. Grant: from the Old French for "to promise" or "assure," from the Latin for "to believe." A name taken on by a man who wants to appear trustworthy. Grant: to cede, to yield. To agree to fulfill, to acknowledge, to bestow. In this case, the name of a man who does not intend to fulfill his obligations as a husband and father, to acknowledge his children, to write to them, to call, to pay a nickel. I searched for him decades later. Eighty years after he abandoned his family, forty years after my father killed himself, I scoured old phone directories and census records, looking for a sign. Year after year, in the Bay Area, there are no Forhans, but there are a few Fred Grants, unmarried and without a distinguishing middle initial. Or perhaps there is only one Fred Grant, continually on the move. In 1937, he's on Larkin Street, near Nob Hill. Later, he's on Hyde, then Castro, then Cayuga, then Post, then Polk. He's listed as a lodger. He lives in apartments. He's a bartender. A gardener. A printing press operator. He might be my father's father. He might not be. Nat Forhan has disappeared into Fred Grant, and Fred Grant into the vast anonymous crowd.

Wherever he is, he is not there for my father's third birthday party, or fourth or fifth. He is not there when his three young sons decide to play near the water, at the west side of Lake Union in the middle of the city. They walk down to the narrow shore from a houseboat they are living in with their mother and, probably, her new boyfriend. The gasworks, where the boys' grandfather worked as foreman for two decades, is visible a mile away, its tanks and trestles and smokestacks stark against the blue sky at the northern edge of the lake. He died a month ago, their grandfather Forhan, at only sixty-four. Have they heard about this? Had they even known him? And do Eddie and Jim, in the midst of their play, notice how long it is taking Skippy to return from the houseboat with a jar of ice? Whatever they are up to, they need that ice, but Skippy is only five, easily distracted. What's keeping him this time?

He does not come back. After collecting the ice and running down the gangplank that connects the house to the shore, he slips. For too long, no one notices he is missing. His brothers believe he is on his way back from the house. His mother believes he has returned to his brothers. Later, when the sheriff's bloodhound, King, arrives, the dog needs little time to sniff his way to the end of the gangplank and stop there. Skippy's body, a few hours later, is hauled up from the lake bottom.

For almost forty years, until his own death, my father rarely spoke about Skippy. A couple of times when I was young, while driving past Calvary, the Catholic cemetery near our neighborhood, he'd say, "My little brother's in there." Or maybe I have that wrong; maybe it is only my desirous memory putting those words into his mouth and placing him behind the steering wheel. Maybe it was my mother who pointed at the simple chain-link fence and said, "You know, your dad's little brother's in there." My father certainly never told us the whole story, or even part of it—but for all of those decades he kept a newspaper clipping about the drowning. I discovered that only when I began writing this book, and my mother said, "I have a small box of some of your father's old things. There's nothing special in there, probably, but you're welcome to give it a look." Before I held the newspaper article in my hands, I'd heard so little about Skippy, the poor drowned boy, and his name sounded so unlikely—too cute to be true—that the whole sketchy story seemed the wispiest of fairy tales. But it happened.

Skippy was buried in the graveyard where his grandfather had been laid to rest the month before. They were placed acres away from each other, with a hill between them. According to cemetery records, the address of the person paying for Skippy's burial was that of Bernadine's in-laws. Maybe Ellen Forhan, Skippy's grandmother, took it upon herself to pay. Maybe even Nat—Fred—did, if he had the money. The plot cost ten dollars and the box, made of cedar, five. A five-foot box. As Seamus Heaney says in a poem: a foot for every year.

14

Not long after Skippy's death, Bernadine and her two remaining boys moved again, this time to an apartment on the north side of the lake, in the Fremont neighborhood. The gasworks were only a few blocks south, and Nat's oldest brother, Jim, lived only a block away. If Bernadine and her young sons had strolled a few blocks toward the lake and turned left, they soon would have passed the business Jim had recently started: Forhan's Tavern, serving sandwiches and fish and chips and Schlitz and Olympia beer. It was a nondescript one-story building near the water, close enough to the shipyard to do a bustling business. Did Jim's brothers frequent the place, plunking themselves on stools at the long bar, sipping free Schlitz? I imagine four of them lined up, fists gripping glasses, complaining about some new boss or old wife, suppressing some sorrow with a long swallow or a wisecrack. Maybe Fred Grant, up from California, wandered in now and then. And what about Bernadine? Did she ever slip through the door of the tavern, let her eyes adjust to the darkness until she saw the face of a Forhan, and ask, "Where is Nat? Where is my husband?"

Maybe she didn't care to know where he was.

By the fall of 1939, Bernadine had moved with her sons out of Fremont to the northern edge of downtown. A new boyfriend was the cause, a divorced Scottish truck driver. In the spring, when the census taker came around, Bernadine lied that she, too, was divorced. It must have been the easiest thing to say. She could not have been very healthy by then, after years of dealing with her diabetes. In the meantime, Eddie and Jim had changed schools, as they must have several times already. Perhaps they had gotten used to not getting used to anything.

Across the street from their new home stood a bronze statue: a tall, robed Chief Seattle, that noble, resourceful man who watched his people's ways—the hunting, canoeing, berry-gathering—supplanted by the customs of Christian missionaries, fur traders, and hard-drinking lumbermen; Seattle, who gave up his land and removed himself and his tribe to a reservation; Seattle, who in his youth took on the power of the Thunderbird through a vision quest and who, in his older age, was baptized Catholic; Seattle, whose entire life was given over to transformation and accommodation. Grave-faced, the chief raised his right arm to the Forhan boys in welcome.

Then their mother was gone: fallen into another diabetic coma, then gone for good. At thirty-one, Bernadine was dead.

My father was eleven. His little brother, Skippy, was four years in the grave. His father was nowhere. Now, too, was his mother.

He still had twelve-year-old Jim. The family had shrunk to the two of them. On a sunny September morning, they stood on the sidewalk outside of Sacred Heart Church, two blocks from where they had lived with their mother and her truck-driver boyfriend. They had just attended Bernadine's funeral. Now what? Mourners shuffled past them to their cars and drove off. At last, their grandparents, the Careys, appeared in the church doorway and approached them. Eddie looked up. "Where am I going to live now?" he said. "Who's going to take care of me?"

"Why, Bud," his grandmother answered, "you're coming with us. Didn't you know that?"

No, he did not know that. Nobody had told him.

Bernadine was buried in the Catholic cemetery where Skippy lay. Would my father have doubted that the two of them were together in heaven now? Probably not. He was a good boy and did what he was told—he may very well have believed what he was told, too. He was soon to become an altar boy, solemnly pledging, as his official certificate proclaimed, "to live and die befitting one who has dedicated himself to the service of our Lord, Jesus Christ." Almost until the end of his life, he attended Mass weekly, sidling into the pews with his grandparents and brother, then later with his wife and children, standing to sing, kneeling to pray, muttering, "Thanks be to God, thanks be to God." He professed that the dead are not truly dead, that they will be resurrected.

As a child, if my father could depend on little else, he knew that the church, with its enduring rituals, was unchanging: the hushed gathering at the baptismal font, the splash of water and the murmured prayers; the flickering banks of white votive candles; the sticking out of your tongue at the priest as he lifts the almost weightless wafer to your mouth; the altar boys' little tinkling bells; the intermittently explicable Latin—*Sancta Maria, Mater Dei, ora pro nobis peccatoribus;* and always the bleeding Christ gazing forlornly and expectantly down from where he's been nailed, his mind half in this world, half in the next.

My father would have found, in the church, a version of what he heard at home: that his ceaseless mission was to prove himself worthy. Almost any impulse within him must be scrutinized as a sign of possible trespass. Even an unconsummated thought, a fancy fueled by desire, could be an offense to God, so one had to be careful to keep the mind clean. And as for the hands, any number of things they were capable of could mean damnation: stealing, masturbating, taking another's life, taking one's own.

He would have been taught the importance of honoring his mother and father. But what could that mean, exactly, with his mother dead and his father vanished?

A mile to the west of where their mother and little brother lay, Eddie and Jim moved into their grandma and grandpa Carey's house: a modest clapboard with a brick porch fronted by a tiny raised lawn. The old folks had the dust and calluses of the old country upon them still; they believed in discipline, duty, and honest labor; they had learned, I suspect, to demand little from life and to respect those whose ambitions and expectations were comparably humble.

They tried to track down Nat, the boys' father—and Bernadine's widower, though Nat might not have known that. The Careys had no interest in talking to the heel; they wanted only to know whether he was dead. His mother had died in 1942, and Nat hadn't shown for the funeral. Afterward, one of the Forhan daughters wrote to her brother, "John, do you know *anything* about Nat? Sister Dolorita told us that she knows that he is dead. She told us quite a story, but I do not know whether or not to believe it."

So Nat's oldest sister, who had become a nun, claimed he was dead. The story apparently involved his coming to a bad end at the hands of gangsters; her own sister, also a nun, suspected she was lying. Maybe, for Sister Dolorita, loyalty to her brother trumped the commandment not to bear false witness; maybe she was covering for him so no one would worry about him any longer or come looking for him.

Or maybe the tall tale was an act of charity toward the Careys: an invented story that would allow them to keep Eddie and Jim in their home. It might be no accident that, only three weeks after Dolorita announced the death of Nat, the Careys' legal adoption of the Forhan boys was finalized, the adoption papers indicating that Nat had "deserted and abandoned" his children and had not contributed to their support.

Also, if Nat were dead, he might have left behind a pension or insurance money. Responding to the Careys' inquiry, the adjutant general's office wrote that it had no record of a Nathaniel Forhan having been enlisted or inducted into the military. Nat's life insurance company reported that if the Careys could show evidence of his death while the policy was in effect, they could make a claim for full benefits. In the meantime, the surrender value of the policy was seventy-three dollars. The Careys had no idea when or where or even if Nat had died. They took the money.

When Eddie and Jim lived with the Careys, throughout the 1940s, there was an older boy in the house, too: a teenager, Jack, whom the Careys had taken in just after he was born and whom they would adopt later. There was little money for taking care of three growing boys—John Carey earned only a couple of thousand dollars a year as maintenance foreman for the city transit system—but the money was steady, and my father and his brother learned the value of a nickel and the value of work. If they yearned for a new Stan Musial–endorsed baseball glove, there was the lawn to mow first, every Saturday for a month. When they reached driving age and wanted to borrow the family car, they knew they'd be washing it inside and out first. Every night at the same time, dinner was laid upon the table. Every Sunday morning, the family got gussied up and drove to church. In every school subject, the boys were expected to do their level best. When Bernadine died, my father was in sixth grade at Blessed Sacrament School. He earned high marks that year. Only in singing, for which he received a C, was he unable to summon sufficient zeal.

15

Eddie was not his mother's boy any longer, nor had he ever been his father's. He couldn't have known what it felt like to have a father, except an absent one, a parent who existed only as a vilified name. What did it feel like for him to be a son? What could *son* mean to him? No matter how welcoming and accepting his grandparents were, he might always have felt like an accidental resident of their house, a guest, an interloper. Whether the Careys made him feel this way or whether he brought it on himself, he continually needed to prove to them that he was worthy of having been taken in. Every day, by being good, by doing what was expected of him, and doing so uncomplainingly, he was earning all over again the right to be there. Perhaps this meant not revealing entirely what was on his mind for fear of disappointing someone. Perhaps it meant training himself to say the proper thing, the safe thing, but no more than that. Perhaps, in wanting not to be a problem for his grandparents, he determined that he would keep his problems to himself. He would work hard, be a joiner, be a good sport, a chum. He would help set the table, make his bed, yank weeds from the garden. He would earn an A-plus for conduct and application. He would ace the final, cook with gas, not get his kicks with knuckleheads. He would have the clean kind of fun, be a good hoofer, charm the prettiest girl, glide her across the gleaming gym floor to the year's top hit, about how it's better to have a paper doll than a real girl you can't trust. He might get a smooch or two.

Maybe from Jean, whoever she was. When my mother showed me the box of things my father had saved for decades, among them was a letter he'd received from Jean when he was fourteen. There were no letters from my mother, but there was this one, sent two years before my parents met, handwritten in pen on small stationery, folded twice. Jean begins by asking, "Is your nickname 'Bud'? I got a letter from Ruth today and she was telling me about a parish dance. She said, 'Bud Forhan took a look in the doorway and evidently he thought that it was a flop, too,' or something like that." Jean also notes that she's been to the pictures, seeing an American submarine sneak into Tokyo Bay in *Destination, Tokyo*. She "was nuts about" the flick—"Wasn't it super? Just think, Cary Grant and John Garfield in the same show, together! Wow!"

It sounds like what a ninth-grade girl would write in 1944. Who was she? My mother has no idea—and my father couldn't have known her very well, since Jean was unaware of his nickname. Why did my father save this letter, filled only with amiable teenage small talk and gossip?

Who was this guy?

Was there something about being fourteen and fifteen that he wanted always to remember? Is it possible, poor man, that these were the happiest years of his life? In a high school yearbook photo taken when he was fifteen, my father looks boyish and handsome, with full dark hair and a broad, open smile. The war is on, but its incomprehensible horrors are far away—they appear only as headlines or are contorted for the big screen into tales of providentially ordained acts of heroism, amply rewarded. The rightness of the American cause is unquestioned; Eddie and his classmates are roused by a cheery patriotism and a desire to prove themselves the youthful face of freedom and its necessary sacrifices.

There is much for Roosevelt High School students to do on the home front: train in a drill organization, scour their neighborhood for old garden hoses and fan belts to contribute to the school rubber drive, add brushstrokes of crimson paint to the giant paper thermometer measuring the school's purchases of war stamps and bonds. Girls might join the Junior Red Cross, filling Christmas stockings to send to the brave boys overseas. Boys might join the ROTC—or the swim team; after all, as the yearbook reminded them, "Swimming is one of the first vital requirements requested by our armed forces. Many of our former swimming team members are now instructors of swimming for Uncle Sam."

Eddie decides Hall Patrol is to his liking. He is one of four dozen boys whose duty is to keep order in the halls between classes and during fire drills. Eddie is nothing if not orderly; his grandparents demand it of him, and he demands it of himself. It probably comes naturally to him. Raised amid chaos and loss, he feels safe within systems of rules that can be followed and expectations that can be met.

With the war effort reminding him that there are concerns larger than any one person's private woes; with geometry, Latin, and world history homework keeping him occupied; and with the Careys requiring that he do his part at home, he might feel that life makes a kind of sense, that everything is in its place, that everything has a place, and that he does, too.

And pretty, convivial girls are a pleasant consequence of living in such a world. In a photo from this time, one that he kept in the box that he saved for decades, my father, in swim trunks, is standing on a beach, his hair long on top so it swoops down the side of his head in a thick wave. He is tussling with a girl who wears a backless one-piece striped bathing suit. This is play, but there's a fierceness in it: they are facing each other, but she is bent at the waist, head down, curly brown hair falling forward, and he grips the back of her neck with both hands, feet planted, as if preparing to toss her to the ground. She is reaching up, grabbing his hands, trying to pull them away. Her face cannot be seen, although I know she is not my mother. But I recognize the boy: he is my father, smiling grimly.

16

My parents were trained, mainly through circumstance, to depend on themselves, not on others—certainly not on their fathers. A father was a person who deserted his children, and happily. Home was a borrowed room and a shared bed, then a trunk full of clothes lugged to another address, then another.

Growing up, my parents knew as the primary determining forces in the world only depression, then war; they understood that, as a matter of survival and of honor, a person was expected to labor and to sacrifice. They were also not many generations removed from their Irish and Scandinavian forebears—close enough to the old country to be steeped in the immigrant ethos of toil, perseverance, and the modest ambition to make a steady living. They came from people for whom family and religion were the central social structures, even if those structures were sometimes maintained so heedlessly and mechanically that they existed more as pretense than as reality. A family ostensibly meant love, self-sacrifice, and a bulwark against outside forces that might harm it, yet family often meant dissembling, bitterness, and division. Religion ostensibly meant humility, rigorous self-scrutiny, and awe before wondrous and indecipherable mysteries, yet religion often involved an unthinking practicing of rituals out of mere habit or fear of disapproval. Maybe that is why the cultures that produced my parents, cultures that valued family and church—the cultures that produced me—also bred silence and shame.

Those forces might have been at work within my father when he chose not to speak to his new bride about his mother. Maybe he was embarrassed about the series of apparently shiftless, shady men she lived with after her husband disappeared. Or maybe his memories of her were so few and confused that he felt it was hardly worth bothering to share them.

After Nat left her, Bernadine did not marry again. She didn't even seek a divorce. My mother wondered about that after marrying my father. Why didn't Bernadine break all ties with Nat finally? It was the 1930s, and Bernadine was neither highly educated nor highly skilled, so she couldn't be expected to find a way to support herself and three small boys. Her plight was remarkably similar to that of Ange's mother, Esther, who found security in a new marriage. Why didn't Bernadine at least consider remarrying and giving her children the stability that might have come from a permanent stepfather? When my mother asked, my father snapped, "She would never get a divorce." He would speak no more on the subject. Bernadine was Catholic. Bernadine was his mother. No more was necessary to know.

But how much more about her did he know? He must have recalled, as a blur, those early years with her: the series of homes, the parade of men who stepped tentatively and temporarily into his father's shoes, some of them with articulate fists as well as mouths. Maybe he remembered lying in the dark and hearing, from the next room, stern, reproachful words, a chair scraping on linoleum, a slap, a slammed door. Maybe he remembered being held gently by Bernadine, sung to by her in some dim evening light. Maybe he remembered her being sick again, hospitalized, and he and his brothers tangling as they tried to sleep together in an unfamiliar bed at their grandparents' house.

Bernadine, it seems, was reckless in her romantic life, heedless in

her choice of men, and careless with her health: she was less than diligent in monitoring and treating her diabetes. Nonetheless, in death,
she became the poor, sainted Bernadine. In the home of the grandparents who adopted my father and his brother, she and the scoundrel
Nat lived on invisibly, as names spoken with a quick glance upward
and a hasty prayer that their souls receive the justice due to them. In
this home, Eddie at last was part of a permanent, stable family, one in
which he was raised, in the immigrant way, the American way, to grin
and bear it, to tough it out, to leave his worries on the doorstep, forget
his troubles, come on, get happy.

That's what he would do now, with his young wife and the baby
who would be born to them soon. His old life, the only one he'd
known, the life of loss and uncertainty, was over. Who his father was,
who his mother was, did not matter. Even his older brother was fading to a mere idea—an ill-defined thought, perhaps, that might waft
occasionally through my father's mind. Jim, having shared with my
father the same series of losses, might have been the person best able
to understand him, the person he most needed as he began to navigate
adulthood. But Jim had married, moved to California, and started a
lifetime career in the marines; in the next few years, my father would
see him once or twice, but then Jim would go silent, as their own
father, Nat, had. He would become another absence, another shadow.
When my father began his new life as husband and father, the journey
he had taken to arrive at this moment—through a childhood of pov-
erty and abandonment and displacement, through an adolescence of
cautious, self-conscious deference to the grandparents who had taken
him in—did not matter. It was this new life he cared about, one solely
of his own making, like a robe of silk he might sew and slip into, con-
cealing the self that had suffered and didn't care to talk about it.

17

Ed and Ange moved into student housing, and my father became a college man, unlike any of the Forhan men before him. Many of his uncles—his father's brothers—had not even finished high school; they had honored the family tradition of turning to common labor: they were mechanics and truck drivers and filling station attendants. My father would not be a Forhan in that way, nor in his behavior as a husband and father. He would do his duty. He would be responsible. His life was his own, to make as he desired. He just needed to set himself to the task.

And he did, taking a job in the student union cafeteria and studying hard. He wanted that business degree, that sharp suit and tie, that briefcase, that desk, that secretary, that steady, respectable, growing salary.

Halfway through Ed's first university term, the baby was born: a girl, my oldest sister. They named her Theresa Lee, after two saints, the first one sanctified by Rome, the second one—the baby's kind and gentle stepgrandfather—by my mother.

Although Ed was distracted by his studies and Ange by motherhood, and although their first winter together was Seattle's worst on record—repeated harsh arctic blasts and snowfall that shut down the city—they were happy, mainly, according to my mother. They were making something: a family, a future. Both knew their roles and flourished in them. Ange's was to keep the household running smoothly. On her first Mother's Day, she received from Ed a mass-manufactured greeting card, on the front of which was a drawing of a harried housewife wearing a pink knee-length dress, a blue frilly apron, and black pumps. She was removing a hot pie from the oven with her right hand and gripping the handle of a pot of steaming vegetables with her left. The printed message:

> *Though you keep busy 'round the house*
> *And take things as they come,*
> *Please take time out on Mother's Day*
> *To love your old man some!*

On the inside of the card, the wife had her hands full still, holding a broom and a mop and her husband's shoulder. The gift for her on this special day: a plea that, in the midst of her interminable, mindless labor, she devote some attention to her needy husband.

The same quaint and frightening pre–Betty Friedan world of gender expectations gave birth to this store-bought Valentine's message my mother gave to my father:

> *Some husbands ask for homemade pies*
> *And then refuse to eat 'em—*
> *Some husbands boss their wives around . . .*
> *And now and then they beat 'em . . .*
> *But mine is such an angel,*
> *So different from the rest . . .*
> *That I'm gonna buy a pair o' wings*
> *And sew them to his vest!*

Being neither a cloddish ingrate nor a bully and abuser, Ed must have been heaven-sent. Of course, to buy those wings, Ange might have had to ask him for a temporary increase in her household allowance.

Before Theresa—Terry, as she was called—was a year old, Ange was pregnant again. She herself was still a kid, only eighteen, and not long before had been living cheerlessly in the house of her mother, a woman whom she had come to understand existed in a kind of permanent Norwegian bleakness and rigidity. In leaving that home, Ange had entered a taxing life of her own, but, still, it was her life, and it had some fun in it. She had no desire to return to that house in Wedgwood, but, in this summer of her second pregnancy, this summer of 1950, she began to fear that possibility. In late June, North Korean forces invaded South Korea. Ed, a member of the marine reserve, was called up to active duty. He would be going overseas, almost certainly.

My father was not stupid; he had known that joining the marines meant possibly getting shot at. Still, he had enlisted in peacetime, and he had done it not out of a blundering or starry-eyed patriotism, not out of a desire to sacrifice himself for his country—or for another country, across the ocean, that he likely could not identify on a map. He had enlisted out of shrewdness and necessity, as a means of putting himself through school. Now he had a wife and child and another baby on the way. To the military, that did not matter: he was a soldier; if called upon, he would go. As for Ange, she was not eager to see Ed leave her yet again, especially when this time there was a chance that it would not be him, but his boxed body, returning to her on a troop transport. Also, with Ed gone, she would not be allowed to live in student housing, and she didn't know how she could face returning to the home she had escaped from.

In the midst of their worry, with my mother four months pregnant, my parents decided to be kids again, without plans or obligations, if only for an afternoon. They rarely visited the Careys, Ed's grandparents; they entered that house only when formally invited for dinner, and they weren't invited often. But on an August day, the sun dazzling and the sky a boundless blue, they pulled their bicycles out onto the sidewalk and, one of them carrying Terry, wheeled their bikes a mile and a half to the Careys' house. They were not expected. When they arrived, Ange handed the baby to Ed's grandmother. Would she watch Terry for a while? They were riding their bikes to the lake. Grandma Carey said yes—she must have understood that there could be no other answer.

This little outing was important enough that my parents brought their camera along. They were already remembering the day in advance. Ange took a photo of Ed standing on the wooden porch steps of his old home, posing between his grandparents. Ed is goofily attired, as if he has woken abruptly from a deep sleep and found himself unexpectedly on an island vacation but without the full wardrobe. He sports wrinkled bathing trunks, a light short-sleeved shirt, dark dress socks, and street shoes. At his side, his grandfather wears the grim, contrived smile of the imposed upon.

Then my parents were gone, flying off on their bikes, as if in a last burst of youthful abandon, down the gradually declining hill to Green Lake. They took photos of each other there, future proof, as they posed on their bicycles on the dirt track that edged the lake. Four years earlier, they had come to this lake in their white clothes, looking giddy and innocent and filled with the promise of teenage love. The Ange of this photograph, in her one-piece strapless bathing suit, white ankle socks, and saddle shoes, seems little changed. She looks like the fresh-faced college girl who, in a different life, she might have been— a young woman with her whole enticingly undefined life ahead of her, although she is already vaguely plump around the middle, someone else's life, again, growing within her.

18

Ed had one chance to stay in Seattle and avoid Korea: he could apply to the air force ROTC program at the university, but he would be accepted only if he excelled in the required exam. If taken, he would avoid active duty as long as he was enrolled in school.

About two hundred men passed the exam. Ed was in the top thirty of them. He had dodged a bullet. Maybe more than one.

That winter, instead of being hunched in a ditch in the snow near Toktong Pass, he was home for the birth of his second daughter, Patty. And he was home for the phone call—the one from his father.

Nat Forhan—Fred Grant—was alive after all. A decade before, his sibling, Sister Dolorita, had stretched the truth about his being in the grave; he had only acted as though he were. Now Nat had tracked down his son. For what reason? Purposefully or not, he had waited, conveniently, until my father was of age—that is, no longer a legal dependent of Nat's—to inform him that he was still among the living.

Ed agreed to meet him, and he would do it alone. If my father felt any particular emotion about the prospect of seeing him—anxiety, anguish, irritation, curiosity, anger—he did not show it to my mother. He just went, taking the short walk north to the Duchess Tavern, a popular haunt for university students, where father and son had arranged to reunite. At home, Ange waited for his return.

Only recently, I have unearthed photos of Nat from around the time he reunited with my father. He is in his forties but looks sixty. In one, he stands in a front yard with a few of his siblings. His brothers are dressed informally, in white T-shirts and narrow suspenders, while Nat, hair graying, wears a dark double-breasted suit and tie. He stands with arms folded across his chest, squinting into the brilliant sunlight. He might be the relative just in from out of town, the one who long ago hopped a train, made his fortune, and knows not to talk too much about it.

In another picture, posing again with siblings and their spouses, he stands slightly stooped and stiff-legged, as if favoring an old battle injury. In a suit coat and tie, he stands to one side, slightly apart from the others, his hands behind his back. He looks almost not there, ready to be cropped out.

For almost the entirety of my father's life, Nat had been a phantom, one whom it was bad luck to mention. Ed had seen him in his mind's eye only. Now he would see him in the flesh. What had he come to ask, or to offer? An explanation, perhaps. But what explanation would satisfy? What would a man say who had forsaken his son?

Maybe he'd had no choice. Renowned detective that he was, he had been called in to lead the search for Lindberg's baby. He had fought with the Spanish loyalists; had served as a leader in the French Resistance; had, with a cocked revolver, gotten within six feet of Hitler, but the trigger had jammed; had helped plan the landing at Normandy; had toiled shoulder to shoulder with Gandhi; had piloted a cargo plane during the Berlin airlift.

Or no. Intensely desiring a life for his children more prosperous than his, he had shipped off to Sierra Leone for some secret dealings, none of them shady, had traveled to Singapore, to Shanghai, to Santiago, for years and years, keeping only pocket money for himself, slipping all other profits into a suitcase—this one. *Open it, son, plunge your hands in, those are gold coins, all of them, and all for you.*

Or he'd been imprisoned on a bum rap. It wasn't his knife. He hardly knew the man. Dodging the searchlights, he'd clambered over the prison wall, slicing his palms and shins on the barbed wire, spent twenty years undercover, seeking the real killer. *I've found him, it's settled now, I'm a free man, free at last to be the father I couldn't have been to you before.*

Or he was sorry, so sorry he could hardly speak of it. No man had been as selfish as he, as thoughtless, as heartless. But he had changed. He understood. He wanted to speak now of the past, of Bernadine, of his fierce, undying love for Ed and for his two other sons (*Skippy! Poor boy!*). He could not make it up to them, he knew—oh, how he knew—*but son, please, son, I am on my knees, hands clasped before me. Let us begin again, take me back, take me back, though I am an unworthy thing deserving only of your contempt.*

Or Nat had no time to explain himself. Ed entered the tavern, looked once into his father's conniving eyes, and socked him in the jaw. Decked him, stalked off.

Or Nat volunteered no meaningful explanation, and he and my father engaged in awkward small talk. That is what really happened. That, at least, is what my father reported to my mother when he returned home that night. He had sat for two hours with his father, and they had spoken superficially. Ed had talked about his wife, his two girls, and his college courses, Nat reacting courteously but not appearing especially curious about his son's life. He expressed no interest in talking about the past, although he did point out that if Ed had been trying to find him, any difficulty would have been the result of him living in San Francisco under an assumed name.

Ed had not been trying to find him.

When my father returned from his reunion with Nat, my mother asked if he would like her to meet his father, too. Would they be seeing each other again? No. No such plan had been made. Ed was content with that; he was finished with his father. He would not see him again, and, for the rest of his life, he would hardly mention him. During that second half of his life, how much did he think of Nat? Did he ruminate over the things his father had said to him in their one brief meeting? Perhaps not—the topics of conversation had been safe and forgettable ones. What else does one talk about with a stranger?

19

A year after Patty, their second child, was born, my parents had a third daughter, Peggy. Terry Patty Peggy: my three older sisters arrived within two and a half years of each other. My father was twenty-two, still an undergraduate, and my mother was twenty. Ed was continually distracted by schoolwork—perhaps contentedly so, considering the bustle of diapering and feeding and squealing and rocking and cooing that he otherwise would have been in the midst of. They lived in student housing, and any extra income they could scrounge up was welcome. Amid the cooking and cleaning Ange was doing for her own family, she began taking in the laundry of university medical students, washing, starching, and ironing for a quarter a shirt, more than enough for a loaf of bread. They nonetheless had time for fun: parties and barbecues with other young couples, with Ed often at the center of the action, cigarette or beer in hand, holding forth, gregarious and quick-witted.

Nineteen fifty-three, when my father was preparing to graduate, was not a bad year to look for a job. America was working; the middle class was expanding. Families found themselves able to buy a house, a car, a television, a washing machine, and my parents were riding that wave of increased prosperity. Before Ed had even earned his degree, he was hired as an accountant by Price Waterhouse and inaugurated into the life he would lead for twenty years—the life of business: the closetful of conventional suits in blue and gray and charcoal; the starched white collars and slim ties; the hurried breakfast and quick peck on the wife's cheek; the fedora, the briefcase; the sun-splashed hood of the sedan on the drive downtown; the swift, purposeful stride down the sidewalk and through the building's glass doors; the glance at the Timex on the wrist before the elevator doors slide open; the loyal and indefatigable secretary—*Three messages for you, sir, and don't forget lunch with Mr. Ramsbottom;* the leather chair and ledger; the calculator; the cabinet; the smile; the firm handshake; the ride home, in thick traffic, in time for dinner, or maybe not.

A life of work. A life elsewhere, away from home. For my father, that often meant not just in his own office downtown but in other companies' offices out of state. In his early years of work, he would typically spend three weeks out of the month traveling, doing field audits. He would fly out on a Sunday, return home on Friday, then fly out again two days later.

By the end of the year, Ed might have seemed—if you didn't look too closely—a personification of the pride and strength and limitless potential of postwar America. He had earned his degree, passed his certified public accountant exam, been appointed a second lieutenant in the Air Force Reserve, and even, for his distinguished military service, been awarded the good conduct medal and the World War II Victory Medal. He had enlisted a year after VJ Day, and his most memorable accomplishment in the military had been to get caught sleeping on guard duty in the Hawaii sunshine, but he was nonetheless honored for his wartime service. It was a matter of happy timing: President Truman didn't officially announce an end to the hostilities of World War II until the last day of 1946, and anyone on active duty before then received the Victory Medal. He had made it by three months.

For my parents, I imagine the next few years were a blur—a happy blur, mainly, according to my mother's memory—of working, of watching their daughters learn to walk and then run, of lugging their belongings into a house, a house at last, even if it's a rented one: there's Dad, struggling valiantly in the snow to maneuver his car backward downhill and around the corner to the new house, a trailer packed with all of their possessions hitched behind him, Ange flailing her arms in the streets to guide him. Then there's the next home—a snug one of their own, with a mortgage, a modest front lawn, a small back-yard emptying into woods. It's a weekday morning, the bustle of get-ting everyone off to school; then, the sun dipping beneath the trees, Dad's home from work, leaning back in his armchair with the newspa-per, then the girls, fresh from the bath, are in their pajamas, and Dad chats with them before they're tucked in—about Terry's arithmetic homework, Pat's plans for her sixth birthday party, the boo-boo on Peg's knee. Now it's Sunday evening, Dad's at the airport gate, waving goodbye, now it's the next Sunday and he's back there waving again; he'll be gone all week, somewhere in Alaska, in Oregon, in Califor-nia, but he'll return for the weekend, when he'll sleep, maybe sleep all day—*You kids pipe down now.* Then the girls are in the backyard, ready to perform their well-rehearsed play, and the neighborhood mothers are there, and a couple of fathers, and, look, there's Dad, he's up and sunlit and settling into a lawn chair. Later, the kids in bed, he's at the dining room table with a pack of cards, teaching his wife his favor-ite game: here's how you shuffle, here's how you deal, here's how you know what you have and what you're willing to give up, here's how you make your face a mask—but she doesn't get it, she's not taking to it. Then the whole family's at Sunday Mass, backs straight and firm as they sit in the pew, the three girls in sweet pastel dresses and lace head coverings. Now the girls are wearing buckskin and feathers or long dresses and bonnets made of gingham—it's the neighborhood Pioneer

Days celebration, it's the kids' parade, children pulling wagons down the blocked-off main boulevard, hula hoops taped to each wagon as a frame for a sheet; it's a Conestoga wagon—and, as the horse to lead it, a dog. Then the girls are curled in their beds, mid-summer, their thoughts dissolving into sleep, soft music floating toward them from next door, from the tennis court the neighborhood parents are dancing across—a burst of grown-up laughter rises, then dies away. And it's morning, and Mom's in the kitchen, clearing the last of the breakfast dishes, while Dad's outside—he has picked up a turtle that has emerged again from the woods, the familiar neighborhood turtle, and Dad is squatting, showing it to his daughters, saying, "Look, he won't bite, you can touch him if you're gentle—feel his back, his belly—now let's set him down and give him a chance to find his way home again."

20

Amid this continual activity, how much could my parents have been learning about each other? Through most of their courtship, an ocean had divided them, then they had married young and abruptly, and, from the start, their marriage had been devoted almost entirely to work, not the work of understanding each other—of sharing their fears and griefs and desires—but the work of finishing school, beginning a professional life, paying the bills, and raising children.

Suddenly, they had another project to work on, a permanent one. When he was twenty-six, my father began, unaccountably, to lose weight. He seemed to be eating plenty, and he was always hungry, but he was getting noticeably skinny. He was always tired. Always thirsty, too. My parents decided he should see a doctor.

Just back from his appointment, he met Ange in the kitchen. "I have diabetes," he said. Diabetes: the disease of his father's family and the disease that had killed his mother. He must have thought back to his boyhood then, the years of Bernadine being chronically ill, often gone from the house, lying in a hospital bed. A diabetic is unable to properly produce insulin, the hormone needed to convert sugar and maintain an appropriate level of blood glucose. Who knows how Bernadine was living in her last years, how much she knew about how to treat her illness, and how conscientious she was about doing so? Was she getting regular insulin injections? What was she eating? Was she drinking? How much? She was poor, maybe jobless, with little money for health care. If the amount of sugar in her blood rose too high, she would have become tired or restless or oddly unresponsive. To a young boy, she might have seemed as though she wasn't his mother anymore. With too little sugar in her blood, she would have become confused, maybe drowsy, maybe irritable, strangely loud—and, if one of her sons didn't know to plead with her to drink some apple juice or eat a handful of candy, she might have fainted, even gone into a coma. Maybe my father remembered rising in the morning, wandering into his mother's bedroom, and being unable to shake her awake. Maybe he remembered having to call his mother's parents or knock on a neighbor's door for help.

My parents understood immediately what this diagnosis meant: their lives would have to change now, and permanently. They took classes at a hospital and learned about the necessity of controlling Ed's diet and constantly monitoring his blood sugar levels. He wasn't supposed to drink alcohol—but if he did, each drink would have to count toward his carbohydrate intake. And he had to give himself daily insulin injections. The household of my childhood is the one in which Dad was in the bathroom jabbing himself with a needle and Mom was in the kitchen with the little scale, measuring every gram of what my father would eat.

They were instructed on the danger of neglecting these rituals: the risk of diabetic shock and coma, heart disease, kidney disease, blindness, amputation. When my father traveled, as he often did, my mother was worried: was he controlling his diet, taking his insulin? If he had a diabetic reaction—becoming manic, confused, physically uncoordinated—who would be there to help, to peel him an orange or buy him a scoop of ice cream? Would he be able to help himself? When he was home, my father, at least for the first ten years or so after his diagnosis, was assiduous in the treatment of his illness. Also, meticulous accountant that he was, he was careful each year to deduct from his income tax the costs of this regimen: the blood glucose testing tape, the insulin, the needles, the antiseptic alcohol, even the cotton balls—up to two dollars a year by the 1960s.

Meanwhile, his list of exemptions for dependents kept getting longer. My parents were 1950s Catholics—they weren't thinking much about birth control. If they ever employed the rhythm method, it didn't succeed for long. In 1957, my older brother, Kevin, was born. Over the next decade came me and Dana, then our little sisters, Kim and Erica. Terry Patty Peggy Kevin Chris Dana Kim and Erica. Eight children: a throng of an Irish Catholic family. We arrived in clusters, subcommittees of two or three born close together: Terry Patty Peggy. Kevin Chris Dana. Kim and Erica.

We were raised by people who had seen, from the example of their own parents, that mothers and fathers were distant: absent from the family or remote emotionally. My parents were kind people, capable of gestures of tenderness. But they were also overwhelmed, and those gestures were memorable because they were infrequent. The essential tools my parents brought to the raising of a platoon of children were those that helped them keep the house in order and the children safe: their perfectionism—their own ambition to do this thing well, to do anything well that they put their hands to; their natural intelligence; and their skill at organizing. In our house, things got done. Our mother ensured that we were on time to baseball practices, to birthday parties, to Girl Scout meetings. On school mornings, our sack lunches were prepared and sitting in a row on the counter, organized from oldest child to youngest, waiting for us to grab them and head out the door. A quick lick to her handkerchief and a scrub of our cheek guaranteed that we were unsmudged in public. We were all tasked with making our beds and keeping our rooms tidy, the cleaning of much of the rest of the house being divided formally among us: somebody vacuumed the rec room while another scrubbed the bathroom and another raked the leaves. Because she was there, my mother took on the role of disciplinarian. She spanked, a wooden spoon being her favored implement.

Our father was not often home, and, when he was, he was typically busy with a project of his own: a gutter had come loose and needed renailing; the basement door, if planed a bit, might shut more smoothly; the Ford could use an oil change. His main jobs were to make sure our home, the physical thing itself, was in working order and to take care of us financially: he paid the bills and taught us the value of a dollar and of a nickel. In these things, he was expert. In helping us to fathom and navigate our inner lives, he was not. In this way, he was a typical father of his generation and perhaps a typical Irishman, deft at employing his charmingly wry wit to deflect attention from what unsettled him, what he could not possibly begin to talk about. But I suspect that his particular skill at silently, implicitly discouraging discussions of feelings was sharpened by his own childhood series of losses and fears that he had been expected to resolve or forget. He must have been hiding painful, disquieting feelings—from his children, more harmfully from his wife, and, most disastrously, from himself.

He probably wasn't revealing much to his grandmother, either, who was not, herself, inclined to speak inquisitively, with tolerant and genuine interest, about others' feelings. My oldest sister, Terry, remembers Grandma Carey as being affectionate toward our father but exhibiting no noticeable warmth toward our mother; Ange, after all, had married her favorite grandson, taken him away, and presented him with a slew of children to be responsible for—children who were sometimes too loud and who put their fingers, slick with slobber, on things that didn't belong to them. As a little girl, Terry once opened a drawer in a table at Grandma Carey's house, a drawer where Grandma kept her cigarettes. For years afterward, Grandma reminded our mother that Terry ought to be watched closely. "That one—she's always after my cigarettes."

By the time I knew Grandma, she was in her seventies: minked, rouged, slow-moving, and seemingly without mirth, both her daughter and her husband long dead. She persisted, until the end, in calling my father Bud. She was the only one to do so then, as if my father had never left her house, as if Roosevelt were still in his third term. Grandma Carey was another of my father's constant obligations. He was expected to visit frequently, to fix the leaky sink and broken toilet, to drive her to the doctor, to speak to the neighbor about that yapping dog; one summer he spent days with a ladder and drop cloth and bucket, painting her house. A few years later, he sold it for her—his childhood home, if he thought of himself as having one—and helped her move into a Catholic retirement center in downtown Seattle. He paid her bills, listing her as a dependent on his tax return. He was happy to help. He did not question it. He could not forget how, years before, she and his grandfather had adopted him and his brother and given them a home, a stable life. In her last will and testament, Grandma Carey bequeathed her entire estate, such as it was, to my father. She made no mention of Jim, the Forhan boy in whom the Careys had been disappointed—he was the one who, like his father, had disappeared. Jim had divorced his wife after only a few years of marriage, and since then neither my father nor his grandmother had heard from him. Only years later, when Jim remarried, did my parents learn what had become of him. He was stationed at a marine base in North Carolina. And he still couldn't summon an interest in talking with my father or his grandmother. For a decade thereafter, though, Ange and Violet, the two women who had married the Forhan boys, remained in contact; they shared birthday and Christmas cards, filling each other in on the respective families' news. Apparently, that was enough for my father and Jim. They heard through their wives about how the other was doing and never bothered, themselves, to pick up the phone or put pen to paper.

Grandma Carey never wavered in her high opinion of my father, and he never faltered in his efforts to prove her right. According to my mother, he knew—he *felt*—that he owed his grandparents, that he would never stop owing them. No one had given him such security before. Why should he believe that he deserved it?

Work. Keep working. Get the next thing done, then the next. My father was good at that: earning his paycheck and earning, perhaps, a right to believe that he was worthy—of trust, of love. Still, he understood that he couldn't continue working in the way he had been, traveling three weeks out of the month—not with his diabetes to control, not with so many children in the house, not with his aging grandmother to attend to. When he was offered a new job, he took it.

The company, Alaska Lumber and Pulp, was a fledgling one. While at Price Waterhouse, my father had done AL&P's audits and impressed its executives enough that they asked him to serve as their assistant treasurer. This new job might be easier, my father thought. True, he would have to learn something about Japanese etiquette—the bowing, the gift-giving, the refusing to refuse a drink: AL&P was a Japanese company, and all of its directors and officers lived in Tokyo; to rebuild after the war, Japan needed timber, and Alaska had it. Also, my father's responsibilities would be considerable: overseeing all of the company's financial activities in the United States, ensuring that the accounting records were accurate and acting as liaison between the company's owners and the bankers from whom they would be seeking loans to keep them afloat. However, he would be able to stay home more. He would manage an office in downtown Seattle and travel only occasionally to the company's main operation in Sitka, Alaska, to supervise the financial operations there.

In the fall of 1959, a year after my father assumed his new identity as local boss, international underling, translator, and negotiator, I was born, entering a world in which, it might have seemed, truth was becoming harder and harder to discern, being gladly and easily distorted by fiction or subsumed by it. Congress was investigating the TV quiz shows, discovering how scripted was their spontaneous drama. Richard Nixon was a teen idol: in Los Angeles, a swarm of college students clamoring for his autograph had driven him to seek refuge in a women's restroom. The top tune in the nation was an assemblage of fabrications and mutations: a song written in German and adapted from a two-hundred-year-old tale first written in English, meant to be sung by a fictional character in a musical but performed now in an English translation by an American who went by a stage name, not his given Italian one—a singer who believed, even now, the lie that his grandparents were his parents and his mother was his older sister, a singer who was a teenybopper rocker but, on this record, was reinventing himself in the image of Frank Sinatra.

And Bobby Darin's "Mack the Knife" totally, authentically swung.

I was christened Christopher: Christ bearer. It was there in my name—I would hold Christ in my heart, as the saint I was named for had held Him on his shoulders, carrying the exalted toddler across the swollen river. By the time I was ten, though, Saint Christopher's credentials were being formally questioned, and, when his story was judged legend, not fact, the Vatican took away his feast day. I, too, would be drained of some sacredness, my name becoming, for my schoolmates, Chriscross-Applesauce, Christopher Robin, Chris Piss. But, in my adulthood, to junk-mailers whose computer program prints only the first six letters of a long name, I sometimes am back in church, with pride of place above the altar: Christ Forhan.

21

Sitka. I heard the name often in my childhood. It was the place my father flew to and then returned from, weeks later—a place I couldn't picture, except I knew it was very far away and had a pulp mill, whatever that looked like. Sitka was on the west side of an island, looking out to the Pacific. To get there, my father had to travel on a small plane from Seattle a thousand miles north to Juneau, overshooting his ultimate destination, then board a seaplane and reverse direction, going south the last hundred miles to the coast, landing in the water, and motoring up to the dock. Sometimes he traveled to Wrangell, two hundred miles from Sitka, to the company's lumber mill. *Sitka. Wrangell.* These were words my father carried back to us, as if in little leather pouches, from the edge of the world, to speak at the dinner table, words with jagged music in them, initial syllables falling swiftly like an ax—*Sitka, Wrangell,* consonants closing the throat: words almost absent of meaning but with mystery glittering in them, the mystery of what my father did in those places, of what the air smelled like there, of who the people were. At five, at seven, at ten, I could have only the vaguest understanding of what my father did for a living. I might not even have cared much. Fathers went to work; that's what they did. Up and down our street, morning after morning, Jenny's dad, William's dad, Pete's dad, Tommy's dad—each gripped the top of the steering wheel with his left hand, craned his neck to look behind him, backed down the driveway, shifted gears, then drove off, turning at the corner and disappearing. They each might as well have been going to the same office. But my father sometimes was gone for days and days, leaving us for Sitka, for Wrangell, leaving us with room to imagine anything we might about those places, leaving us with time to begin feeling that he, hardly ever here, was hardly real himself.

Sitka and Wrangell—Alaska in general—remained illusory: words, not places. They were postcards my father sent home from his travels: a totem pole beside a grinning, squinting Eskimo; a team of huskies pulling a sled through snow; a log cabin, solitary among looming firs and spruces; and, once statehood was official, the flag: gold stars of the Big Dipper against a deep blue background.

That gold was Yukon gold, the elusive yearned-for thing we heard about when our father recited "The Cremation of Sam McGee." This was one of the first poems I knew, and I loved it. Or I loved the few minutes my father sometimes spared in an evening, my pajama'ed brother and I sitting together on a bed, when he pulled up a chair and opened his book of Robert Service poems. Maybe he'd owned the book for years; maybe he'd had it as a child. More likely, he'd picked it up recently on a whim at an Alaska tourism office. It was "The Cremation of Sam McGee" we wanted to hear, always. We were tickled by the wild, morbid comedy of it, and he was, too. We loved that we were chuckling about the same thing our father was; we loved the words of the poem in his voice, and we loved his voice in our ears. *There are strange things done in the midnight sun / By the men who moil for gold.* The brisk but steady rhythms, the frequent rhymes, all exact and landing squarely on the beat: these surely appealed to Kevin and me. But it was the story—what child doesn't love a story?—that mattered most. A prospector from the warm clime of Tennessee has never had it so cold as he does in the Yukon, so cold that his dreams of riches are overcome by dreams of death and of the relief he might feel if his partner keeps a promise to cremate his remains. *'Tain't being dead— it's my awful dread / Of the icy grave that pains.* The promise is kept: Sam's pal builds a fire in the furnace of an abandoned boat and stuffs Sam's frozen corpse into it. He leaves, but then he can't help himself— he returns to take a peek. There, in the blaze, is his friend, smiling, imploring him to close the furnace door, saying, *Since I left Plumtree, down in Tennessee, / It's the first time I've been warm.*

A man happy at last only in death, amid the flames devouring him: Dad and Kevin and I sat silently for a moment, grinning in the glow of it.

Part III

Empty Plate

22

My parents voted for the Catholic and the New Frontier. As JFK and Jackie were preparing to move into the White House, my parents were boxing up their belongings and transporting them to a new home, the one where all of their children would grow up. About a mile away from their old house, it was more than twice as big and cost twice as much, but, with the higher salary of my father's new job, they could afford it, even if they would otherwise have to scrimp. Since the house was brand-new, they'd had a hand in designing it. Instead of their old one-car garage, they now had a carport big enough for two vehicles. With five children already, and Dana due to be born around the time of the move, they made sure to include six bedrooms—three on the top floor, three on the bottom. The oldest children would each be given a downstairs bedroom, and the youngest would live upstairs in rooms across the hall from our parents. As the years went by and new babies were born, the younger children, one by one, moved downstairs into the bedrooms the older siblings left behind when they moved out. The new house had three bathrooms: one for my mother; one, off the master bedroom, for my father; and one, downstairs, for the children. That bathroom featured a long counter with three sinks side by side, each with a medicine cabinet built in to a mirror extending the length of the wall. With their three oldest daughters soon to be teenagers, my parents anticipated traffic jams.

The house was on an unpaved dead-end road in the northeast section of the city, where only in the last few years had lots been cleared for construction. There were still large thickets of trees in the area and ponds with tadpoles flitting about in them. Only three other families lived on the street, but as our house was being constructed, three other homes were as well. Young couples who had started their families a decade before were doing well enough to dream about and build their own homes, to clear the pines and wild blackberry bushes from their own chosen plot of land and stamp it with a new address. During the first ten years of our life on that secluded street, there was rarely a summer undisturbed by the rumble and grind of backhoes and bulldozers and the multiple short reports of hammers. After ours, another dozen homes rose up—another dozen mothers bustling about in kitchens and laundry rooms, another dozen fathers, in late afternoon, pulling into driveways, sitting at the wheel in a haze of cigarette smoke.

Before we moved in, my father spent weeks driving alone to the unfinished home in the evening, after his workday downtown. The builders had agreed to take five percent off the purchase price if he did some of the painting and tiling himself. So my father stowed in the family car what he needed—the cans and brushes and rollers and drop cloths and saws and pencils and tiles and tape measure—drove to the house, and went at it, solitary, happy. He was never more serene than when confronted with a project to accomplish: a physical predicament that he could solve through mathematical calculations, tiny, inconspicuous adjustments, and a steady hand. By trial and error and much corrective sanding, he learned how to slather and smooth mud onto drywall. He worked and worked, accompanied only by the fresh echoes of the empty house, while my pregnant mother remained in the old house, caring for their five children, awaiting his return.

One night, he didn't return. He had gone to the new house to spend the evening laying tile on the ground floor. Three hours went by, then four, then five. My mother couldn't pack up her children and drive to check on him: he had taken the only car. She couldn't call him: there was no phone in the new house yet. Even if there were, would he answer? He might be lying unconscious on the partially tiled floor, having slipped into a diabetic coma. He might be—my mother didn't want to think of this—dead. She tucked us, one by one, into bed, then lay down in her own bed. There was only silence, no sign of her husband. She drifted off. When she woke, she was still alone in bed and certain something horrible had happened, something tragic, and she had been unable to prevent it. As she prepared breakfast for the family and saw Terry, Patty, and Peggy off to school, she was intent on remaining outwardly calm. Finally, with the three girls gone, she bundled me into a stroller and headed out the door with Kevin, who was three, toddling beside her. "We're taking a morning walk, Kev. Isn't this fun? It won't be a long walk, not too long. Make sure to keep to the side of the road." My father had been gone probably fourteen hours. We walked the mile toward the new house, where she would deal as best she could with whatever crisis we encountered. There were neighbors across the street; she could run there and plead with them to call for an ambulance.

When we reached the house, my mother lifted me out of the stroller and walked with Kevin toward the basement door. She eased it open. On the floor, kneeling, pushing a tile into place, was my father—looking, my mother said later, "happy as a clam." He glanced up, puzzled. "What are you doing here?" he said.

This was the house where everything happened, the house of my first and most indelible memories—indelible, perhaps, because they were half real and half created by imagination, the earliest of them forged when reality and imagination were hardly distinguishable. Gaston Bachelard says our childhood house is "our first universe," that which "shelters daydreaming," the enclosed space that retains its shadows. This space of my childhood is the dark nook beneath the stairs, behind the water heater; it is the one floor tile, set there by my father, that bubbled and buckled and would not lie flat; the rough stone wall around the upstairs fireplace, rising to the high ceiling, enough narrow footholds jutting out of it for us to climb, if we were patient, to the top; our parents' bedroom, at the end of the upstairs hall, in the daytime— the strict quiet, the king bedspread wide and cool and untouchable in the dimness; downstairs, the closet of my older sister with its menagerie of stuffed animals, emptied when she left the house and I fell heir to her room; the closet in the downstairs rec room, the kids' realm, filled with boots and skis and sleeping bags and tennis rackets and boxes of old documents, including, we discovered once through snooping, a photo of our parents on their wedding day, a photo dated only six months before our oldest sister's birthday, and that's how we knew our parents had lived a life before us, a life they didn't speak about; the concrete laundry tub, uncoupled from its plumbing and sunk into a pit in the backyard to make fires in; the flat carport roof, strewn with pebbles, upon which we were allowed to set foot once a year—when Dad lugged the box of Christmas lights up and we followed him, creeping to the roof's edge and kneeling, untangling the red and green bulbs so he could string them up; the wooden stairs to the back deck, fat slats we could sit on, slipping our skinny legs between them to dangle down as we ate our summer lunch, the milk in the glass slowly warming, absorbing the flavorless taste of sunlight.

This was the house in which, at two years old, lying in the dark, my charge being to fall asleep, I was given for company unnatural voices—deep and rolling, high and howling, as of wild giants quarreling. My parents had brought a radio into the room and tuned it to the classical music station. But it was not Bach or Chopin I was hearing; it was opera—voices wailing and moaning in no tongue I could understand. Gradually, terribly, I descended into sleep, as Tosca hurled herself from the parapet, as Don Giovanni was dragged down into the everlasting flames.

It wasn't long before I heard music that drew me toward it, music that we children chose for ourselves. "She Loves You." "Thank You Girl." "I Want to Hold Your Hand." "All My Loving." In 1964, my older sisters were fourteen and thirteen and twelve: they swooned for the Beatles. Considering their age and gender, they were duty-bound to do so. Weekend slumber parties meant entire nights of those Capitol releases spinning in the rec room while I lingered in the hall, trying to be a part of the party without being told to go away. I yearned to join the world of that room, a world without parents, a world that seemed built upon a single article of faith: abandonment to joy—a joy made manifest in sudden shrieks, giggles, and urgent whispers. I was the kid brother, the littlest one—cute, like Paul, if I was lucky. We were all expected to choose our favorite Beatle. It was Paul I wanted to be: maybe I'd discovered that the teenage girls lounging in their pajamas in the next room liked him best. Maybe, in the Beatles cartoon I watched on Saturday mornings, Paul engaged in the funniest high jinks. Maybe I liked his singing. My older sisters wanted to date the Beatles, but we three youngest children, Kevin, Dana, and I, wanted to be them. That's what the family badminton rackets were for. They were our guitars. One of our sisters acquired an array of mop-top paraphernalia: Beatle boots, Beatle dolls, Beatle wigs. And there were plenty of real beetles crawling around outside. When we spotted one, we classified it by species. Those with narrow, angular features: George. The more rounded ones: John. Those with evident goofiness or asymmetry: Ringo. And the cute ones were Paul.

What our parents thought of all of this, I don't know. They had their own life upstairs, the adult one, without music.

I recall them talking sometimes—about money, about my father's work, about what the mayor was up to. I also recall silence: the hush in which my father recovered from his workday, in which he leaned back in his big vinyl armchair and scanned the newspaper, in which he smoked and smoked—sometimes Camels but mainly Tareytons, the crisp white package marked with two bold vertical crimson bars, like highway lanes. Sometimes the silence was heavy with tension, with an unspoken accusation and complaint that my mother, busy in the kitchen, was considering voicing, and with the recrimination my father was silently preparing in return. Probably he had returned late again from work. He knew that dinner was served at six. He had promised to arrive by then. Where had he been? Was his family that unimportant? Did he have that little respect for his wife?

Sometimes he would be so late coming home that dinner was long over, the dishes scraped, washed, and dried, the children in bed. Sometimes he would not return until the next morning. What could he have been doing all night? Certainly not poring over the company ledgers. Amazingly, my mother—at least as she tells it—did not ask. My father did not explain himself, and she did not insist that he do so. Maybe, when this pattern first developed, she asked him questions, but she eventually became weary of doing so. Her own father—the first Ed she had known—had long ago instructed her, through his actions, that a husband's way is to be distant and untrustworthy. As my parents' marriage progressed, how little my mother must have learned to expect and how little therefore to demand. My father knew that his behavior distressed her. He must have known, as the months and years went by, that it was making her less inclined, less able, to be generous and forgiving toward him. But if it crossed his mind that he might explain himself and express regret, he did not act on that thought.

Unable sometimes to address him directly, my mother could nonetheless communicate symbolically. More than once she left his dinner plate, empty and forlorn, fork and knife beside it, on the table for him to notice when he walked in. Might that silent, accusing place setting rouse some feelings of guilt in him, even inspire a change? For my mother, this subtle, probably futile act of retaliation was a show of power—the little she had. My sister Peggy recalls a moment when our mother confronted our father about his absences and irresponsibility. She was in the kitchen, and he was sitting nearby at the dining room table; she told him he had to change. If necessary, he had to get help. Peggy, only eleven or twelve, ever cheerful, went up to our father and hugged him. "You can do it, Dad," she said. "You can do it." He hugged her back. "I can't," he said. "I just can't."

He had established a pattern of doing superior work in his job while acting, sometimes, like a ghost in his own house, as his own parents had been ghosts to him: his father a rumor, his mother an absence that ached, then faded into a sweet, unspeakable, useless love, fixed and distant.

One night, my oldest sister, probably fourteen, was a few miles away from the house, babysitting for a young couple who were out on the town. With three small children in their beds, Terry heard something that made her breath stop: an odd noise, the kind that teenage babysitters in unfamiliar houses are wont to weave into horror stories before they realize the noise is nothing.

But this wasn't nothing. A man had broken into the house. He was not imaginary; he was there.

He demanded that Terry take off her shirt. Then he fondled her breasts. Terror-stricken, she sat rigid, able to think only of what might happen next, what violence.

And then he ran off.

When she had steadied herself, and steeled herself, she got up and made sure that every door was locked tight. It was almost midnight. She called home. My mother answered; my father was asleep, and the phone did not rouse him.

"Ed," my mother said, shaking him. "Ed, wake up. Something's happened to Terry." He would not rise. Groggy, he lay in the sheets. How much of my mother's pleading did he hear? How much did he understand? However much of what she said sank in, he was unpersuaded that he should rise, dress, and go to his daughter. So my mother went alone.

She stayed with my sister for two hours, stayed while the police arrived and took Terry's report, stayed until the owners of the home returned. Then she drove home with her shaken daughter.

My mother explained to my father what had happened. He seemed content that the problem had been resolved; he needed to hear no details.

Later, as Terry sat scanning mug shots that the police placed before her, asking her if this was the man, or this, it was her mother, not her father, who sat beside her, who tenderly rubbed her back with a palm.

23

As a boy, I knew I was Irish—or half so—because when I asked my parents what I was, that's what they told me. The other half, they said, was Norwegian and Swedish. By the 1960s, in my family, that meant little more than feeling a frequent hankering for sweet pastries and having a grandmother—Esther—who, when a day of shopping had gone on too long and she plopped herself down and rubbed her feet, muttered, "Uff da." When the mayor said a stupid thing: "Uff da." When her husband, Lee, played his favorite Bix Beiderbecke record too loudly once too often, then again: "Uff da." If my mother ever used the phrase, it was a self-conscious mimicking of her own mother. As for us children being Irish—well, one of my sisters could plunk out, on our borrowed piano, a plodding but recognizable "When Irish Eyes Are Smiling." But I imagine a lot of people's sisters could do that.

One of my father's aunts, it turns out, was an enthusiastic piano player; as a teenager, she needed little prodding to seat herself at the family piano and play a rollicking version of "The Isle of Capri," belting out, "Lady, I'm a rover. Can you spare a sweet word of love?" This was Marie, who would soon give up secular pleasures to become a Dominican nun. Three of her sisters did the same thing. In an astonishing photo from the early 1960s, these four Forhan women—Sisters Dolorita, Lucille, Pauline, and Marie—stand shoulder to shoulder, dressed in full white habits, rosaries dangling at their sides. Their hair and ears are hidden by white coifs and their foreheads by bandeaus. Each wears glasses and is plump-faced, even jowly, and brims with personality. Lucille and Pauline purse their lips, each hinting at a smile, as if contemplating the love of an inexplicable God or thinking of the same slightly steamy joke. Dolorita looks puckish, her head turned slightly sideways as her wide eyes size up the camera. Marie is a pudgy version of my father—or the old character actor Vincent Gardenia. It is as if, with so much of them concealed by white cloth, the sisters' faces appear exaggeratedly filled with life.

Decades after my father died, craving an explanation of him, I searched for answers in the lives of our shared ancestors, the people of whom he never spoke, including those nuns and their six brothers. As if to unsubtly fulfill the Irish stereotype, while the Forhan girls were joining the convent, the boys were taking on work as manual laborers—shipyard workers, meatpackers, mechanics, truck drivers—and drinking, marrying, gallivanting, and abandoning their families. Nat, my father's father, was one of them.

I have discovered that we—Nat, my father, and I—are not of the Forhan's toothpaste Forhans, whose popular gum-treating formula allowed them to marry illustrious Nebraska cattlemen and Italian counts and ride out the Depression in sleek Rolls-Royces. We are undescended from the Forhan Boys, vaudevillian strummers and crooners in blackface, nor may we be linked to Simon J. Forhan, the "Killingly Komical Komedian" who, in the 1880s, led the Forhan Comedy Company on theatrical tours of the Midwest and eastern seaboard. Instead, we are of the Forhans who, in the middle of the nineteenth century, driven by famine, fled southern Ireland and, massed and huddled, crossed the ocean to farm and railroad and drink and brawl and barely scrape by, to keep the gasworks going, to blacken their fists as mechanics and steamfitters or keep their hands clean as brides of Christ, to take their stories with them into graves marked only by grass.

These older Forhans, silent now: what can they tell me about my father? They were immigrants, Catholics, farmers, slave owners, soldiers, itinerant railroad workers: labels that say something, but not much. I might propose—maybe this is all I can say credibly—that these people are recognizably American. The bare facts of their lives, arranged as a narrative, tell of the rough-hewn, makeshift quality of the country, the colliding of idealism, drudgery, sacrifice, promise, chance, and heartbreak. That's the big story, an old tale told in broad strokes. What can that story say about my father, who never knew these people, possibly never heard of them?

Oh, to be like that young woman I met in my twenties, not long after I moved from the west to New England: an American of my own age, an apprentice poet, who spoke easily, knowingly, and not a little smugly of her Irish ancestry. She seemed to slip into a light brogue as she did so, and her blue-gray eyes glimmered like the sun-dappled Atlantic as she spoke of her most dear possession: the cable-knit fishing sweater worn first by an eighteenth-century ancestor in County Galway, cherished by each succeeding generation until it was delivered at last into her grateful hands. Listening, I felt as though I were from nowhere, from nobody. What were my treasured family heirlooms? I could think only of the gilded metal ruler, a promotional giveaway stamped with a local insurance company's logo, that, in 1971, my father had brought home from his downtown office. "Want this, Chris?" he'd said offhandedly. I had taken the ruler, and I own it still. Sometimes my own young sons ask to play with it—a handy stand-in for a light saber or a magic wand, this advertisement for an obsolete business that was my father's gift to me, that one day might be my gift to them.

Mine was an American family, whatever that might mean, and a northwestern one at that, putting down roots in the fresh soil of a city settled only a century earlier by errant, enterprising lumbermen for whom cultural heritage meant little and profit meant almost everything. By the time the Forhans had meandered their way to the far upper-left corner of the country, and by the time my parents were raising a family there, the Irish in us—or the external cultural signifiers of Irishness—had become lost or attenuated. The Catholicism remained; that is, we went to church. But the religion was more important to our mother, who had been baptized into the faith after she married, than to our father; his participation—as, ultimately, some of his children's—seemed perfunctory, drained of meaning. The immigrant's habit of hard work remained: the absolute doggedness, as if the continual labor that once had meant the promise of a life of leisure, or at least of comfort, had become the life entirely. But the work—the diligent attention to whatever was the task at hand—seemed sometimes to arise from an unthinking sense of duty, or, rather, it seemed a distraction from thought. We had rituals of pleasure, real pleasure. However, our special meals meant not ancient family recipes but bags of burgers and shakes from Dick's Drive-in or Mom's famous spaghetti sauce, the flavors taken from a store-bought envelope of factory-mixed herbs and spices. We celebrated Christmas and Easter, but a holiday that made us children feel equally in accord with the eternal and inscrutable was the annual telecast of *The Wizard of Oz:* that opening of a farmhouse door to a Technicolor elsewhere, that giddy dancing toward a dark wood. The culture we were steeped in was the culture of things newly brewed: a half hour of TV each evening (*My Favorite Martian* or *Batman,* on our lucky days), hula hoops, Gary Lewis and the Playboys' *Golden Greats,* capsules filled with astronauts splashing down in the Pacific, lime Jell-O dotted with floating pear chunks, backyard badminton, report cards in slim golden envelopes. The part of our lives that was older—the part that had been passed down to us stealthily, ineluctably, through generations of anonymous ancestors—was our personalities, those impossible things.

24

My three oldest siblings could have been sisters in a fairy tale. Unless they had been triplets, it hardly would have been possible for them to be closer in age: when the youngest of them was born, the oldest was only two years old. As small children, they were always together. Family photos from the 1950s show Terry, Patty, and Peggy, as toddlers, sitting side by side in the park grass in identical sleeveless summer dresses; kneeling together in a half circle on the carpet at Christmas, grinning in identical flannel nightgowns; standing stiffly, pretty maids all in a row, in identical rickrack-trimmed dresses and bonnets and ankle socks, their white-gloved hands gripping identical Easter baskets.

Yet, from the start, they were very different: three points of a triangle joining to make a single shape but straining in separate directions. Terry was the only blond among us—that bit of our Scandinavian ancestry, a gift from our estranged paternal grandfather, blossoming just in her. Ten years older than I, almost to the day, she was the firstborn, with a first child's ease and confidence and ambition, the kind of girl whom teachers praised as having leadership potential. She signed up for things. Whirling around the maypole of Camelot in her high school's musical, she sang bold and clear—the only one of us who could truly sing. I see her sitting in the spring sunlight of our backyard, guitar in her lap, her long blond hair glowing, a collection of her high school friends around her, all of them joining in, earnestly working to harmonize, maybe on some Peter, Paul and Mary song. Terry had a clean-cut, likable high school boyfriend, Brian, who wouldn't last, who couldn't, because she was off to college, happily headed toward a shining horizon.

Patty couldn't shake us, though she seemed to try. She was dark-haired, as the rest of the Forhan children would be, delicately pretty, and, unlike her siblings, diabetic: she shared our father's disease. When she was very young, she suffered from chronic problems of the skin, which erupted in rashes and cracks and scabs; my mother could not hold her without hurting her. Maybe that early isolation, that sense of being different from—and distant from—the rest of the family, contributed to Patty's painful adolescence. With the wild inconstancy of her teenage moods intensified by insulin instability, she tangled continually with Terry and raged at our parents, becoming so erratic and unsettling and unhappy a presence in our household that she fell into the habit of running away, finding sanctuary in the homes of her boyfriend or of schoolmates. Eventually, at a loss for what else to do, our parents agreed that Patty should live in another home, with a foster family. Nonetheless, when she lived with us, I was happy to have her there: an older sister who seemed to promise that there was another life, one filled more with fun than with responsibility. She is the sister who, when I was seven and she sixteen, gave me a summer Saturday on the town, the two of us boarding a bus and traveling the eight miles downtown for a burger and cotton candy at Seattle Center, where the World's Fair had been; for a monorail ride to the middle of the city, where at Woolworth's we posed for a strip of black-and-white photos in a booth, Patty with the sly hint of a grin, her straight dark hair hanging low and flat along her brow, I with a wide, toothy smile, my plaid shirt buttoned to the topmost button; and for a walk along the waterfront, where, as a grand finale, we wandered through Ye Olde Curiosity Shop, gazing at whale bones and totem poles and shrunken heads brought back from the Amazon and a pin that had, we were told, the Lord's Prayer carved on its head. Patty is the sister who returned from school one afternoon and surprised me with the offer of a piece of chocolate and then, when she saw that I'd tasted the grasshopper hidden within it, shrieked with laughter. She is the sister who began to go steady with a mysterious boy we rarely saw and then, at eighteen, married him, then had a baby, making me an uncle before I'd finished fifth grade. That marriage didn't last, nor the next one, nor the next, and Patty, at fifty-one, became the first of my parents' children to die, collapsing in the kitchen of her small apartment while readying herself for another day of work. In her final years, she had begun to speak of the value of family, claiming that there was nothing more important in a person's life, saying she regretted the years she had wasted being angry for no reason. She took a late liking to poetry; she wrote to me with questions about a Yeats poem that bewildered her. For years, she had many steady, loving friends. At her funeral, we met them.

The third child, Peggy, was Patty's opposite: quiet and mild-mannered, a beaming girl in a plain pageboy haircut, content to exist in the midst of us, happy to live in the family home, not bothering anyone or feeling bothered herself. When, at twenty-one, she moved out of the house to an apartment she shared with a friend, she had to be nudged, gently, by my mother to do so. No burning ambition—for a career or adventure—seemed to drive Peggy. She was a calm, solid force in the family, a peacemaker. To Kevin, Dana, and me, she became a partner and confidante, joining us in Chinese checkers and tick-tack-toe and creating, with me, a secret code, a cipher, by which we communicated, slipping notes beneath each other's bedroom doors. "We meet for a game of gin rummy in thirty minutes," my message might say. Hers: "As to your question, the capital of Delaware is Dover. You are hereby charged 25 cents for the use of my brain."

I looked up to my three older sisters. They were old enough to seem of a separate generation. They had their own experiences of our father, certainly, and their own feelings about him, but I wouldn't have known what they were. I had arrived late, born into the family after the best of my father's years. The father in my older sisters' minds was someone I'd never met. In the years when they were teenagers, when they must have been grappling, as teenagers do, with their relationship with their parents, redefining it as they redefined themselves, I was elsewhere: in my younger child's head, in my younger child's life, attending more to my toys and coloring books than to whatever distant, mysterious experiences my sisters were having. Each night I slipped into bed long before they did, before the kind of conversations between older children and their parents that take place in the darker hours of the evening.

During these years, when Kevin, Dana, and I were in elementary school, our father often had good days and good weeks; he was home with us and acting as we had heard a father acts. On a warm Saturday, as our cousins and we scampered and squealed through the backyard, he stood at ease, beer in hand, monitoring the burgers sizzling on the fire-pit grill, chatting and chuckling with Bob and Earl, my uncles: mustered, the men who had married the three Peterson girls. On a Sunday, Mass attended, the paper read, my father fiddled at his workbench in the basement and paused to show us how to grip a hammer properly and aim squarely for the nail head. He wiggled a rotting fencepost out of the ground and replaced it. He sharpened the mower's blades, greased the axle, and made short work of the backyard grass. (We noticed his labors; we defined him by them. In my eighth year, for Father's Day, I presented him with a handmade card, a crayon drawing on the front depicting him in a father's uniform—fedora and tie—and me, in a striped shirt, leaning in to his shoulder, red hearts floating all around us. Inside, I wrote, "Dear Dad I hope you have a nice time today. Me Kevin and Dana moad the lawn for you.") Occasionally, he drove us kids in the station wagon a couple of miles down to the railroad tracks near the shore of Lake Washington, to the blackberry thickets, and handed each of us a bucket to fill. He drove us to the local Elks club—we had joined for the use of the pool—and held us up in the water, tugging us along by our fingertips, teaching us how to stay afloat. He filled the car with camping equipment—musty rolled-up tent, Coleman stove, cooler, and sleeping bags—and drove us a few hours to the rain forest on the Olympic Peninsula. On one of those trips, Kevin, Dana, and I had helped him set up our tent at a public campground and lay out our cooking gear. Dad was pacing slowly, smoking, perhaps contentedly examining a job well done—there had been this to do, and he had done it—and I was traipsing through the nearby woods, among the monstrously large moss-covered Douglas firs, their roots knuckling up from the ground, the bouquets of ferns bursting out of the dirt. I was barefoot. I was Peter Pan. I was Huck Finn. I was shrieking—I had stepped on something horrible: slimy, thick. My father sprinted toward me in long strides, while a dozen other campers, strangers to us, stopped what they were doing, turned, and gawked. I had planted my naked foot on an enormous slug, bigger than a roll of quarters, yellow-green, its antennae waving blindly, its sloped back moist with juice.

"Look," I said to my father, and pointed. "That slug. I stepped on it."

In an instant, his concerned expression melted into the look of someone who would be relieved not to know me. "Grow up," he said. "You embarrassed me. Don't do that again."

A half century later, myself a father, I understand his annoyance: my scream had promised a danger greater than a slick slug—it had stirred in him a parental concern that turned out to be unwarranted. But why, after all these decades, do I recall the incident so clearly? Maybe because it is among the few moments when my father seemed truly to reveal himself, with me as the sole cause and the sole audience. I saw him reduced, perhaps, to something fundamental, to a code he lived by: whatever unsettling feelings you express, you'd better have an unassailable reason for expressing them. You'd better be in an emergency.

25

Day by day, the world of our home, the structure of activities, felt predictable, and safely so—our mother's doing, mainly. With so many children in the house—six or seven under one roof at the same time, the oldest maybe a grumpy adolescent, the youngest a toddler searching for sharp, shiny objects to shove into her mouth—our mother had no choice but to keep things organized, although the structure admittedly appealed to her innate sense of order. Every day, the vacuum came out; regularly, too, the furniture polish, window cleaner, floor wax. When I think of my mother in the 1960s, I think of her with a dish towel in hand or a pot holder or a washrag or a tiny knife, whittling away at the waxy buildup on the kitchen's linoleum floor. I picture her going about the unending business of keeping the dirt and clutter away, of keeping disorder at bay, and doing so beautifully, all while being beautiful herself, her figure trim, her long dark hair curled in the latest style—in her, still, was the pretty teenager my father had fallen for. But that had happened two decades before. Now she was managing a house full of children, and, with her husband gone all day at work and sometimes for days at a time on business trips, she was doing so almost entirely alone. Dinner was at six, and grace preceded dinner. Cups of dessert—maybe cubes of Jell-O wiggling beneath whipped cream or a healthy dollop of chocolate or butterscotch pudding—were arranged in a row on the counter that separated the dining room from the kitchen, so we could eye them as we nibbled our peas and carrots and hamburger patty. The first one who cleaned his plate had first choice of the cups—one, we could swear, held slightly more than the others. Anyone at odds with his Brussels sprouts, who poked at them dolefully, had to sit and sit as, one by one, his siblings finished and excused themselves from the table and our mother filled the dishwasher and wiped down the counters and dimmed the kitchen light, but not before setting the timer on the oven clock. "You have seven minutes to finish those vegetables, and you won't leave the table until you do." Bedtime was seven-thirty and then, when you were a year older, seven-forty-five, then eight. The oldest children helped take care of the youngest, and the youngest were trained, like their siblings before them, to pick up after themselves, to keep their rooms tidy, and to spend Saturday mornings after breakfast taking a broom or vacuum or bucket and rag and can of cleanser to the rest of the house. A neighboring mom complimented me once on my ability to scrub, saying I used that "Forhan elbow grease." Word had gotten out about our family's can-do attitude. Each weekend, our reward: one can of pop—grape, please—and one Hostess snack—cherry fruit pie, thank you. Thank you, thank you, God, to whom we were taught to give thanks, for our mother's Scandinavian sweet tooth, her love of Sunday pastries, and her one strange day a year—her day of shameless extravagance—when, with the buckets of wild blackberries we'd picked, she baked pie after pie after pie and presented each of her children with one and said this is your dinner, this whole pie is yours, no vegetables, just eat this pie till you've had enough, and if there's some left, have at it again tomorrow. She was the unsleeping center of energy in the household, her gift for organization and economy giving shape to our days and weeks—comfortingly so. Every birthday party, every Thanksgiving and Christmas and Easter celebration, was planned and executed with panache and efficiency. Every Sunday morning: church. Every Ash Wednesday: soot on the forehead. We children were taught to be obedient, to say *please* and *excuse me,* to answer the phone not by saying hello but by reporting to the caller that he had reached the Forhan residence. And we were coming to understand that there were things it was best to keep quiet about: bewildering desires, feelings of guilt, unusual opinions, the compulsion to crack a joke, then another, then another. No one told us that; we just knew it, eventually, and with certainty. Mom or Dad might be angry; an argument between them might be simmering, for all we knew; they might be weary and harried from overwork—it was better not to risk their wrath or a withering look of moral judgment. It was better not to say too much. Something might happen.

The world of children and the world of adults existed side by side, but they were separate. Taunted on the street one day, teased by three older boys who circled me, raised their clenched fists, and would not let me leave their block and walk on to my home, I watched one car after another drive slowly by, one adult after another decline to stop, step out, and save me from my tormentors, adults who saw us but did not see us. The bald old man I sat behind in church, ears sprouting gray hairs, shoulders flecked with dandruff: he might have been a thousand years old and have journeyed to Mass from his home beneath the sea.

My parents' bedroom, at the far end of the upstairs hall, was miles away, and what they said to each other there I could not know, although sometimes, as I sat at the dining room table or stood in the nearby kitchen, I heard raised voices, a sudden shout, an accusation, a verbal sneer, then silence—nothing for the rest of the night—or I heard the yanked-open door and saw my father walk purposefully out of the hallway, past me and down the stairs, face stricken, teeth clenched, one time weeping loudly, and then I heard the downstairs front door click open and shut and his car engine stammer to life.

Dad would escape by driving away, out of the neighborhood, to who knows where. My older sisters had their secret teenage lives; they had the phone or friends' homes to flee to. We younger kids—Kevin, Dana, and I—would escape with our neighborhood friends to the top of the street, to the dead end, into the woods that grew thick there, that sheltered us as we split into two platoons to play war games, as we arranged snapped branches with broad leaves into huts' that we hid in to eat our wrapped sandwiches, as we squatted and slid on our dirty tennis shoes down the steep hill toward the shadowy, deep ravine.

The summer when I was five was especially dry and hot, and we seemed to live in the woods then, the children from our own street and older ones from the next street over: the boys who were menacing and mysterious because they were twelve and thirteen and had constructed a sophisticated tree house far off the ground in which they convened and smoked cigarettes. One day in late July, it was ninety degrees; for weeks, no rain had fallen. I ambled with Dana, who was four, up the street to the woods. I was the older brother, the tacit leader on this outing. We found ourselves gazing up at the older boys' tree house. We had no thought of climbing to it: we wouldn't have known how to begin, and we weren't going to try something that dangerous. I spotted, on the ground, a small piece of folded cardboard. I bent to pick it up. It was a book of matches. "Let's light one," I said to Dana.

"No," she said. "Anyway, you don't know how to."

"Of course I do."

"No, you don't. Let's go."

I opened the matchbook. Three or four matches remained. I pulled one out. It was easy. "Let's light it," I said.

"I don't know. Can you even do it?"

"Uh-huh." Actually, I wasn't sure. Dana was right: I had never lit a match. But I had seen my father do it, scraping the red end quickly across the black stripe. I tried it. Between my fingertips, the match flared.

I dropped it. I didn't know what else to do. I hadn't considered that, if I succeeded at lighting the match, I would be responsible for the flame.

Dana and I gazed at the ground where the match had landed. The flame was bigger now; a small dry bush had caught fire. Then a ragged patch of tall grass next to the bush was ablaze, too.

We turned and raced out of the woods, looking for someone to tell, for anyone who could help. Across the street from our house, in the neighbors' yard, our older brother, Kevin, and a couple of his friends were playing football. "There's a fire in the woods!" we yelled.

"Yeah, sure," they responded, laughing. "Fire in the woods! Fire in the woods!" They resumed tossing the football to each other.

We needed to knock on a door, to find a grown-up. We rushed to the next house up the street, the Younies', and pounded on the door. It opened. Mr. Younie—a distant, even intimidating presence, with whom we rarely traded words—looked quizzically down at us. After a few breathless words from us, he strode swiftly toward the woods. A moment later, he returned. "You kids go home," he barked.

Once I was home, where could I hide? Where could I make myself invisible, pretend that what had happened had not happened?

I don't know where Dana went—maybe immediately to our mother. I fled to the smallest room in the house, the one least likely for anyone to look in: my father's bathroom, the one that adjoined my parents' bedroom. Only he went into that room, and he wasn't home. It was cool and shadowy and smelled of soap and aftershave. On the counter near the sink were his shaving brush and razor. On the back of the toilet was his beige leather pouch in which he kept his insulin, syringe, alcohol, and cotton balls. To my left was the shower; I thought to click its glass door open and hide inside, to become a shadow behind the opaque glass, but only my father ever stood in that space. Hiding there would feel like a second transgression. I sat in the corner of the room, on the tile floor, and huddled, my back against the cabinet, arms around my knees, head down.

How long did I wait? Ten minutes? Two hours? I wanted to be undiscovered forever. I knew that eventually someone would find me, that I would have to become a part of the family again, that I would never get my old life back, the life that had been mine that morning, the one in which I had not yet been touched by disgrace. As my father before me had, I was being raised to be a good boy: dutiful, respectful, careful, hardworking. But maybe I wasn't good, or as good as I should have been. For a few minutes, anyway, I could be alone and apart with the fact of my sin, even while the siren outside proclaimed it.

I do not recall who found me or how I explained myself or whether I tried to. I do not recall being scolded or lectured by my mother or father, although I probably was. What I remember is being an exile from the world of children: I remember the lesson on fire safety, presented by an actual fireman, that all of the kids of the street attended the next week in a neighbor's basement. I remember, as soon as I entered the room, kneeling behind an armchair to hide. I remember the fireman asking the assembled children if the boy who set the fire in the woods was present. I remember being pointed at: "That's him. Behind the chair." I remember, on another day, standing at the big picture window of our home, watching the children of the street, in a replanting ceremony to which I had not been invited, parade solemnly in single file to the scene of the crime, each with a sprig held tenderly in his hand.

I was no longer of their tribe. I understood what I had done. I had burned down our woods.

Almost forty years later, I found a report of the fire that appeared the next day in the local newspaper: "4:19 p.m. 3816 N.E. 96th St. Grass fire caused by child with matches; no loss."

26

It would be comforting to remember my father as a drunk, to diagnose him as an alcoholic and be done with it, to imagine him, in those hours after work when he should have been home with us, hunched at the end of some dim downtown bar, giving in to temptation. When he arrived home late, maybe whistling overzealously, tromping up the stairs to the dining room, my mother sometimes smelled alcohol on his breath. She began to think he might have a drinking problem.

An enthusiasm for alcohol was, after all, a family tradition. On his mother's side were Irish immigrants to Canada who had a lucrative business in home liquor, running the stuff over the border to Detroit during Prohibition. A great-uncle suffered a flurry of neighborhood attention in 1895 when he was arrested for operating a still that the local newspaper reported was "capable of producing ten gallons of spirits daily, and bearing evidence of having been used very recently." An ancestor on his father's side was Daniel Shawhan, a farmer and distiller in Kentucky who made a whiskey so smooth and popular that the grateful citizenry named a Bourbon County town after him. The oldest of my father's Forhan uncles was a tavern owner, while the youngest was a loquacious, convivial guitar-picker prone to vanishing for days at a time and being tracked down in the shadowy corner of some pub in Seattle's skid row. His own sons, my father's cousins, struggled with the bottle, too, one of them coming to a lurid end, strangled in a cheap motel room by a transgender ex-con whom he'd propositioned drunkenly.

But my father—did I ever see him drunk? Not stumblingly so. I don't recall him often with a drink in his hand—a beer at a ball game, a mixed drink at Christmas, but not much more than that. I saw him manic, charged up, speaking in a rush of uninterrupted syllables, physically reckless, insensibly knocking a water glass from the table with an elbow, becoming unbalanced while climbing a ladder in the backyard and tumbling from it. But this behavior was caused by diabetic reactions—by low blood sugar. I saw him lethargic, unable or unwilling to rise from the couch as the hours of some Saturday wore on toward dusk. But he was tired from overwork. Or maybe depressed. Or maybe, by 1967, with seven children in the house, he was incapable of facing the chaos. Maybe that's why, when his workday was long over, he found something other to do than come home. What that something was, who knows. Was he closing down all of the bars? Was he cheating on my mother? When I was seven and eight and nine, neither of these possibilities crossed my mind; I knew nothing of the snares and lures of adult life. I just knew that my father was often gone when he wasn't supposed to be, and this made me nervous and my mother fretful and testy.

But she kept the household going, climbing out of bed early enough, even if she'd stayed up late wondering where my father was, to get the children fed and off to school. My three oldest sisters attended a Catholic high school, each morning donning their uniform—the plaid shirt and white blouse—and slipping their textbooks, protected by covers made from brown paper bags they had scissored, folded, and taped, into a canvas bag they cinched shut. Terry remembers leaving the house on those mornings and knowing, from the empty space in the carport, that our father had not come home. This was the space where his bright red Volkswagen Beetle should have been, his humble little rounded insect of a car. Riding in the Beetle, you felt each bump in the road and heard the wind whipping past you. "The tin can," my father called it.

One morning in March 1967, as we kids slid from bed and gathered upstairs for breakfast, the red car, again, was not in the carport; our mother, again, was methodical, efficient, in getting us ready for school. The five oldest of us headed out the door. Dana, a year younger than I, would not be going to her kindergarten class until the afternoon, so she was there when the tow truck pulled up to the house, the passenger door swung open, and our father stepped out. She was there to see him wearing the suit he'd gone to work in the day before, but he was disheveled now, tie undone, hair in disarray, blood streaming down his face. He was shaking, nearly weeping. Dana remembers our mother leading him to their bedroom, making him sit on the bed, and stepping into his bathroom to soak a washcloth in warm water. "Go to your dad, Dana. Talk to him," she said.

Dana did move toward him, reluctantly, but couldn't murmur a word. "I didn't want to," she remembers. "He was not my dad."

He had begun driving home that morning after the sun rose. Two miles from our street, he had lost control, spun off the road, and rolled: the car was crushed—only the driver's compartment remained intact, unmangled. Anyone sitting elsewhere might have been killed.

The next day, cleaned up, calm, on the mend, our father explained to us children what had happened. It was an unfortunate accident. It couldn't have been helped. A car had veered toward him, and he had swerved to avoid it.

Later, an alternate story began circulating among us: he had driven off a freeway overpass on purpose. He had tried to kill himself. One of our older sisters must have told us that, and we believed it. *We believed it:* we did not doubt our father could do such a thing.

This is what he told our mother: he had been drinking. He was drunk. In front of him, suddenly, a woman and her child were crossing the street. He nearly hit them. He could have killed them, could have killed himself. He was aghast at what he had done.

After the accident, my mother says, he shaped up for a while. He bought another car, the last he would own: a white 1966 Dodge Dart with red interior—handsome but unassuming, used but solid. Reliable.

Two months after he crashed the Beetle, the Seattle-Tacoma chapter of the National Association of Accountants elected him as its president. In his life away from us, our father was doing well, or at least successfully preventing his peers from thinking otherwise. And what did he think? Perhaps, when he left home in the morning, he felt relief—able, with the voices of his wife and children silenced, to sink into his own thoughts at last—and he felt dread when he returned. Or maybe the dread existed no matter which direction he drove.

For whatever reason, he soon returned to his undependable ways, often failing to arrive home on time for dinner. We sat at the table, pushing our mashed potatoes and peas around on our plates, waiting. Kevin, ten, Opie-ish—a hint of red in his hair, freckled, gangly, getting to be all elbows and knees—and precociously witty, could ease the tension with an ironic quip and sly grin. Dana, six, a cherubically cute prankster, her dark brown hair in pigtails, preferred slapstick: the exaggeratedly twisted face and, when our mother wasn't looking, the wide-open mouth revealing half-masticated cube steak. My habit was to gaze innocently at nothing while kicking her fiercely beneath the table. Kim, in her high chair, drooled and whacked happily with open palms at her Cheerios. We hoped to hear our father's Dodge muttering to a stop in the carport, and then, as the minutes passed and our mother grew gloomier, we hoped not to.

27

A benefit of my father working for a lumber and pulp company was that he kept us supplied with free stacks of cardboard and reams of paper that he lugged home from the office. On the paper, I painted watercolors of houses, front walks curving away from them and off the page, wood smoke swirling from their chimneys. I lay them on the floor to dry, the paper puckering. I drew a crayon portrait of my new pet gerbil, LBJ, named after the most famous person I could think of. LBJ was an agreeable roommate, keeping to himself, sleeping amid his wood shavings, crouching in the corner discreetly emitting pellets, making his wheel squeak forlornly in the night. In his portrait, I drew him huddled behind the bars of his cage near his hanging water bottle—above him, on the wall, a portrait within a portrait: the Sacred Heart of a black-bearded Jesus, orange flames bursting from his chest.

As the weeks went by, Christ and I watched over my gerbil. Then, one morning, I noticed that LBJ's left eye was purple and swollen. Was this normal? I told myself that it was, that gerbils' eyes are prone to bulging grotesquely and that the problem would go away. I wanted it to; the eye was not easy to look at. But what if it didn't go away? That would be my fault, wouldn't it? LBJ was my gerbil; he was my friend—I was responsible for him. In a perverse misapplication of that responsibility, as day gave way to day, I kept the fact of LBJ's condition to myself. I did not tell my parents, and I did not offer aid to him. I hadn't a clue how I might do so. Instead, I waited, I temporized, my shame and secrecy feeding each other. Like a small version of my father, perhaps, I was ignoring a warning sign because it was easier to do so: easier merely to hope for the best and say nothing than to admit that I was inadequate to solve the problem alone, or to admit that I might be the problem. LBJ's bulge grew larger, more freakish, so I understood that he was truly suffering and that his suffering was indeed my fault, so much so that I could bear to glance at him only occasionally and then chose not to look at him at all, shielding my eyes with my hand when I fed him or changed his water. Finally, one day, no rustling noises came from his cage. LBJ lay still on his side in the corner. I prodded him with a pencil. He did not unstiffen, to my relief. With a trowel, I dug a deep gerbil-sized hole in the corner of the backyard and deposited him in it, marking the grave with an upright Popsicle stick.

I had not been able to reveal to my mother or father that my pet was sick, let alone that I had allowed his condition to worsen because it repelled me. I had begun to nurture a protective privacy, a silence within which I might hide and ward off censure. Instead of speaking freely and spontaneously about what I felt and thought, I preferred to show off the parts of myself that I felt safe in revealing, the unassailable parts: my artistic flair and high-mindedness. I was beginning to try my hand at verse. My earliest extant poem is an occasional one, written for my mother when I was eight:

There are daisy's that grow,
and tulip's sometimes too,
but ofcourse they'll never do!
So there's the carnatain.
Because Mother's day is a celebratoin.

The poem was cunningly original, I thought: my best effort yet.

My imagination was glutting itself not only on the poetic implications of nature, and not only on tales of superheroes and villains of the Wild West and knights and kings, but on the stories shared with me by nuns and priests. As my father had been once, and his father before him, I was a Catholic schoolboy, sitting rigidly in my seat each morning, hands folded before me, in my uniform of salt-and-pepper corduroy pants, white button-down shirt, and navy blue sweater, the school insignia sewn over the left breast. It was here—with Sister Aida, white-habited and black-shoed, looking down upon us as she patrolled the rows of desks—where I practiced my penmanship, penciling *O* after *O* after *O* and, when it was time to try a whole sentence in cursive, was instructed to try my hand at this: "O my God, I am heartily sorry for having offended thee."

God was watching me. Like Santa Claus, He was tough on criers and pouters. He likely didn't approve of my wobbly penmanship. He seemed generally unpleasable—strict and particular, having concocted a dauntingly long list of sins, venial and mortal, for me to steer clear of, and those were on top of the nasty original blotch on my soul that I had earned just by being born. But God was also capable of extravagant generosity, most of all in His final gift of eternal, ecstatic life in heaven alongside Him, although I would have to earn that reward every day, every minute, throughout my entire life, and He would never apprise me of how I was doing. I would have to die and be surprised.

I believed in heaven as an actual place, a geographical location. One day, during art hour, our teacher asked us to draw our private vision of it. On that rough grayish paper we used for everything in school, with bright-colored crayons, orange, yellow, and green, I drew something that looked suspiciously like the Emerald City: slender, tightly gathered towers soaring skyward, sparkling with stars. Beyond that, I had only the fuzziest sense of the place. Would ice cream be served?

Would we be issued wings and, if so, would they be feathered? Assuming Dana would also be present—a big assumption, considering her general and intensifying brattiness—would she and I be together on the same family cloud, bound eternally, or would we be free to roam independently? Would kickball be played, or would we only lounge eternally in the glow of God's love? And what would that feel like? I wanted specifics.

More relevant to me and real, because I had seen them, were the remote, secret places of television: Maxwell Smart's underground headquarters, which you got to through a phone booth concealed behind five sets of doors; the Batcave, sheltering a sleek black convertible and blinking computer consoles; and the scrubby, prehistoric world of club-wielding cavemen into which two astronauts, falling backward through time, crash-landed their capsule.

Christ had done something like that, hadn't he—fallen from a far star and awoken in the desert, burbling, wrapped in swaddling clothes? Christ I could understand better than his father because I could picture him—or, rather, because he was pictured for me. He was there in my slim children's missal, the gilt edges of its pages sleek and gleaming: gazing upward, his face full of tender yearning, tawny hair falling in gentle curls upon his shoulders; standing atop a rock, palms uplifted, preaching to his kneeling, rapt apostles; or, barefoot and robed, riding up, up, and away on a shaft of golden sunlight streaming through a hole in a cloud.

But church was filled with riddles. I was told that, as the priest mumbled, waving his hands like a wizard over the silver tray of wafers and the chalice of wine, Christ himself was present there before us. But I never saw him. I looked and looked. And what about this business of the Communion wafers being Christ's body? Every picture of him I had seen indicated that our Lord was no giant; after all of these hundreds of years and all of these Masses in all of the churches of the world, by now he should have been entirely punched through with holes.

Nobody told me I might think of it as a metaphor. True, at seven, eight, or nine, I had limited capacity for abstract thought. But someone could have tried. Did all of these Catholics—did my parents, my older sisters—really believe all this literally? When, on my own, through years of careful observation and deduction, I had determined that Santa was a pretty fiction, and I had begun to consider that the same might apply to the biblical miracles and the empty tomb, I did not feel free to speak my thoughts. When I was fourteen, a confirmed doubter being asked to proclaim in front of the congregation that I was a believer, I felt alone with my awkward secret; it would have been a great gift, though a highly unlikely one, for some priest to take me aside and whisper, "You know, it's only the *symbolism* of the stories that matters, really." I was years away from being able to think of the strange and glorious Christian story as a poem, a way of expressing indirectly, in images and words that humans comprehend, those things that, by definition, transcend comprehension.

What did my father—the lifelong Catholic, the altar boy—think? I do not remember asking him. Perhaps when I was three or four I posed, as children do, rudimentary theological questions to my parents: What is God? When you die, where do you go? But what I remember of my parents' conception of faith is just one thing: they went to church, and they required their children to do so. My mother had come to Catholicism late, at seventeen, because she married my father. But he, like generations of Forhans before him and like his children after him, was born into it. Is it possible he doubted this faith he had not chosen? He was a practical man. His job was to make things add up. Did the story of Christ and the concepts of sin and salvation in which he professed belief make sense to him? Maybe it didn't much matter. Maybe he was a Catholic in the way he was an orphan and grandson and father: it was something that happened to him, so it was something that he was, not something to think about. And because he was Catholic, he weekly expressed, in ritual and song, his understanding of his insufficiency, his sinfulness, his duty to be humble and strive to reach the ideal of absolute love and sacrifice embodied by Christ.

Like my father, I was told that Jesus was conceived by a ghost and that, because of him, when you're dead, you're not really dead. And I believed it. In second grade, wearing dark slacks, a white shirt, and a clip-on bow tie, I took First Communion, sticking my tongue out so the priest could set a thin bit of our Lord upon it. He tasted kind of good. The next year came my first confession: the ritual of opening, with quivering hand, the polished wooden door, then stepping into the small dark box of a room, lowering myself onto the creaky kneeler, waiting for the little window to *shhh* open before me, the dim figure of the priest leaning at his ease on the other side, his ear toward me. Regularly afterward, groups of us children were brought from the classroom into the church to do this. Peering at the blurred outline of the priest as he waited for me to speak, I had to think, and fast. Had I hit my sister? Talked back to my mother? Dillydallied and daydreamed and not made my bed? I didn't think so, but I had to say something; I would tell the priest that I had done those things. Given a penance of two Our Fathers and five Hail Marys, I got up off my knees, then exited the confessional as if floating; it really did work—I felt absolved, scrubbed clean. At the front of the church, I knelt before the altar, bowed my head, and murmured my assigned prayers. But the relief was only temporary. I felt deflated when I thought of what I had been taught: that there would be a lifetime of this—decades of monitoring my misdeeds and loathing them, of pleading for another chance, of asking for forgiveness that, stained from the start, I might not deserve.

Even in my twenties, long after I had left the church, Catholicism remained in my muscle memory. If I would not, as my father did, continue to practice the public rituals of the faith into adulthood, I none-theless would find myself unable to shake it entirely: certain habits of mind and body had been shaped by it. In graduate school, I worked for a summer in a candy store in a Maine resort town. One afternoon, in a moment when I hadn't anything else to do, I grabbed a broom and started sweeping. A customer remarked, "You're Catholic, right?"

I looked up from my work. The woman was smiling.

"I was raised Catholic," I said. "How did you know?"

"I recognize the sign: doing more than you have to because you know you can never do enough."

28

In third grade, I was a good boy. My grades in deportment and attention were exemplary. Regularly, I promised to do my best to do my duty to God and my country, to be square and obey the law of the pack: like the other boys I knew in school, and like my brother before me, I had joined the Scouts. I was a boy; it's what a boy did. "Do you like to pretend you are someone else sometimes?," I had read in the *Wolf Cub Scout Book.* "Well, Cub Scouts in their meetings pretend they are cowboys, space cadets, firemen, policemen, knights, and almost any kind of hero." This sounded promising. And I admired the uniform: the smart blue pants and shirt, the gold belt buckle, the neckerchief, the cap. In it, I was unimpeachable. This is a boy, the uniform said, on the side of right, a reverent boy, a courteous boy, a boy aware already of what will make him, one day, a respectable man: a knowledge of knot-tying and pocketknife safety.

Week by week, in my official Scout book, I checked off accomplishments that proved me a worthy member of the pack: I played catch with someone twenty feet away. I showed three ways we give respect to the flag. I wrote a fifty-word essay on what I liked about America. I practiced my religion as I was taught. I explained what to do in case there was an accident in the home and one of my parents needed help.

I was practicing my reading, too. Sister Aida was fond of the Dictionary Game: at our desks, each of us sat before a closed dictionary. She called out a word—*disciple, tabernacle, resurrection*—and the first student to find it in the dictionary raised his or her hand and read aloud the definition. I often found the word first: I was becoming proficient in spelling, at least.

Outside of school, I read everything that entered my line of sight: cereal boxes, Richie Rich comics, mattress tags. There were few books in our house; my parents had sprung for a set of Funk & Wagnalls encyclopedias and a few *Reader's Digest* condensed books, but there were no Jane Austen novels, no collections of Shakespeare, and I doubt I would have cracked their spines if I had discovered them. Instead, I let the language of advertising flow into me unimpeded. Riding in a car, I made a silent game out of trying to read every word on every billboard and business sign as it passed. *Eat Energy-Packed Hansen's Sunbeam Enriched Bread. Dag's Beefy Boy Burgers 19 Cents. Nixon's the One.*

When I wrote, I did so primarily to convince people that I was admirable. In a flamboyant effort to please Sister Aida, I wrote a seventy-word illustrated novel about an insect who knows nothing but then goes to school to learn and becomes so smart and appreciative of teachers that he opens a school of his own.

Only once that I recall did I use writing privately, as sheer self-expression, as personal catharsis. I had been bullied—as many in my third-grade class had—by a boy named Leslie. Maybe his girlish name made him surly. He was stocky and blond, his head flat as an anvil, and, when he wasn't scowling, he smirked. As all of the students in the class paraded single-file out of the building to the playground, he was fond of stepping swiftly out of line and shouldering someone hard toward a wall, like a hockey player checking an opponent against the boards. On hot days at recess, he grabbed the sweater I'd wrapped around my waist and tossed it into the bushes. In the classroom, when I rose from my seat and walked to the pencil sharpener, he followed, then stood behind me, poking me repeatedly, rhythmically, in the lower back with his pencil tip. One morning, outside of school, when he was certain that no one was watching, he spat at me, the bubbly white stuff hitting my pant leg and dribbling down. This was too much, finally: I reported to Sister Aida what Leslie had done. I don't recall the punishment he received, but it was not enough for me. Later that day, sitting on the asphalt playground, leaning my back against the wall of the gym building, I lifted my pencil to the red brick and wrote, slowly, deliberately, pressing down hard, "Leslie is a moron."

I lowered my pencil and looked up. Striding stern-jawed across the playground directly toward me was one of the older nuns. She reached down, yanked me up by the elbow, and pointed at the wall. "What's this?" she demanded.

"I don't know."

"Yes, you do." She spied the pencil in my fist. "Is that yours?"

"No."

"You're staying after school today, and you're going to scrub your handiwork off this wall."

So I did. But writing those words—pushing my pencil lead emphatically against the brick, making palpable my unequivocal judgment of Leslie's mental capacity—had been exhilarating. He had spat on my pants, so I had spat on his character. I had felt something real and expressed it. Still, I had hoped to do so anonymously, the vandalizing of church property being a sin and all.

29

"Tell us about dinosaurs and why they're gone."

"Tell us about the ocean—the deepest fish, the ones we never see."

"How does radio work?"

There were times when we younger children had our father completely to ourselves. He had returned home in time for dinner and was in a buoyant mood, and, after we ate, Mom was happy to finish the dishes in solitude or to grab a few private moments on the living room couch with a magazine while he gave us his attention. One of us—Kevin, Dana, or I—or maybe all of us together, conspiring, would say, "Can we have a staying-up night?" Dad would say, "Sure," and that meant we wouldn't be going to sleep, not yet, not when we were supposed to. Instead, we would put on our pajamas, gather downstairs on somebody's bed, and ask our dad about anything, anything at all that came into our heads, and he would explain it to us. He seemed a bottomless repository of knowledge. I picture Dana lying on my bed on her stomach, bare feet in the air, chin on her fist, Kevin and me sitting cross-legged near her. Our father, in slippers, lies on his back along the length of the bed's edge, hands behind his head.

"Tell us about airplanes, about how people first learned to fly."

"Why are there volcanoes?"

"What was your mother like?"

No, we didn't ask that. It wouldn't have occurred to us. Our father's past was mentioned so seldom that he might as well not have had one. We did not ask him about himself; we asked him about the world outside of himself, the one we were convinced he had become expert at navigating. In these moments, past our bedtimes, time didn't matter; only our father did. He was ours alone, and, for the half hour or so that our talk lasted, he seemed happy to be so, looking each of us in the eye in turn, earnestly, patiently explaining to us how planets and moons orbit in interlocked patterns, grinning at the wonder of it, asking if we understood. The world we knew—our rooms, our house, our school, our street, our friends—seemed cramped and circumscribed, but it was surrounded by another world: the truer one, a world unbounded and fathomless with secrets. My father, I sensed, knew them all.

Maybe every adult did, and growing up meant learning the secrets one by one, taking a series of hesitant, or sudden, steps into the bigger world and finding it fitting or frightening or baffling to be there. You light your first match, the flame blossoming abruptly from your fingertips. You take possession of a pet and agree to take care of it. You find yourself standing alone in public, a grown-up stranger's eyes fixed upon you, expectantly—as I did when the family visited a California amusement park and filed into a row of seats to watch, onstage, someone we'd seen on TV: Andy Devine, a movie cowboy sidekick and kids' entertainer. He strolled the stage with a microphone, a hitch in his stride, and, in his raspy, angular voice that suggested chronic delight, cracked jokes and recounted tales of old Hollywood. He had a big, rubbery face, bushy-browed and jowly. As I watched him, I thought about how I was watching him, how I was having an experience. This was a star—he'd been on *Flipper* and *Batman*, for Pete's sake—and he and I were in the same room at the same time. I felt myself, in the moment, recording my memory of the moment.

I leaned toward my father and asked if I could borrow the camera.

"The camera?" he whispered. "You?" I nodded, and he handed it to me. It was heavier than I'd expected.

I stood up and shuffled sideways past the long row of knees, then walked down the main aisle twenty rows to the lip of the stage. I lifted the lens to my eye and pointed it at Devine. He noticed me, sidled over, still talking, and posed for a good shot. I continued to hold the camera in front of my face. It occurred to me that I didn't know what to do next. How did one work this thing? Was there something, perhaps, I was supposed to know about flashbulbs? I stood still, and Devine stood still, pointing his face at the camera that was pointing at him. Then he squinted quizzically, shrugged, pivoted, and strolled toward the other end of the stage. I returned to my seat and handed the camera back to my father. He grinned and shook his head. My siblings rolled their eyes.

It was a risk to hold in my hands any unfamiliar complicated object, or even a simple one, such as a baseball bat. I had taken the Cub Scout oath because all the boys were doing it; the same assumption—that any organized activity my peers were volunteering for must be a requirement of boyhood—compelled me to join a Pee Wee baseball team. The best part was the uniform: a bright orange T-shirt, the team name—MAPLE LEAF—inscribed in black on the front. The rest was a mix of boredom, bafflement, and ineptness. Every game, all game long, I stood in right field, inert, my hand clammy in my glove, listening to the distant, wind-muffled sounds of other boys hollering at each other. For the season, I went hitless—bat and ball never made contact—and the team went winless: 0–11.

It was only after practice, when I trudged across the diamond and through the opening in the chain-link fence, then headed home alone, that happiness, even exhilaration, began to take hold of me. It might have been that, as with the moment after I left the confessional, I felt the joy of a dreaded thing being over. But it was more than that: it was my being alone, walking home, but having a while until I would arrive and so, for a time, being unaccounted for, accountable only to myself, living my life in secret, accompanied only by whatever dog chose to tail me for a block and by my own meandering thoughts or the scrap of a tune I'd begun humming without being aware of it. The distance from the ball field to home was only a little more than a mile, but anything might happen on that walk. One afternoon, practice ended under menacing slate-gray clouds. A block into my walk, with a thunder crack, the sky opened. Hail, swift and sharp, pelted me. It hurt. But I liked the chill of it and the feel of hailstones melting inside my shirt, trickling down my back. I liked that I was caught in something vast and wild and mindless but something natural, something that happens, something that will end eventually.

On another afternoon, under a cloudless sky, I gave myself a project: I would count each step the whole way home. *One, two, three . . . ten, eleven . . . one hundred and five, one hundred and six . . . one thousand and ninety-nine, ten thousand, ten thousand and one . . . ten thousand and ninety-nine, one million . . .* When I arrived home, I made a proud and excited announcement to the first person I encountered: my father, leaning back in his vinyl-covered recliner in the living room, studying the newspaper.

"Dad?" He looked up. I had his full attention. I was ready to startle him with how smart I'd become, how attuned to the workings of the world. "I just walked home from baseball, and I counted every step. Guess how many it took?"

"I've no idea."

"Two billion and four."

"You don't say," said my accountant father. Then he looked back down at his paper.

30

In 1969, after a dozen years in a difficult job, after eight children, my father must have felt overtaxed, maybe panicky, as if he had lit a match and distractedly let it burn to his fingertips. But it was not his habit to confess such a thing, maybe even to himself. Whatever pressure he was under at work was beginning to show there; he was slipping up, by his own admission to my mother. Maybe he was missing meetings, missing deadlines. At home, as my mother told me years later, he was behaving strangely, erratically, not taking care of himself. I had only a nine-year-old's sense of this: he was Dad, and he was unpredictable, and sometimes this made me wary of him. Terry and Patty were out of the house by now, but six of us remained, including the two little girls, Kim and Erica, only three and one. We were a huge brood, and our mother, without a dependable husband to help her, was overwhelmed. But she kept our clothes clean and pressed and patched; she packed our school lunch boxes and set them on the kitchen counter each morning, ready for us to grab them as we headed out; she was always there, with a box of crayons and colored construction paper for our art projects, with bandages for our wounds

For several evenings in a row, our father would return home from work in time for dinner; he would engage with our mother in civil, occasionally droll conversation over the lasagna or scalloped potatoes, and that meant life was good for now. That meant—who knew?—that our parents might begin to be happier with each other and then permanently so. They would make plans to go out one night, just the two of them, and then keep those plans, Dad dressing in a sharp blue suit, slapping on aftershave, and brushing his hair neatly, with a perfect part, Mom donning her best dress and a string of faux pearls. They would dance the evening away, and the sixteen-year-old boy my father had been once, the boy whose eye had been caught by my mother on a high school dance floor, would come to life again. He would glide and spin with cheer and conviction, even though—as my mother saw it—he was a much less able dancer than he thought he was, with defective rhythm. What could that matter when he had that patented move, the magic flourish at the start of each dance: he would slide his big wing-tipped foot forward in a theatrical sweep, his wife, in his arms, deciding to keep quiet about how silly it looked. Sometimes, on a weekend evening after dinner, suddenly in the mood for a show, Dad would pull down from a closet shelf the heavy slide projector, set it up in the rec room, roll down a white screen, and show old family photos. *Click.* "That's the Olympic National Forest, Mom sitting pretty on a fallen tree." *Click.* "That's the big snow of—what was it, '56? It took days to dig the car out." *Click.* "Oops—a blank." *Click. Click.* "Those are the girls at Yellowstone. Old Faithful's behind them."

Then, one night, without having called to warn our mother, our father would arrive home from work hours late, long after the family had eaten. He would find, in the dark kitchen, in the warm oven, his dinner wrapped in foil and, in the living room, my mother sitting alone, resolving this time either to hold her tongue or to let him have it. Then the next night, and the next, he would not come home at all. After arriving the following morning, he would sleep all day. He was there but not there, a husband but not a husband, a father but not a father. If my parents both were home and both out of bed, they kept a distance from each other, speaking, if at all, with stiff courtesy or thinly veiled resentment. They must have become experts at reading each other's tone: the accusation delivered as ironic apology, the agonized plea for empathy expressed as sarcastic gratitude. We children could read the weather of any room our parents were in. We sensed when a squall was about to erupt and retreated to the solitude and safety of our separate bedrooms.

Typically, though, our parents did not scream at each other; they seethed and brooded. There were shouting matches and slammed doors, but more prevalent and unyielding was the simple heavy tension in the air, the tension of the unsaid, maybe of the unsayable. We all walked quietly through that house, a tightness in our chests.

In 1967, after my father had crashed his car, my mother urged him to seek counseling. But he refused. He was a hard worker; he was disciplined. And he wasn't the type to spill his guts to a stranger. If something needed fixing, he would fix it himself.

But he couldn't, or didn't, and my mother began to realize that a time would come, maybe soon, when he would be of absolutely no help to her, when the responsibility for the children would be hers alone. She made up her mind: she would go back to school. She had always regretted not having been able to finish college, and now she felt not just a vague wistfulness about it but an urgent sense of necessity. Somehow, eventually—because of the end of her marriage or the end of her husband's ability to function in the workplace—she would have to earn a salary. She would need a degree and marketable skills.

My father didn't object to her going to school; he just didn't understand why she needed to, and he didn't want to pay for it. As long as she could pay for the tuition out of her household allowance, he told her, she could do as she pleased. She began taking night courses at a community college. Like many other older women with families in the late 1960s, she found herself sitting with pen poised above an open notebook in freshman composition and Psych 101, among slouching, lank-haired students half her age. Before leaving home for class—before donning her long plaid coat, wrapping her hair in a sheer scarf knotted at the chin, slipping her purse over her shoulder, and grabbing her books—she would set out food for our dinner, with notes attached: instructions for when to put the dishes in the oven, at what temperature, and for how long. Peggy was fifteen, the oldest of the children still in the house, and she was happy to help, happy to babysit her five younger brothers and sisters while our mother was taking notes on Freud's patients' dreams.

My mother probably didn't see herself as being swept up in the women's movement—she was being swept up by the exigencies of her own uncertain marriage and by her determination to make the most of the nimble mind she had been given. But it turned out that women of her age across the country were having a similar experience: they had been married for two decades, devoting their creative energies and affections to their homes—to their husbands and children; now those children were older, maybe off on their own, their husbands were inattentive, undependable, or gone, and the constrictive social world of the 1950s and early 1960s was crumbling.

Around the time my mother began going to school, she began visiting an attorney. The two acts seem related: they were calculated steps—maybe desperate ones—designed to improve her life and the family's life. And maybe save her marriage. Sifting through letters as I walked from our mailbox to the house, I noticed long, slim envelopes addressed to my mother, sent by a law firm. Kevin noticed the letters, too; they lay, menacingly, for days on the Formica countertop of the kitchen. It was probably Kevin who explained to me their significance: Mom and Dad might be divorcing. He deduced that before our mother told us.

The thought of divorce terrified me: I could not bear to lose what I was used to, even if it was untenable instability and unease.

Decades later, my mother told me that she did file for divorce but that she had no intention of going through with it and concealed this fact from my father. She needed to file in order to be granted a legal separation; she wanted him out of the house, out into the open air, away from the family, away from her, where he could think more clearly, where he could learn what being alone, as the man he had become, felt like. Filing divorce papers must have been excruciating for her. She was no longer keeping their problems between the two of them. She had gone to an outside party for help—and her strategy was, in effect, to gain leverage over her husband by making him believe she was willing to divorce him. She had to use that lie to shock him into admitting the truth that he needed help. His wry humor, the goofy wisecracks that had served as a defense against trouble and had charmed her in their early years, wasn't working anymore. It had become wearying: a sign of him ignoring their problems—ignoring his problems.

When he was served the papers, according to my mother, he was stunned. He and she were Catholic; they believed that marriage is for life; they had vowed so before a priest twenty years before. His own Catholic mother, Bernadine, had not divorced Nat even after years of him being missing. From the first time, years before, that my mother had broached the topic, my father had refused to consider that Bernadine might have benefited from ending her marriage. A separation from his own wife? Maybe a divorce? The possibility apparently hadn't crossed his mind.

My mother told him that if he would get help, she would not proceed with the divorce. She wasn't merely asking this time; she was giving him an ultimatum. There was something wrong in his head, something haunting him. If he wanted the marriage to survive, he needed to see a psychiatrist.

So he did. And he left the house, moving into a small, nondescript apartment a few miles away. If someone asked where our father was, our mother instructed us, we should say he was on a business trip.

The trip lasted almost two years. He had become such a phantom, flickering and fading at the edges of the family, that I don't recall our home feeling much different when he was gone. It was just less tense, and instead of wondering every evening whether my father would return home in time for dinner, I sometimes wondered whether he would ever return. My mother never visited him at his apartment. Once or twice, it was arranged that we children would visit him. I recall being dropped off, with Kevin and Dana, for a weekend hour or two at his apartment. The place was impersonally furnished: off-white walls without a picture upon them; a cheap sofa upholstered in some solid color—lime green or burgundy; a spare coffee table of dark wood, nothing on it but the gifts he had bought us to mark our brief reunion: one big Time-Life illustrated nature book for each of us—*The Universe, Early Man, Animal Behavior.* We knelt around his coffee table, turning the pages, muttering, "Thanks, Dad." Then Terry picked us up and drove us home.

In that apartment that might have been anyone's or no one's, in that sparsely furnished new life in which his obligations had been reduced to just his job and himself, what did our father feel? Maybe overwhelming relief. He had lived with his mother and brothers, then his grandparents, then a platoon of marines in barracks, then his wife and their expanding brood. For the first time in his life, he was alone, absolutely alone. He could wake when he wanted, sleep when he wanted, gaze at the TV all night if it pleased him, eat what he cared to eat, even if it was only hot dogs, canned beans, and frozen dinners. I suspect that he didn't—as my mother had when he was home—weigh each gram of his food with care to ensure a proper blood sugar level. He didn't have to ensure much of anything anymore. He had no yard or house to maintain; if the bathroom faucet dripped, he could call the landlord or, hell, just let it drip. When he arrived home from work, whenever that was, he arrived not to tension and questions but to silence and solitude. He must have felt the power of that. Perhaps, with his life stripped bare, he was able to sense, with clarity and force, what he cared about most, what he needed, what made him feel alive. Without the daily requirement of playing the role of husband and father, maybe whatever was at his core, most truly and crucially, revealed itself to him. I wonder if he looked at it, if he had the courage to do so.

Occasionally, he drove to our house, staying only a minute, long enough to pack a few of us children into the Dodge and take us away somewhere: to a movie, the ice cream parlor, a baseball game. The first summer of the separation was the summer of Woodstock, of men on the moon, of Chappaquiddick, of Manson—but, for me, it was the summer of the Pilots, Seattle's major league team, in their first season. If we could be in the big leagues at last, playing the Yankees and Red Sox, anything was possible. "Go, go, you Pilots, you proud Seattle team," the club's rousing march of a theme song went. "Go go go go go go go go go!"

And they did go: bankrupt, then east. After one year, the Pilots moved to Milwaukee and changed their name. But, for a summer, my tenth summer, even with my family changing, maybe splitting apart forever, I was young enough to have faith in what felt eternal—and still does: that shock of green, the vast sunlit field, as we stepped up the concrete stairs and into the stands; the players in their blinding white uniforms and dark blue caps; the old, stooped usher who studied our father's ticket stub, a ball of sweat hanging from the tip of his nose, wobbling, refusing to fall; our dad with us in the bleacher seats, with a bag of peanuts in the shell and a big beer in a paper cup; and down in the bullpen, fists in their jacket pockets, the Pilots' pitchers—among them Jim Bouton, taking mental notes on the memoir he was writing.

This was the summer the family vacationed, fatherless, at Ocean

Shores, a little Washington beach town. It was chilly and cloudy. My mother in a heavy coat and scarf and six of us children in long pants, we knelt on the beach, heads down, scooping up wet gray sand. The weather didn't matter: we'd driven a long way, we'd come there to have fun, by God, and we were going to play in this sand. We huddled close together, each of us working on his own project, digging a trench or holding packed sand in two hands, trying to make something of it.

This was the summer I was old enough to go to summer camp. It was a Catholic camp—there would be no avoiding Mass. But it was set on a lakeshore, so boating and canoeing were promised, and hiking, and a daily trip to the canteen for a candy bar or bottle of pop of my choosing, and campfires at night and ghost stories. For comfort, I brought along my own pillow with a tiger-print case, black and orange stripes. On the first day, I stepped from the bus with my suitcase and pillow and entered the cabin I would share with a dozen other nine-year-olds. A tall blond boy, slack-jawed and sneering, grabbed the pillow from me, scurried to the open back window, and tossed it out. "Tigermaster!" he yelled. "Tigermaster! Hey, Tigermaster!" The other boys laughed, stopped what they were doing, and gathered near him.

What should I make of this? My cheeks warm, I walked out the front door and around to the back of the cabin. The pillow lay in the high weeds. I picked it up and brought it back inside. The boy yanked it from my hands again and, to the others' glee, held it out the window for a moment, then dropped it, chanting, "Tigermaster! Tigermaster!" Trembling, suppressing tears, I asked him not to do that anymore and retrieved my pillow. He did it again. Then he grew weary of it, plopped onto his bunk, and stared at nothing, flicking his tongue against his top lip.

Later that first day, my assigned counselor, a wiry, crew-cut high-schooler, observed in front of the assembled boys that my hair—which had begun to creep over my ears, Brady Bunch–style—was too long, didn't they agree? Did they have a hippie in their midst? He promised them he would scrounge up some scissors and, that night as I slept, sneak up on me and do what the barber had neglected to do.

I was a Forhan, mired deep in the habit, when unnerved, of retreating into rigidity and good manners; I requested that he not do that, please. Each morning after that, at the bugle's call, I rose immediately and made my bed neatly. After each meal, I brushed my teeth with vigor. I asked the counselor if he needed assistance carrying those dodgeballs. On the last evening before going home, I received an official commendation: the counselor had named me honor camper, the most obedient boy in the cabin.

I had successfully kept my head down—including literally. Throughout the week, whenever I walked toward the boat dock on the lakeshore, I avoided raising my gaze to the top window of the big main lodge. With hushed voices, shaking their heads, the counselors had warned us about a former colleague of theirs, a young man who had worked at the camp a couple of years before, someone who had been quite a jovial fellow, immensely popular, but who had gone absolutely mad. Stark raving. He'd been separated from the rest of the camp, confined to the attic of the lodge. If he got loose, he'd be dangerous. It had happened once already, and the consequences to an innocent camper who'd found himself in the madman's path were something they didn't care to discuss. Occasionally, throughout the week, one of us boys would glimpse, he thought, the silhouette of the insane man materialize in the window, then vanish.

Stay where you are, I thought as I walked past the lodge. *Just stay where you are.*

31

My father was miles away, but who needed him? Who needed parents at all? Our little street was the children's street, the children's world. Squeezed between Puget Sound to the west and Lake Washington to the east, the city of Seattle had rapidly developed northward, and our secluded dead-end street in the far northeast corner of town was lined on both sides with houses now. At the closed-off end, where I had once dropped that lit match, there were no woods at all anymore: just a tract of upturned dirt, a vast construction site, where a final few houses were rising shoulder to shoulder around a cul-de-sac. Adults had bought these homes. Adults would live in them. But we didn't have to think about that. Where once, stepping into the rich shade of dense trees, we imagined we were vanishing into the frontier wilderness, we now called to each other across wide concrete slabs sprouting rebar. We gaped at colossal bulldozers and backhoes, ponderous single-minded beasts, inexorably erasing the landscape we knew. And we loved them: their hugeness, their grinding and grunting, their smokestacks puffing black exhaust, their treads with thick muck stuck to them. Who needed parents? We befriended a bulldozer operator, Nels—someone who would greet us with a grin and a salute as we stood, rapt, at the edge of the work site, who would load up his arms with a pile of scrap lumber and hand it over to us, telling us we ought to build something, too. One evening, the construction crew gone, dusk settling in, my friend William and I strayed, as if pulled by some deep invisible current, up the street to the work site. Nels' bulldozer sat empty, idle. We clambered up and in, plunking ourselves down behind the wheel. We were grown-ups. We were tough and taciturn construction workers. Then we saw what we had half hoped we would not see: the key in the ignition. What choice did we have now? William reached forward and turned the key. The engine sputtered awake. We leaped from the bulldozer, leaving it running, scampered off, and told no one.

Up and down the street, there were yards to frolic in, expanses of grass on which we gathered and had no parents. At dusk in summer, we played a game in which one of us, dubbed the "ghost," tried to tag the rest of us and imprison us in his dungeon. Stepping hesitantly across the grass, holding our breath, or fleeing full-tilt, we played and played as darkness rose and swallowed us. No parents. On drizzly afternoons, in dim basement rooms, we played Twister and Hands Down and Rock 'em Sock 'em Robots or, with a mouthful of Cheez-Its, stared at afternoon reruns of *Gilligan's Island* or *The Jetsons*. No parents. On sunny days, anyone's yard might be good for Slip 'n Slide or Simon Says or fireworks—a children's world, world without end, world of utter fun, except on the day, waving a lit sparkler, I misjudged my reach and slashed Kathy's chest, leaving a thin pink scar, like an embedded worm. Our street was a gradual, steady incline, ideal for picking up speed on a sled or a bike, ideal for rides of unabated pleasure, except that morning when Jennifer, at the bottom of the hill, steered her hurtling Yankee Clipper into a parked truck, and her spleen exploded, and her dad jogged from the house and picked her up and carried her, limp and moaning, to his station wagon, and except that Saturday when my feet couldn't find the spinning pedals on my five-speed and I stopped my momentum by slamming my head against a mailbox, then woke on the couch, my mother's palm warm and soft on my forehead.

One afternoon, in the backyard next door, I met a gangly, sandy-haired high school boy, Bill, who introduced me to a new game: pickle-ball. It was cartoonish and amusing, a kind of cross between Ping-Pong and badminton involving a paddle, a net, and a Wiffle ball. The neighbors were holding a party for the man who had invented the game: a moderate Republican—there were such things then—running for Congress. The house was full of his well-heeled supporters, and their kids, including Bill, decamped to the backyard. I didn't stand a chance against Bill on the court: he was four years older and an old hand at pickleball. However, the budding and permanent passion of Bill—who had come to the party with his parents, Mr. and Mrs. Gates—was computers.

Kevin liked to fiddle with machines, too. In his downstairs bedroom across the hall from mine, he sat contentedly for hours among wires and switches and capacitors and batteries and bulbs and circuit boards, teaching himself how they functioned and how they connected. He was testing reality with his own hands, his own mind, trying to get to the bottom of it. Kevin was the one who, two decades later, would prepare for every Christmas by inventing and painstakingly constructing an original gift for his girlfriend—some intricate gizmo with little purpose but to charm: a miniature scene of skaters on a pond who would move when it was plugged in; an alarm clock that, when it went off, played one of their favorite Graham Parker songs: *I want to wake up next to you. . . .*

I had been lucky, when Patty moved out of the house, to inherit her room: the one beneath our parents' and therefore identical in size and shape—the largest of the kids' rooms, half buried in the earth, with a window that offered a ground-level view of the backyard: the wooden steps that led down from the deck, the small irregular rectangle of lawn, the raised plot of cherry and apple trees. I kept to myself in that room, listening to Top 40 music on my transistor. It did not occur to me that any other music mattered—or that there was any other music. The songs were playing nonstop on the radio, after all, and playing nonstop in my head, making a pleasing shape, and some sense, of reality: "O-o-h Child," "No Matter What," "Cracklin' Rosie." After saving my lawn-mowing money and a few months of allowance, I had enough to buy a thirty-dollar portable record player at the drugstore. That gave me a reason to buy records: mostly 45s, starting with "Indian Reservation" by the Raiders. From friends and church bazaars, I bought used records by the Beatles and Three Dog Night and the Turtles. My enthusiasm had a scholarly, or at least archival, component: I set aside a college-ruled notebook in which to transcribe the lyrics of my favorite songs. I wrote about how the world is a ball of confusion. I wrote about how a poor, dying man burdens his son with a reminder that he is the only one left now to ensure that the family survives. With Casey Kasem counting down the top hits each week on the radio, I felt the necessity of ranking the records in my bedroom—of determining my personal cosmology. I still own my single of "Penny Lane" and "Strawberry Fields Forever" with a small numeral *1* written in pencil on the picture sleeve.

I had been issued an acoustic guitar—even that late, with the 1960s over and the folk boom having waned, it was almost compulsory that middle-class adolescents own a guitar on which to strum Pete Seeger tunes. With the aid of a beginner's book, I learned a few chords. And I started writing songs that sounded like what someone would write if he were pretending to write songs. A blue-collar anthem:

> *I'm a workingman, I get a workingman's pay,*
> *Even though I work an eleven-hour day.*
> *O Lord, O Lord, there must be another way.*

A piercing insight into social injustice, inspired by a poster:

> *There's a child, she's hungry,*
> *Hasn't had any food for days*

And she's about to die.
But people don't realize what's going on.
They don't want to take the time.
But who's going to save the children?

A lament in which, if I remember correctly, I was imagining myself as a black person:

Yesterday I came to this town.
People stood and stared, they didn't make a sound.
They just said, "You'd better leave. We don't want any fight."
They just wanted me out of their sight.
But I don't want any sympathy, I don't want any tears.
I've been unaccepted in many places over the years.
It seems I've gone this road before many times in the past,
So I'd best get out of here and hope this time's the last.

Most of my melodies made prominent use of the E-minor chord, a heartsick sound I could make with only two fingers.

I did not share the songs with anyone. Maybe I feared they weren't good enough. More probably I kept them private because they *were* private: I sensed that, in them, I was most nakedly myself, most free to try my feelings on for size without risking censure, even if that meant pretending to be a black man.

I was recognizing, more and more, a distinct difference between what I felt and what I did, between what I imagined and created behind the closed door of my bedroom and what I professed to care about in public. I was discovering what mattered most to me and keeping silent about it.

32

For my eleventh birthday, I had a date with my father. I hadn't seen him in weeks, maybe months, but we arranged that he would drive to the house after dinner and take me out for the night. My mother had decided I was old enough to dress smartly for the occasion—old enough, she said, to own a decent overcoat, so she bought me one: calf-length, charcoal gray. Before my father arrived, she made sure that I put on my best shirt and pants and that I polished my shoes. On our way out, my father and I paused in the doorway of the house so she could take a photograph. What did my parents say to each other in that moment? Probably something brief, safe, and not impolite. In my new coat, I looked stiff and small and affected; I looked like an idea. *Little Dad.*

What did my father and I do first? Stop off for an ice cream sundae, maybe, and for harmless, perfunctory talk about how school was going? I remember only that I felt pleased to be with him after so much time apart, and hopeful—he was still my dad; his life still intersected with mine—and I felt a little awkward, conscious of the formality of the occasion, of its being a plan that we were executing. How did my father feel? Pleased, too, maybe, and hopeful and a little awkward. The central event of the evening was a trip to a downtown movie theater to see *Beneath the Planet of the Apes,* about a world turned upside down, with apes—the self-styled superior species—ruling humans. We watched the movie's astronaut hero journey underground in search of his lost colleague, Charlton Heston. We watched the astronaut struggle to communicate with his companion on the quest, Heston's beautiful, mute female mate from whom he'd been separated. But we witnessed no stirring, permanent reunion of the lovers—only, in the end, a battle between an army of apes and a race of mutant humans who worshipped a doomsday bomb, the one that could eradicate the planet. In the last scene, Heston, shot and dying—Heston, a believer in amity, rationality, and forbearance but seeing no solution to the interminable stupid stalemate between civilizations—with his bloody hand pushed the button on the bomb and blew up the whole damned dirty thing.

We stood up. I tugged my new overcoat back on, and my dad drove me home.

The next month, a second Christmas passed without our father in the house, and then my parents began speaking to each other on the phone, calmly and kindly, not as antagonists but as partners with a plan. My father was saying the right things. He had changed. Partly with a psychiatrist's help, he could see things more clearly. His health had improved; the psychiatrist had prescribed medication, and he was taking proper care of his diabetes. Still, when my mother asked about the particular source of his troubles, he spoke vaguely, dismissively. What was his condition, exactly? Had there been a diagnosis? How could she help him? "I'm fine now," he would say. "Let's leave it at that." She called his psychiatrist. "I'm sorry, Mrs. Forhan," he replied. "Everything you're asking me: it's confidential. I can't speak to you about it." If her husband seemed newly stable, even chipper, she would just have to trust that there were reasons for it. She would need to have faith that he would stay that way.

"Okay," she told him, "you can come home."

He had done what my mother had required of him: he had sought professional help, and now he was better. After he moved back in with us, he stopped seeing the psychiatrist and stopped taking medication. He was a grown man, a responsible man: he could do the rest himself.

My happiest memories of my father during the next couple of years involve a single ritual: from time to time, having returned home from work and shared dinner with the family, he would say, "You kids interested in seeing the Sonics tonight?" We always were—*we* almost invariably being Kevin and Dana and me. Peggy was usually content to stay at home with our mother and help take care of Kim and Erica, who were too young for evenings out.

The Sonics were Seattle's professional basketball team; they were in just their fourth year and had never come close to having a winning record, but they were the only major pro team in town and were a plucky, endearing bunch of underdogs. On the roster were a thoughtful, soft-spoken point guard doing double duty as coach; a floppy-haired sharpshooter; a backup forward with a good jump shot and a bad stutter; and a twenty-one-year-old phenomenon and renegade, undrafted and underage by league rules, who'd leaped to the team from another league and, to set foot on the Sonics' court, needed the permission of the Supreme Court. The first thing I remember doing with my father after he came back to the family was driving down the freeway on a February evening in his white Dodge, along with my brother and sister, heading for a game. It was a special game we were going to: the team had designated this Tom Meschery Night. Meschery was a power forward—a fan favorite—who had announced his retirement. He was a bruiser, a brawler, a fearless enforcer under the boards, and there was something exotic about him. He was an immigrant whose Russian parents had escaped their homeland during the Bolshevik Revolution; he sported a thick handlebar mustache; and he was a fledgling poet. The year before, he had published a collection called *Over the Rim*, on the cover of which he was pictured in game action, crouched tigerlike. Forty years after Tom Meschery Night, I was talking with the poet Mark Strand, who taught in Seattle when I was young, and I mentioned Meschery. "Oh, I knew Tom," Mark said. The two of them had struck up a friendship when Meschery was with the Sonics, and Mark later advised Meschery that he owed it to himself and his writing to attend the Iowa Writers' Workshop, which he did.

On that February night in 1971, as my father and brother and sister and I entered the Coliseum, we were handed two souvenirs: a paper program entitled "A Poet in Motion" and a false handlebar mustache made of thick black construction paper, shaped so that we might slide two hooks into our nostrils and it would stay there.

Later, in his warm-up outfit, Meschery strode onto the court to receive his gifts of thanks: plaques and trophies, a set of crystal, a color television, an electric typewriter, a round-the-world trip for him and his wife. As we watched him walk to mid-court to be honored, I lifted my false mustache to my nostrils and attached it; the paper pinched and tickled. Kevin attached his mustache. Dana, too, and our father. I gazed around the Coliseum, row upon row, section upon section: ten thousand mustachioed people, men and women, boys and girls. It was stupid; it was beautiful. For a moment, all of us were poets. All of us were big-hearted rebounders.

33

In Scouts, I was now a Webelo. "We'll Be Loyal Scouts," the name meant. I enjoyed the natty uniform: the golf-style cap and the three woven strands of gold, red, and green on which I pinned my activity badges—the little tree for forestry; the interlocking gears for engineering; the sleek sedan for traveling.

I liked the evenings when my father—with a plan and the tools and skills to complete it—stood at the end of his workbench downstairs, eyeing a small rectangular block of wood in the grip of his vise. He was helping me prepare for the Pinewood Derby; each year, the Scout pack set aside a Saturday for pitting each boy's miniature custom-made car against the others', letting gravity pull them down a long, sloped track in the church gym. Each Scout brought a car he had built with the help of his father: they had carved and shaped the block of pine with saw and rasp, measured its length and width, weighed it to the gram, sanded it, spray-painted it, set it aside to dry, then added a second coat, attached axles and plastic wheels, delicately applied decals, drilled holes, and filled them with lead weights so the car was swift but not so heavy as to break the rules, which were rigid and many.

Every year, the car my father helped me bring into being seemed perfect, impossibly so: aerodynamically sleek and gleaming, its wheels spinning freely at a touch. Every year, the car flamed out in the first heat. For the hour that followed, my father and I slouched in metal folding chairs along the wall, watching with polite interest as heat after heat narrowed the field to the eventual winning car, to the smiling dad and son who must have known something essential that we did not. Maybe they had cheated. But winning wasn't everything: the true satisfaction was in the preparation, in the construction of a car you could be proud of regardless of how it fared in competition, my father might have said, and didn't.

Most of the time, in Webelos, I was on my own. And the whole thing—the uninterrupted succession of pleasant rituals—started to give me the creeps: buttoning up my uniform shirt and tugging on my cap; sitting in den meetings with a dozen other boys, pledging and praying with them, proclaiming in unison, in song, what we should do if we were happy and we knew it; hunching with them over a long table, cutting and gluing colored construction paper into Christmas ornaments and spraying fake snow on them from an aerosol can. I was part of an organization, of a scheme for growing up and becoming an honorable citizen, that didn't feel right because—well, I was starting to sense, because it was organized, and because it was a scheme.

My father was a joiner. He had signed up for the society of altar boys, for the marines, for the Air Force Reserve; he had graduated from college; he had joined the National Association of Accountants—he had become his chapter's president. The first ten years of his life had been ragged and structureless, his gone father, drowned brother, and dead mother instructing him in the fragility of families and of plans. But the path he traveled after that was through institutions of certainty and stability. It might be said that he worked hard at playing it safe, employing his considerable intelligence and industry to succeed at tasks that were clearly defined and unquestioningly valued by whatever social group he made himself a part of. One of those groups was us—the big Irish Catholic family he created with my mother, a family he must have hoped would be different from the one he knew as a boy: dependable, permanent. One reason to believe so was the woman—the girl—he had chosen, by luck or some mix of conscious and unconscious design, to be his wife. My mother, unlike his parents, would stick it out with him; she was strong and steadfast—permanently loyal to the ideal of marriage and to the actual marriage she was living in, however profoundly it might test her. As my father pursued, indefatigably, his safe, conventional path, it defined him as an accountant, a successful professional, a faithful parishioner, a husband, and a father. I wonder, within those selves, where the fatherless, motherless, brotherless little boy was. What had become of little Eddie, of Bud?

In organized groups—a baseball team, a Cub Scout pack, a congregation at Mass—I was beginning to feel vaguely false, peripheral, simultaneously in the group and outside it, observing it, observing myself, or only a part of myself, within it. Maybe my father felt that way, too. In fourth grade, because my friends were doing it, I chose a musical instrument to learn and joined the school band. By sixth grade, though, I had wearied of the clarinet. I was tired of lugging the thing around, the black case bumping against my leg; tired of the saliva, all that licking of the reed; tired of the beginner's repertoire—"Arapahoe Warriors," "Go Tell Aunt Rhody"; tired of the gruffness of Mr. Holbrook, the band director, tall and angular, with shaggy blond hair and a confident willingness to wear black-and-white large-checked pants. He had the habit of seizing my instrument from my hands and, with his wide mouth and big jaw, blowing into it so I could hear how a real clarinetist plays, then returning it to me with his spittle still on it. I realized that I had only been pretending to be a clarinetist—it had seemed an appealing and acceptable identity, so I had tried it on. I quit and asked my mother to return my rented instrument.

Kevin felt restless in groups, too: he had made it to Webelos but not beyond. I followed his lead. When I told the Scoutmaster I was quitting, he was bewildered. "But you're a good Scout, a model Scout," he said. "You're a Tenderfoot now. You could be Eagle Scout material."

No, I couldn't. I was a boy who liked to shoot free throws in his backyard by himself and to sit on his bed with a guitar and to curl up under the covers at night, transistor pressed to his ear, listening for the next thing he might decide he loved, alone.

34

Bins of glittering nails; sacks of grass seed; hammers, wrenches, and handsaws hanging on hooks; a row of bright bicycles, pink, blue, and yellow, the scent of their new rubber tires an intoxicant; jars and jars of hard, striped candy in cellophane—strawberry, root beer, coconut, sarsaparilla: this was McVicar's hardware store. This was my father, who was the reason I went there. When I try to bring him back to life in memory, he is squatting in an aisle at McVicar's, gazing at a jar of putty in his hand. He is standing between two sawhorses on our patio, letting a metal tape measure snap back into its case as he picks up a pencil to mark a spot on a two-by-four. He is hauling a bucket of dark gray paint up a ladder that leans against the house. He is recruiting Kevin and me to help him with a summer project. In the backyard, he has built a long wooden vat in which to dip dozens of narrow boards and stain them before he fashions them into a slatted roof for our deck. We slide a little wire hoop over the end of each board, lower it into the vat, then lift it, lay it on a drop cloth and let it dry, then do it again, giving it a second coat. "Good job today, boys. Let's clean up and head on in."

Near the carport, in the storage shed, my father kept the supplies he needed to maintain the family cars: motor oil, spark plugs, Turtle Wax and chamois rags, brushes and sponges, an air pressure gauge, a tin of grease, replacement bulbs and air filters, a low rolling wooden creeper to slide beneath a lifted car. On the top shelf in this shed is where, one summer day, I found a battered, well-thumbed paperback novel. It was called *The Seven Minutes*, and on its cover was the gauzy image of a naked woman on her back, knees raised and spread slightly, her right arm lifted to her head. What was this book doing in the shed? Was my father hiding it there? Or was this merely the kind of thing he liked to read, and he kept it outside while working so he could make a few pages of progress during cigarette breaks?

"That's how long it takes to have sex," my brother told me. "Seven minutes. That's why it's called *The Seven Minutes*."

It was Kevin who had revealed to me, a year or so before, why men have penises and women vaginas. I had scoffed; the notion was preposterous. But then I began to think about it—and I have rarely stopped thinking about it since.

Of course my parents had sex. One remark that I overheard confirmed that they were still at it, whatever *it* was, exactly. Not long after they reunited, they slipped back into a familiar pattern, engaging in tense, silent standoffs interrupted by fragile, tentative truces and occasional eruptions of enraged denunciation. One evening they were arguing in their bedroom, loud enough that snatches of angry language carried through their door and down the hall. "Even during intercourse . . ." I heard my mother complain.

Even during intercourse *what*? If I heard the rest of the sentence, I don't remember it. It was enough to have heard my mother say *intercourse*—enough to make me stop what I was doing, or stop whatever I was pretending to do as I tried to ignore that my parents were fighting. She did not say *fucking*. She did not say *making love*. She said, "Even during intercourse." The word she uttered after that phrase must have been an accusing *you* or a lamenting *I*, but in the passion of her fury she employed the clinical terminology of a junior high health textbook. Maybe it was because of her Scandinavian reserve. Maybe it was because of her Catholicism. Maybe it was because she knew her children might be listening, so she was wary in her choice of words, even in her rage. Maybe it was because she'd never had sex other than with her unreliable and secretive husband, and she could not recognize what they did as fucking or making love. Intercourse, though: she could testify to that.

It was as if there was something essential in my father's mind—something essential in his life—that he would not share with his wife, let alone with his children. Sometimes, sitting with him in his car as he held the wheel, we felt him being both there and not there, both with and without us. One summer he hired Peggy to work in his downtown office, cleaning and organizing the storeroom where his firm's records were kept. Every afternoon he would drive her home, and Peggy would sit nervously as he steered and accelerated erratically and as, manically and strangely, he narrated the drive, as if he had to confirm for himself what he was doing or as if he could think of nothing else to say to his teenage daughter: "There's Third Avenue. There's Fourth. And here's the road we take—here we go, turning left." When they reached the freeway, he would sometimes drive too slowly, forty miles an hour, traffic whizzing past on both sides. *It's better than going too fast*, Peggy would tell herself. *It's okay. We'll get through this.* Had he been drinking? Was his blood sugar low? Or was his mind simply off by itself somewhere?

One steamy summer morning, he drove several of us kids miles out of town to a berry farm. We spent an hour or two in the fields, fanning out, choosing a row and kneeling in the moist soil, picking strawberries, plunking them into wooden baskets, the sun warm on the backs of our necks. Then we loaded the baskets into the car trunk and headed home, along a two-lane highway, up a mild incline. Sitting in the front passenger seat, I felt that something was wrong: the car was gaining speed too quickly, then continuing to accelerate, my father silent, sitting stiffly. I peered down; his foot was pressed to the floor. Should I say something? Probably not: my father, not I, was the one who knew how to drive, and he was not a person whose behavior you questioned out loud. And then we were careening off the road, the car lurching, bouncing, slamming into a ditch.

For a moment, there was silence. Then, from behind, Kevin spoke. "Dad, are you all right?"

"Yes."

"Chris, are you all right?"

"Yeah."

"Dana?"

"I'm okay."

"Everyone's okay?"

"Yes."

I don't remember how the police were informed of the accident, but an officer arrived, and my father explained to him what had happened: he'd had a diabetic reaction. The officer radioed for a tow truck. "Oh," he added, "and bring a Hershey Bar"—my father needed a quick intake of sugar. We waited and waited, leaning against the car or sitting in the roadside grass, my father drumming his fingers against his knee, waiting for chocolate.

Later, it occurred to us that, the entire time, the trunk of our car had been full of sweet strawberries.

Especially when he was away from home, away from a regulated schedule and quick access to the right foods, my father risked such plummeting: becoming stubborn and irritable and reckless, hands shaking, vision blurring, mouth shutting tight or chattering away.

Kevin remembers one evening, when he was fourteen, accompanying our father to the neighborhood movie theater two miles from home. After the movie, as they were walking to the car, Kevin noticed our father acting strangely: speaking quickly and as if to himself, gesturing with exaggerated, erratic movements. They got into the car and started driving through the dark streets.

"Dad?" Kevin said. "Are you okay?"

"Yes, yes. I'm all right. I'm all right." But he was swerving in and out of his lane. Then he was driving down the middle of the street, in the turn lane.

"Are you sure, Dad? Are you okay?"

"I'm okay. Just read me the street signs. Help me out. Tell me where we are."

"One-hundred-seventeenth Street . . . One-hundred-fifteenth . . . One-hundred-thirteenth . . ." Kevin was panicking. "Dad—"

"Just read me the street signs!"

Street by street, with our father frenzied, angry, near-blind in the dark, and with Kevin terrified and desperate to stay calm—or to appear calm—they managed to find their way safely home. Our father pulled the car up the driveway, shifted into park, and said to Kevin, "Threw a scare into you, didn't I?"

My brother fled into the house.

Our father must have felt sorry about what had happened, maybe a touch ashamed, but he didn't say so to Kevin. He wouldn't have; he probably wouldn't have known how. What he did do was ask, a week later, whether Kevin wanted to see a movie again. Maybe it was his way of apologizing. Or maybe it was his way of pretending that nothing had happened: of erasing that frightening ride home and replacing it with a second one in which he was a different Dad, calm and responsible.

"A movie?" Kevin said. "I'll see." Then he sought out Peggy to ask if she'd like to come along.

Another father might have recognized the fear he had put into his son, might have recognized that he owed him an apology and an explanation. Another father might have talked with him calmly, reasonably, about the challenges he faced as a diabetic and the difficulty of maintaining the proper level of blood sugar. He might have said what he could to reassure his boy.

Our father punished Kevin for his fear. "If you need your sister to come with us," he said, "then we won't go. If you're afraid to go with me alone, forget it. I don't want to take you to the movies."

On our many after-dinner excursions to Sonics games, I recall no frightening driving. I remember the rousing feeling of freedom as Kevin, Dana, and I rushed to finish our dinners, grabbed our coats, then stepped out together into the twilight. I remember how, after backing the Dart down the driveway and into the street, our father pulled the lighter out of the dash and touched it to the tip of the Tareyton between his lips; I remember the smoke filled the car—the pine-scented air freshener, a flat green cardboard tree dangling from the dash, unable to compete with my father's exhalations. I remember we watched the Sonics lose to the Bulls and beat the Bucks and lose to the Lakers, for whom it was the thirtieth win in a row; afterward, I lingered among a throng of fans outside the locker room on the chance that I would glimpse a star, and I spotted Wilt Chamberlain, in street clothes, striding swiftly toward me, looming large, a giant, then his plate of a hand steered me out of his way. I remember that this made me feel rapturously irrelevant. I remember we cheered the Sonics' beloved player-coach, Lenny Wilkens, on a special night when the team honored him; I remember, eight months later, we cheered him again, cheered him after the Sonics had stripped him of his coaching duties and traded him, outraging the fans—we stood and applauded when he came back to town with his new team, we cheered him to victory over the home team that had betrayed him, we did not want ever to stop cheering. I remember the comfort, while our cheering lasted, of knowing that I was feeling and thinking what my father surely felt and thought. We were believing in something, experiencing something, together, at the same time. Yet I remember, through all of this, all of these evenings out, not a single topic of conversation with my father, although we must have talked, we certainly said something. I remember, at the end of these evenings, with the post-game show on the car radio, he drove us back up the freeway, then nosed his Dart into its place in the carport, crushed his cigarette out in the ashtray, turned off the ignition, and announced, "That's all she wrote," the engine ticking.

I wanted to be Lenny Wilkens. I wanted to be Spencer Haywood, Jerry West, Oscar Robertson, Walt Frazier. I was skinny and butterfingered, with no natural athletic gifts, but I had a dream. I would one day be a Sonic: that was an identity I would happily be defined by; that was a group I would join without question. In our backyard, where my father had sunk a four-by-four wooden pole into cement, with a backboard and basket bolted to the top, I dribbled and drove and shot for hours at a time and, because of the wacky configuration of the court, inadvertently developed a grotesque and largely useless one-dimensional game. The court was our patio: an asymmetrical strip of concrete with a large patch of gravel on one side and, on the other, an overhanging deck. I could not drive to the basket from the left: that was the side of the gravel and a rocky incline up to the lawn and a set of concrete steps. I could rarely complete a layup from the right: that's where the deck was. I practiced against Kevin, but, unless he was in a rare, giving mood, he always beat me. He was two years older and almost a head taller; when he had the ball, all he had to do—so long as he wasn't made weary by the tedium—was dribble and dribble and dribble, backing patiently and deliberately into me until he reached the basket, then turn and lay in the ball over my head. When I had the ball, the complicated series of obstacles—the deck, the post holding up the deck, the gravel, the patio concrete's cracks and divots, my lanky brother with his long arms raised—allowed me only two options: a sudden underhanded reverse layup from the right or a wild, blind flick of the ball over my head from the left. Out of necessity, I perfected those shots. When I played in the backyard against someone shorter and slower—ideally, my six-year-old or four-year-old sister—I was a phenom: I was Connie Hawkins; I was Earl Monroe. When I played on a regulation court, on a real team, I ran around without design, my arms outstretched, my palms open, wondering why no one was passing me the ball.

I was in Maple Leaf Elementary now, a public school. What with my parents' separation and my mother's uncertainty about the family's future, she had decided to save the tuition money. At Maple Leaf, I met a new best friend: Paul Ringo. Two Beatles! What were the odds? All I had to do now was meet someone named John George. Paul's father was the pastor of the Lutheran church across the street from school, but nothing about Paul indicated that he had Jesus on his mind. Instead, he thought about the Beatles (natch) and Creedence Clearwater Revival and the Grass Roots and the Nitty Gritty Dirt Band. For his eleventh-birthday party, Paul sent me an invitation that read, "There's just a few things coming my way this time around now"—James Taylor lyrics appropriated for the purpose of reminding his friends to bring presents.

Also on Paul's mind, thankfully, was basketball. He, too, hoped to be a Sonic. We got into the habit—the obsession—of playing against each other after school on the playground court. We went head-to-head in an unending championship series; one of us might be ahead in games won, 43–25, but he couldn't get complacent. No one in this series was ever conclusively the victor. Always there was the possibility of a comeback, a weeklong hot streak, an unprecedented shift of momentum that would make the series interesting again. We played one-on-one, but in our minds each of us was an entire team, with uniforms, logos, arenas adorned with championship banners, and legions of fans who lived and died by our fortunes. The name of Paul's team was inevitable: the Ringo Stars. To document the existence of my team, I clipped a full-page photo from *Sport* magazine: John Havlicek racing downcourt, ball gripped before him in both hands, preparing to pass. From a copy of my recent school picture, I meticulously scissored my head and glued it over Havlicek's. Onto his jersey I glued a thin slip of paper that obscured CELTICS and replaced it with the name of my team.

That evening I showed the picture to my father. Would he be willing to make a dozen or so photocopies at the office the next day? He grinned, nodded, and slipped into his briefcase the doctored photo, the souvenir poster of the Forhan Phantoms.

35

One night each year, the school was not itself: the night of the spring carnival. The fifth-grade classroom became a pond in which to fish for prizes, the second-grade classroom a maze of high cardboard walls, the kindergarten classroom a candlelit haunted house with narrow corridors of black curtains and a bowlful of mushy pasta—human brains to plunge your fingers into. One year word spread quickly about the fortune-teller in my classroom: she was Valerie Harper's sister. Really, I was told: Rhoda from TV had a real sister, and she was there, with beaded headdress and bangles and crystal ball, telling fortunes, or pretending to. I liked it all, the tangle of it: the mingling of the fictional, of Rhoda and the fortune-teller, with the real, the woman who was truly there and truly a TV star's sister—and my classroom that, for this night, was not a classroom. And me, whatever I was.

The grown-up world, inhabited by Valerie Harper's sister and my teachers and my parents and those strangers onto whose porches I flung the afternoon paper in the dusk, remained inscrutable, although I lived within it, or alongside it. I did not fully comprehend the messages it sent. One weekend, a few of us kids tagged along as our dad drove downtown to his grandmother's apartment. Grandma Carey, we were told, had decided to get rid of a bunch of her belongings, little things she had no use for but that children might cherish. She would like us to have them—Grandma

Carey, who normally seemed indifferent to us, even silently disdainful. Who knew what treasures might soon be ours to divvy up: a conch shell with the sound of the ocean trapped inside it? Bright strands of beads? Books about adventurous orphan boys? Postcards from lands across the sea? This day was one of those unearned and sudden gifts of childhood, like the occasional day when our father thought, oh, what the heck, he'd split his big bowl of spare change among us, and we could buy whatever we wanted with the coins, a Big Hunk or candy cigarettes or a Matchbox car. As we drove home from her apartment, Grandma came with us, her big, mysterious cardboard box in the trunk. Then, while she sat in the living room with my mother, chatting, I waited quietly in the next room. I felt myself being mature, being patient and considerate. I kept waiting. I waited and waited. Finally, I could take it no longer. I entered the living room and approached my mother. "Mom," I said, "when are we going to look at Grandma's things and decide who gets what?"

Grandma Carey glared at me. "What a selfish child!" she said.

I understood immediately that I had been misled, that she had never intended to give us a thing. Had my parents misinterpreted her intentions, or had they spoken of them imprecisely enough that I happily misread them to my benefit? Regardless, I felt myself suddenly, and merely, a child: judged unfairly—and helpless to defend myself.

At such a time, the world of grown-ups seemed to be populated by a wholly different species, one whose customs and interests were arcane. There was something important that adults knew, and they weren't telling. At the parish picnic every summer, while the kids lurched along in the three-legged race or potato-sack race or gripped a thick rope for tug-of-war, the grown-ups were the ones on the periphery, the moms keeping watch on us with half an eye, peeling Saran wrap off big bowls of macaroni salad and melon balls, speaking mysteriously to one another, laughing and nodding. The dads were pressing burgers flat on the grill or gathering in a circle in the distance, smoking, flicking ashes, eyeing the trees, or they were slicing twine from bales, strewing hay on the ground, calling the children over to sprawl in it, then circling us, tossing coins toward the hay and laughing as we scrambled for them: dimes, nickels, quarters, sometimes whole dollars; they kept coming—here, then here—a bright coin, then another, descending upon us, spinning, glittering in the sun; we stretched our whole bodies toward them, toward our fathers' offerings.

Oh, to be older, to be the one with a pocket full of change, the one with a lighter in his shirt pocket and a hand on the wheel. The summer of my thirteenth year, the most I could do was be the attentive and clever older brother. Kim and Erica were six and four and bored, standing on the back lawn in pigtails and sundresses, sullenly kicking a rubber ball back and forth, or sitting cross-legged on the rec-room floor, staring at their dolls' fixed smiles. I owned a guitar and knew six or seven chords and saw before me week upon week of nothing but free time, so I recruited my sisters into a band: the Purple People. I would be songwriter, guitarist, arranger, producer, audio technician, concert promoter, and general impresario. We gathered in my bedroom, where I presented Kim and Erica with material to learn—a ballad about a friendly leprechaun who lived beneath a sewer grate, an ode to doors and the varied sounds they make—and, when they had rehearsed sufficiently, I recorded their performance on cassette. The girls played xylophone, bicycle bell, and coffee can and did all of the singing. If Erica, distracted by sudden doubts about the value of our project, forgot the lyrics and collapsed into giggles, or if Kim, overcome by shyness, began to stammer, then whisper, then retreat into a pained silence, I could stop the tape, rewind it a few seconds, embolden the girls with some cheering words, and start again mid-song. Not once, when the tape was rolling, did I join in the singing, pubescent self-consciousness having gathered around me like a fog. Who knew how long these tapes would be around and who might hear them. I would assent to my strumming being heard, but not my voice.

That same summer of 1972, the family spent a week at a cabin on an island in Puget Sound. We weren't roughing it; there was a public swimming pool across the street. One afternoon, I stood in the warm chlorinated water, holding Kim in my arms. She had not yet learned to swim, and I was the strong big brother. I held her in front of me and strode around in the shallow end, my legs cutting easily through the water. "Isn't this fun?" I announced. Then I turned and walked slowly toward the deeper water, the concrete bottom of the pool rough against my feet. The incline was steeper than I'd expected and, because I was holding Kim, hard to negotiate. I felt myself weakening, being overcome by the water. Kim and I were up to our chins. Did she know we were in danger? I hoped not. I didn't call for help—I was too embarrassed. I gritted my teeth, took frantic deep breaths. Desperate for traction, I scratched at the bottom of the pool with my toes. Somehow I gained my footing and enough strength to move us haltingly away from the deep end. Gradually, the water lowered around us. I returned us to the shallow water, where we belonged.

One night that same week, driving the family back to the cabin on a dark road through the woods, my father, silent at the wheel, was taking the turns too fast and hurtling over hills. It was mildly thrilling—and, I realized, possibly frightening to my little sisters. As we plunged down a hill, in order to cheer them, I squealed, "Whooo!"

"Shhh!" my mother said. She looked at me sternly. For a moment, the curtain between the child's world and the adult's lifted; I glimpsed a darkness, an uncertainty I was living in and rarely sensed but that my mother was aware of constantly. Pretending to delight in my father's reckless driving, I had risked encouraging that recklessness. My anxious mother knew better: she was maintaining her vigilant watch over him, her watch over all of us. She was trying to keep us safe.

My mother's every act implied a vision of the world as an orderly, dignified thing. There was a God, a merciful one, whose perfect wisdom was beyond our comprehension, and His spirit breathed perpetual life into the universe, and that life was revealed most powerfully in our capacity to love, and that love, as a daily practice, looked a lot like respect, and that respect extended beyond oneself and others and into one's surroundings. It was my mother who promised that, if I vacuumed the rec room, I could join the family at a matinee movie and then, when I had finished the job, bent down, ran her fingertip across the floor, and said, "There's dirt here still. You'll have to vacuum again." But it was also she who scolded and sent away a man who'd come to the door with a petition to keep "coloreds" out of the neighborhood; it was she who turned to me then and said, "It reminds me of that song you like—'The child is black, the child is white, together they learn to see the light.'" It was she who, when I found a crumpled ten-dollar bill on the street, made me earn the right to keep the money by knocking on every door in the neighborhood and saying to everyone who answered, "I found this money in the street. Is it yours?"

And it was she who ensured that the whole family attended Mass every Sunday. My father, when he lived in the house, came, too, although I rarely sensed that he was as enthusiastic about the ritual as my mother. He seemed to attend as a matter of course more than as a matter of faith.

One Sunday, for some reason, our mother could not attend the same Mass as the rest of us, so Kevin, Dana, and I accompanied our father to church. We paraded silently toward the front and slid into the second pew, facing the pulpit. No one sat in front of us. A few minutes into the Mass, Dana did what she often did, for little apparent reason: she giggled. "Quiet," our father whispered. "May almighty God have mercy on us," the priest pronounced. I stiffened, stared at my lap, sealed my lips shut. Then I giggled, my efforts to muffle the sounds succeeding only in making them burst out more violently. Our father leaned forward, turned his head, and shot us dark looks. "Stop it," Kevin pleaded. "Christ have mercy," the parishioners proclaimed in unison. Kevin erupted in laughter. Our father glowered, fixing his gaze before him. Then the priest stepped up to the pulpit. Dana snickered. Our father's shoulders trembled. He put his hand to his mouth—and he giggled. He was overcome; he could not stop. We all were overcome, giggling uncontrollably. The priest glared at us. "Sorry, sorry," our father muttered as he stood up, and we all stood up with him, biting our lips, staring at the floor, staring at our feet as we walked swiftly out of the pew, into the aisle, and out of the church. Once outside, in the crisp air, the sounds of birds and traffic around us, we exploded with laughter. We laughed and we laughed, and then it was out of us completely, finally, and we wiped our eyes and we drove home and we did not tell our mother.

The energy making mischief within us that morning might have been the kind that spawned *The Daily Nonsense,* the household newspaper my brother published when he was fifteen. *MAD* magazine was a likely influence, too. Kevin was revealing himself to be fiercely smart and sensitive to the absurd and to the use of language as a means of subversion and delight. He sat at the desk in his bedroom and patiently wrote *The Daily Nonsense* in pencil; he had to take great care, since the paper was minuscule—its tininess a kind of apology, an admission of its undersized ambitions: it came in folio form, a single, folded two-inch-by-three-inch sheet of paper. EARTH INVADED! RAY GUNS! one headline screamed. The accompanying article read:

> Mrs. Ray Smith discovered today that the earth in her back yard garden was being invaded by a few slugs. She called her husband (Ray) on the phone.
>
> He was so upset he gunned his engine all the way home.

The weather report:

> Look outside. On a 3 x 5 inch piece of paper describe the weather. Soak the paper in pig fat, stand on your head and say "rats!," salute

General Electric, hold the paper over your head and sneeze. Read it. It will describe the weather exactly.

A political editorial:

The only time Spiro Agnew opens his mouth is to change feet.

While I was squinting and chortling at *The Daily Nonsense* and deciding I admired my brother more than I had thought, and while Kevin was sharpening his pencil and his wit, bending over another little scrap of paper that would be his next issue, our father was coming unmoored again.

He could not be depended upon even to remember a birthday. Our mother's came, and he ignored it or forgot it, so she gave herself a present: a day away from the house, away from him. "Pack some things. Get in the car," she told us kids. "We don't need your dad—we can have fun by ourselves on my birthday." It was as if our parents were separated again; it was as if we were rehearsing for a future in which he would not exist. The day was gray and chilly—autumn, in its first week, already ferociously devoted to its business—but it was the ocean, the beach, that our mother aimed for. We drove three hours and spent all day with our jacket collars up, braving the winds whipping in from the Pacific. Who knows if our father cared that we were gone. Who knows if he noticed.

He had slipped back into the habit of arriving home late for dinner, liquor on his breath, or not arriving at all. He was having trouble at work, although he no longer admitted that to my mother. "Fine," he would say, "everything's fine," when she asked how things were at the office. But on many weekdays he would sleep in, then rush out the door late for work. His secretary would call our mother to confirm that he was coming to the office, then cover for him as best she could while she waited.

But his bosses noticed. After fourteen years on the job, he was neglecting his work. They would not fire him, not yet. They were Japanese—above all else, they valued loyalty. They would try to help him. Was he having trouble with drink? They paid to have him tested at a local hospital that specialized in treating addictions. No, he was told, he was not an alcoholic. Well, he and his bosses decided, he would just have to try harder. He would have to be more disciplined.

In the meantime, my mother—always disciplined, always planning ahead—had earned her degree and, in a Catholic school in a nearby town, begun working as a first-grade teacher. She wasn't being paid much, but she was bringing in something. More important, she had begun a career. If we ever had to survive without support from our father, we could do it. It wouldn't be easy, but we could do it.

In a photo from this time, it is Thanksgiving. My father, at the dining room table, bends over the roasted turkey, gripping a long-bladed carving knife, scraping meat from a leg. His expression is one of absolute attention—attention to doing a dad's work. But he is a man in danger of losing his job, of losing the salary that has allowed him to build this house and feed, clothe, and educate eight children. He is at risk of losing the trust of his wife and the confidence of his sons and daughters. At his office and in his home, he is ill at ease. Now, at the center of our celebration, as he picks up the knife again for the ritual carving, is he thinking of these things? No one would know: he is not the kind of man to speak a word of such thoughts. He is the kind of man who, at Thanksgiving, knows his responsibility is to carve the bird and does so expertly. His hair is long, swept back on the sides, and hanging down over one eye. It has gone almost entirely gray.

36

My junior high school was a sprawling brick prison of a building, its parking lot crammed with portable classrooms to handle the overflowing swarms of platform-soled, hormone-addled children. It was there that my seventh-grade English teacher, a strict, stout German, circled our desks, a whistle on a string around her neck so she could squeal us periodically into submission. It was there that my reward for enrolling in wood shop was to be taunted daily by a squat, muscular black kid in a knit cap who roamed the room, stalking me, whispering that if I crossed paths with him after school, I'd regret it. It was there that I met Al, a fellow twelve-year-old with a long mop of brown hair and a sly smile that veered easily into a smirk. Al was of the opinion that the old folk song "Erie Canal" would be improved if it were entitled "Anal Canal." He explained that for a long time he had been under the misapprehension that girls, unlike boys, had multiple penises, springing from their loins like a bouquet. Immediately, Al and I became best friends, and we stayed so until I went to college.

Al's house, unlike mine, was a glorious confusion, stinking of cigar smoke and boiled potatoes. His dad was an electrical engineer, a tinkerer, so there were gadgets scattered about the house, boxes of plastic or wood half opened, wires and springs dangling out. My own house was tidy and silent; my friends didn't go there. Al's house was a place for lounging around, for clattering down the basement stairs, for blasting the stereo, while his mother smiled and foisted cookies upon us.

As I did, Al and his older brother, Kurt, loved music—but their interest was obsessive, their knowledge exhaustive and esoteric. I liked whatever was poppy and maudlin in the Top 40—I was big into Bread and Jim Croce and Gilbert O'Sullivan; Al and Kurt had given themselves wholly over to dark, weird English bands that specialized in ten-minute organ and guitar jams and released double or triple albums with names like *Lizard Tails in His Majesty's Wardrobe* and *Fables from the Lunar Zoo*. In the unkempt, cramped sanctuaries of their bedrooms—which they seemed not to be under any obligation to clean—were uncategorizable messes of albums and singles and cassettes and reel-to-reel tapes and speakers and turntables and tuners and coiled headphone cords. It was Al who taught me that vinyl records can be washed, carefully, with soap and water—a valuable tip if your collection, as theirs did, came mainly from flea markets. Kurt was a shy Brian Wilson type, holing up in his room all day with his cheap electric guitar, practicing riffs from Yes and King Crimson albums and writing his own songs.

I, too, was still writing songs, although my subject matter had changed. I was walking the school halls surrounded by girls who were different from what they'd been the year before. Suddenly they were lovely to look at and alluringly mysterious: objects of an intense, baffling desire. The girl who won my exclusive adoration was Cherie. She and I had been assigned by our homeroom teacher to take attendance each morning. At the front of the class, with the roster before us on the desk, pencils in hand, we stood side by side, bantering in our few moments together in the coded way of people who share an important and private project. She stood close enough that I took note of the way her chestnut hair curled as it fell upon her shoulder; I observed the tanned skin of her forearm. Her easy, bewitchingly crooked smile, directed toward me, seemed an emissary from some far-off golden land, its fragrant air rich with mystery. I fell for Cherie hard—fell in love, I thought. What else could it be? The passion lasted three years, unrequitedly—lasted that long, probably, because it was unrequited.

Soon after she began haunting all of my thoughts, Cherie started going steady with Brad: handsome and unflappable, with shoulder-length wavy blond hair, a puka-shell necklace, muscles, and a pool. I didn't stand a chance.

Still, if Cherie declined to be the girl in my life, she could not refuse to be the girl in my songs. Her name was fortunate, since it gave me a rhyme for "marry."

I hadn't a clue how to interact with girls. How this could be so with all the females in my house—my mother and six sisters—I don't know. Maybe it was that my early model of womanhood was idealized and untouchable: the Virgin Mary—exquisitely beautiful, eyes downcast, with an air of knowing something I was yet unworthy to hear. Girls seemed to be a separate, prettier, superior species. It was almost impossible to imagine them as living in actual houses, sitting down to dinner with parents and siblings, watching TV, sleeping. To the best of my understanding, they did not shit.

I had learned about love mainly from pop songs, which might be why I was under the impression that someone you desire is obligated to desire you back. When I heard that Debbie, who was Cherie's best friend, had a crush on me, I was flattered—also disappointed, not just because the wrong girl was showing an interest in me but because now, as I understood it, I would have to be her boyfriend. For a while, I tried it. I met Debbie after school every day and held her hand as we walked the two blocks until my route home split off from hers; I bought her a cheap metal necklace with a heart pendant and paid an extra dollar to have her name and mine engraved on opposite sides; when anyone took me aside and conspiratorially asked if it was true that Debbie and I were going steady, I admitted that it was—and I was proud to do so. I had a girlfriend, an official one. I was in the game. I was not regarded entirely without interest by the opposite sex. But I couldn't keep up the ruse for long. I would have to do the brave and honorable thing: I wrote Debbie a note explaining that it would be unfair of me to continue going steady with her, considering that it was really her best friend I was in love with. There would be no negotiation, no trial separation, no mutual effort to rekindle whatever fires might have burned in our first days. I folded the paper multiple times into a small, tight square and, during a break between classes, as Debbie passed me, smiling, in the hall, handed it to her swiftly, with an apologetic, compassionate frown.

I was out: the breakup was clean, with no conversation—perfect.

37

Every waking moment, Cherie flitted at the border of my thoughts or sat smack in the center of them, but I never mentioned her to my mother or father. She seemed safer hidden. Or I was safer. If I were to talk to my parents about this puzzling, consuming desire, I might be judged. I felt pre-accused. I knew that what I felt for Cherie was essentially shameful, or my weakness in the face of it was. Maybe it was the family's Catholicism that made me think this; maybe it was my mother's emphasis on spotlessness, on orderliness of home and of heart; maybe it was the tension in that house, the feeling that the family was teetering at a cliff's edge, so anything unpredictable, anything outside of our established pattern of behavior, any candid expression of raw, unresolved feeling, might upset it. Anyway, how could my mother comprehend what it felt like to be a teenager in love?

And my father? I don't think it crossed my mind that he might advise me in matters of the heart, or in any matter concerning my murky interior world. I remember him then not as a teacher, a guide, a disciplinarian, or a comforter. I remember him as a body—as pieces of a body. He had grown a beard, and the gray hairs in it had gone yellow from his continual exhaling of cigarette smoke. His fingernails were yellowed, too, and his thumbnails had become oddly dented and grooved: he kept picking at them nervously, unconsciously, with the nail of his ring finger.

Although we children were unaware of this, he was continuing to fail at work; his bosses in Japan had tolerated his erratic performance and counseled and supported him as well as they could, but they were running out of patience and debating whether it was time to stop giving him another chance and then another. While trying to hang on to his job, he was also having to tend to his grandmother. A few years before, she had briefly remarried, but her second husband had died, and she was living alone in a retirement center. One spring day, walking on a downtown street, she fell—she probably fainted. Diagnosed with severe heart trouble and showing signs of dementia, she was given a pacemaker and, with my father's consent, placed in a nursing home. My mother was bringing in a small salary to help support the family, but there were still six children in the house, and there were Grandma Carey's medical expenses to deal with, and my father—the central breadwinner, the believer in discipline, industry, and self-reliance—must have been growing dizzy, maybe even desperate, wondering if he was adequate to the demands his life was placing upon him.

To me, he was still just Dad, which meant, most important, that he sometimes surprised us kids by taking us to a ball game or the lumberyard or the boat show. I had little interest in boats—and our family was surely not in the market to buy one—but my father didn't mind wandering the big annual boat show downtown, admiring the gleaming white luxury yachts, climbing aboard them to examine their sleek decks and nifty control panels, saying, "Hmmm," and "Interesting." What I found interesting—my sole motivation for attending—was whatever big promotional gimmick was being sponsored by the Top 40 radio station I listened to. One year the station brought in a world-record-holding high-diver to astonish the crowds by plunging a hundred feet from a platform into a small pool. Another year it carved out a two-ton chunk of Alaskan glacier and shipped it to the boat show to be gazed upon with wonder.

The boat show with the fish: that was the last one my father took me to. For weeks, rapt, I had been listening to excited announcements on the radio about the fish I would receive for free if I attended. This wouldn't be just any fish: it would be a golden koi, the most valuable pet in Japan, the disc jockeys said—prizewinning koi, they announced, sold for as much as twenty thousand dollars. As soon as I arrived at the boat show, taking no chances, I slipped into the line of people awaiting their fish. When my turn came, there were still plenty of fish left—the station had secured ten thousand of them to give away. I was handed a plump, sturdy plastic bag filled with water, a little slip of a golden fish within it. For the next hour, as I walked among the boats on exhibit, I gripped the top of the bag with one hand and supported the bottom carefully with the other. On the ride home, my father behind the wheel in front of me, I sat, my priceless fish on my lap in its plastic bag, and read again the mimeographed note that had come with it:

You now are the owner of an extremely valuable and enjoyable animal. This fish, of Oriental ancestry, will bring you years of happiness with proper care and attention. Your fish will become so tame you can feed it by hand. We sincerely hope you will build a nice pond in your yard so that you may eventually add to your collection and receive the maximum enjoyment.

I did not imagine that I would be building a pond, but, once we arrived home, I did find, in a cabinet, a glass bowl adequate to my needs and transferred the fish and its water into it. The koi, getting used to its new home, looked listless. Throughout the evening, I checked on it, peering at this new member of the family, this delicate pet I would care for in exchange for years of happiness. The fish continued to move sluggishly. Then it didn't move at all. It rose to the surface of the water and floated there, its belly to the ceiling.

Mine was not the only koi that reached a swift end—almost all ten thousand of them died within a day. Their plane trip from Tokyo over the Pacific had been long and the shift in climate sudden, so they were handed to their new owners fatally dazed and frail. They didn't stand a chance.

My father was barely hanging on. Then he fell: in June he was told to collect his things and turn in his key. He no longer had a job.

He had worked at Alaska Lumber and Pulp since before I was born. His severance package was generous: he would be given his full salary for another six months, until the beginning of the new year. When he told my mother the news, she put her arms around him and said, "This is a good thing. There was too much pressure in that job, too much work—it was killing you. Now you have six whole months to find a new job."

Our dad would be home; he would have no reason to stay away. He could begin again—we all could begin again. If the job had been the problem, there was no more problem. In the weeks following the firing, he seemed happier, and so did Mom. They even seemed to enjoy each other. Dad would start looking for work soon, but, in the meantime, this would be a summer of rest and of fun. We planned a two-week family vacation for August—we would travel in our new station wagon down the coast to Disneyland. On the Fourth of July, a few weeks after my father had lost his job, my parents wanted a quiet, leisurely celebration. We boarded a ferry and crossed Puget Sound to a little harbor town, where we would stroll around, duck into a few shops, and stake out a spot on the sidewalk to watch the parade. As my father drove us through town, my mother sitting beside him, I glanced toward the front of the car and saw something I had never seen before: my parents were holding hands.

One Sunday morning at Mass I saw another new thing: my father, robed, standing behind the lectern, the entire congregation watching as he served as that morning's lector. He kissed the Bible, set it down gently before him, opened it to the day's chosen verses, and recited them slowly, steadily, as if he were a man whose daily habit was to contemplate Paul's letters to the Thessalonians. He looked like someone else's dad. Had my mother encouraged him to do this, reminding him that it was time he offered himself in service to his church, to the faith they shared? Or was it his idea, part of his project of winning her trust or of persuading himself that he was a changed man?

Another Sunday, the whole family sat together in a pew, as usual. A guest priest was at the altar, assisting in the celebration of the Mass—he was a visitor for the weekend and had begun work the day before, hearing parishioners' confessions. Not long after the service began, things began to feel odd. This priest didn't seem familiar with the liturgy; he mumbled his way through much of it and interspersed Latin into parts of the Mass that had long been spoken in English. Also, there was something wrong with his hair. Was that a wig?

By the next day, the visiting priest was in jail, two stolen guns and blank checks with our pastor's name on them having been found in his belongings. He was a con artist and convicted check forger who had recently robbed a gun store in Alabama. For years, in cities around the country, he had impersonated a priest. He couldn't help himself, he said. It gave him "satisfaction as a human being."

The following Sunday, one of our parish's priests, a real one, explained to the congregation what had happened. Father Englebert emphasized that, although the visitor was fake, the confessions he'd heard were real: they counted. God's powers are strong enough, he assured us, to work even through an impostor.

38

Our car tilted: it was too low on the driver's side. Otherwise, it was perfect—new and huge and lavishly appointed, a long low boat of a car, a 1973 Plymouth Fury Suburban station wagon, "honey gold," as the manufacturer had it, with faux-wood panels on the side, luggage racks on top, a tailgate that could, as if by a bit of trickery, swing open from the bottom or from the side, and, best of all for us kids, a bench seat in the far back that faced the rear window, a prime vantage point from which to peer at places as they shrank from view and, by gleefully miming the act of yanking on a cord, to signal any trucker to blast his horn.

In the Fury, we would travel down the coast to Disneyland—or, as the youngest of us, five-year-old Erica, put it, "Dinneyland." I know that she said this because I have the tape that proves it. Peggy was unable to make the trip, so Kevin took it upon himself to bring the sounds of it home to her.

On Kevin's lap as we sat in the car, or in his grip as we strolled the aisle of some souvenir shop, was the black-and-silver Panasonic cassette tape recorder he'd received for Christmas. In pushing *record* and *pause* and *stop*, Kevin was packaging our travels, making a shape for them, finding a permanent narrative within the larger, fleeting one. He was sixteen and had become the kind of person so thoughtful about experience that he could not help, in some ways, living slightly to the side of it; for Kevin, to have an experience inevitably meant to observe himself having it and therefore to feel its joy or solemnity or horror but also its absurdity or strangeness or wonder. He was conscious of being conscious; he sensed how easy it is to act as though we understand what can't be understood. This was the boy who had called his minuscule family newspaper *The Daily Nonsense.* He was the boy whose preferred means of terror was to stalk me silently, slowly, from room to room, wearing Buster Keaton's deadpan expression, sitting when I sat, standing when I stood, walking when I walked. He was merely being; what was the harm in that? But I was thoroughly creeped out, while he was entertained. And then there was the dead hand. At any given moment, when I had annoyed him enough, Kevin would raise his long, pale, freckled hand and let it hang limp before my eyes. I couldn't stand it: the raw, simple grotesqueness of it against which there was no rebuttal.

This family vacation would be a beautiful trance, a dream: Dad wasn't working—he was just Dad at last—and we would have him, have both of our parents side by side in the Fury's front seat, or together at a restaurant table, or at the head of a parade of us clicking through the turnstile of some tourist trap; we would have them for as long as we wanted, for as long as it took to wend our way down the coast and back, for as long as it took to forget that things were ever otherwise. We were off to California, where gold glittered in the air and on the license plates, where the land of Mickey and Snow White lay waiting: the place where dreams became real, the place where, just by being there, you were happy.

On the first day, we drove south through Portland, then west to the coast, to Lincoln City and the Sea Gypsy Motel, a three-story building nestled into a kind of low hillside or dune. At ten that night, leaving our father and mother and sisters in their rooms, Kevin and I ambled down to the beach, to the expanse of packed sand black beneath the night sky. Kevin clicked on the recorder; he would begin documenting our journey here. Should we say something? We should say something.

With the waves roaring and the wind whipping into the microphone, we had to shout; we could hardly be heard as we narrated the facts that the waves were roaring, that the wind was whipping, that it was cold and, well, that was about it. "It's just Chris and I. . . ." Kevin announced into the microphone.

"And the *sea*," I added mock-portentously.

We were teenage boys with a tape recorder, a deserted beach, self-consciousness, and an arsenal of dull satirical wit. That's what we were documenting.

The next day, late in the afternoon, after hours of snaking down the curves of the coastline road, our father said, "Here it is!" and drove the Fury across the state line.

"We're in California!" my little sisters sang. "We're in California!"

Our father's words are the first of his that are heard on the tape—the first of only a few. Throughout the trip, he seems to have concentrated, in silence, on driving: on gauging how far we could travel on this tank of gas, on ensuring that he was merging onto the right road, on calculating where the nearest exit was. He might have been enjoying himself, doing the private multiplying and dividing that he was so good at, letting his mind go where it would, regardless of what his children were up to behind him.

"Poor Dad," Erica said. "He always has to drive."

Our mother, in the front passenger seat, turned around regularly to check on the five of us, to ask who was hungry, who needed a potty break. She was the cheerleader, the first-grade teacher by trade, the one who knew how to lasso kids' attention, the one who often broke into song: "California, here I come, right back where I started from!" On the third day, as we wove among the redwoods on Highway 101, she was inspired to lead the family in a rendition of "This Land Is Your Land." Not long after hitting the highway that day, we pulled into the parking lot of Trees of Mystery, a tourist attraction that was hard to miss: its entrance was marked by giant statues, higher than a house, of Paul Bunyan and his trusty companion, Babe the Blue Ox. Paul, in rough black beard, red open-necked shirt, blue jeans, and boots, rested his ax on the ground at his left side while holding his right hand up, palm open: a friendly greeting or a warning to back off.

We climbed out of the station wagon, paid our entrance fee, and took to the trail that wound through the woods—among trees, we'd been told, so strange, so extravagantly large and queerly shaped, that they had to be seen to be believed. We passed a tree that, if we squinted and were generous with our imaginations, could be said to look something like an octopus. We saw the upside-down tree and the lightning-bolt tree. Standing before another, we listened to a recorded voice inform us of its astonishing resemblance to a kneeling elephant. "It looks like a tree with a lot of roots," Kevin said.

Earlier, he had stood beside the road, recorder in hand, capturing the noise of passing traffic. What we are listening to, he whispered, in the awed, excited tone of a jungle explorer who has discovered a new tribe, are the exotic "sounds of California."

A few hours later, our mother exclaimed, "There's the bridge!" The Golden Gate, its orange towers glowing in the afternoon sun, had appeared over the crest of a hill. We were approaching the city that, the last time our dad heard, was where his good-for-nothing father lived. His one short encounter with Nat had happened twenty years earlier. Since that time, how often had he thought about his father? Might he be thinking about him now?

Our dad broke his silence: "I haven't seen as much traffic the whole trip as I have the last hour."

Getting closer to the bridge, he began to read aloud the highway signs, speaking deliberately and quizzically, mainly to himself, in the way that drivers sometimes do, with a mix of attentiveness and distraction: "Toll plaza. Auto toll fifty cents." Then the bridge was under us, only air on either side of us, San Francisco gleaming to our left across the bay, its buildings shimmering white in the sun, spilling over hills and down to the dark blue water.

For a moment, our father's voice changed, his goofy, deadpan Irish humor rising to the surface. "Boy, that's scary! You see that big city over there? *I* don't want to go to San Fran*cis*co." But he did go, checking us in to a motor lodge in the Tenderloin.

The next day, with Kevin again toting around his tape recorder, some of us were growing weary of our brother's project, of the self-conscious drawing of attention to the reality of the reality we were in. My seven-year-old sister Kim, especially, seemed intent on enjoying her vacation without being documented doing it. "Kim," Erica shouted, "watch out! He's going to tape-record your laugh!"

"Kim," Kevin said, "why do you want me not to record your laugh anymore?"

Answering him directly while revealing that she understood she was expected to perform, she sang her reply: "Because I h-a-a-a-te it!"

Why couldn't we just *be* without explaining ourselves? Why couldn't we just talk without thinking about it, without knowing that our words might be remembered forever? Decades hence, would someone be scrutinizing our offhand talk, searching the tape for clues about us, imposing upon our words an unnatural weight?

"It's just a big nuisance to everybody," I said.

Erica backed me up: "Dummy Kevin!"

"It's stupid," I reiterated.

But Kevin was unrelenting. At Fisherman's Wharf, a few of us boarded a helicopter for a spin around the bay, over Alcatraz and back to the dock, and Kevin made sure the tape was running, recording the roar of the helicopter's engine, the *whup-whup-whup* of the blades, the complaint of a foghorn in the harbor. "Okay, Erica," Kevin said as we rose, "what do you have to say?"

Our youngest sister paused. "I don't have to say anything."

But later, with the bustle of a day of touristy thrills and searches for souvenirs almost over, with all of us relaxing at last in a restaurant, we felt more at ease with the recorder sitting on the table before us. Even our dad got into the spirit of the project, assuming the role of narrator. "We're at Borruso's Lighthouse," he announced. "At Fisherman's Wharf." Then he paused. Any more thoughts to share, Dad? "And, by the way, it's overcast. The weather is *not* very good."

Our dad had been a good sport. He'd tried.

We took the fast route the next day, traveling down the interstate so we could make it to Anaheim by evening. We had seen Disneyland on television: every Sunday evening, in living color, Tinker Bell flitted onto our screen and, waving her wand, soared over Sleeping Beauty's castle. The place, amazingly, was real; we knew that—a few of our lucky friends had been there, and they'd returned with postcards and mouse ears to prove it.

"There's the monorail," Kevin said. "See that up there? That's the monorail for Disneyland."

"Where?" Kim complained.

I, too, was disappointed. "I don't see it anywhere."

Then we spied, in the distance, beyond a barrier wall, the craggy white tip of the Matterhorn, the park's little alpine homage. We were there, truly there at last, although I couldn't help feeling let down. Could this be Disneyland if there was a Denny's across the street from it?

Our hotel, at least, looked sufficiently exotic. Shading its main entrance was a high white concrete dome of a canopy supported by four enormous legs; it resembled an alien spacecraft or a giant turtle gutted standing up.

And once within the walls of the park, we were indeed in another world. Riding in little metal gondola cars dangling from cables, we floated to Fantasyland. We took to the water in a jungle steamer, cruising past snakes and rhinos and cannibals and a hippo who rose, dripping, from the murk to roar at us. My father slipped each of us some dollars from

his wallet. I gave one of mine to an artist who had set up his easel in the
open air. He would draw a cartoon caricature of me. It didn't take long. He
squinted at me past the side of the easel, waved his hand across the paper
a few times, then pulled the paper down and handed it to me. The boy in
the picture was a stranger; his mouth was odd and toothy, like a wood-
chuck's. His hair, unlike mine, fell around his ears and down the back of
his head in a series of waves. There was also a wave beneath him: he was
riding a surfboard. I had never surfed in my life, never thought of trying.

In Tomorrowland, I waited with my father, Kevin, and Dana in a long
line winding its way toward a giant microscope. We would enter that
microscope—enter, we were promised, "inner space": we would explore
the parts of us so small that the naked eye cannot detect them. When
we arrived at the front of the line, each of us was ushered into a small
tramcar, shiny blue, like a pill, equipped with a metal safety bar to pull
toward our lap. Then we were moving, one by one, into the dark eyepiece
of the microscope. We heard a voice: our guide, a scientist, reminding
us that, through the creation of the microscope, man "discovered the
fantastic universe beyond the limits of his own meager sight." We saw
nothing; we were in darkness. Then, on the walls and ceiling around us,
large snowflakes gradually appeared; or, rather, the snowflakes were not
large—we had become smaller. We were shrinking, shrinking, we were
hardly ourselves anymore, we were shrinking to the size of a snowflake,
then the size of an atom, then smaller. We were almost nothing: a bit of
black amid a swirl of light specks, uncountable orbiting electrons. To our
side, lurking in the half-blackness, a dim, infinitesimally small particle
of matter appeared. It was shaped, remarkably, like a man. No, it was
a man: he was dressed in Disneyland coveralls and lugging a toolbox.
He was walking alongside the tracks we were riding on, near the place
where the floor met the mesh screen that simulated the microscopic
world we were traveling through. He was heading toward a rip in the
fabric to repair it. But it was too late: I had seen him. I had seen the rip.

39

The next day, Kevin and I were sitting in our hotel room. We shared the room with Dana; our parents and two little sisters occupied another room down the hall. Dana rushed in, looking stricken. She had come from our parents' room. "We're leaving," she stuttered. "Mom is leaving. And all the girls. You're staying with Dad."

"What?" we said. "Why? What happened?"

"I don't know. I'm not sure. Mom's mad. Dad did something. I don't know. I don't want to go!"

Our mother appeared in the doorway. "Kevin, Chris, there's been a change. I'm leaving with Dana and the girls. You're staying here with your dad. Dana, pack your things."

None of this is on Kevin's tape. He didn't bother to use the recorder that day.

It happened within minutes. Our mother and sisters lugged their suitcases into the elevator, and the door closed.

Our father walked to our room and sat on the bed. He spoke to us weakly, as if deflated, defeated. "I can't talk with your mother right now. Kevin, I need you to go down and tell her that I want her to come back."

What had happened? Why couldn't he talk to her himself? Kevin left the room and went downstairs. He found our mother and sisters outside on the sidewalk, waiting for the airport shuttle. "Mom," Kevin said, "Dad wants you to come back. And I want you to come back, too."

Our mother was sorry, but the answer was no. The shuttle came. She boarded it with our sisters, and they were gone.

Our father did not tell us what had happened, neither then nor later. Did we even ask him? Probably we didn't. Our family had become the kind—how does such a thing happen?—that can be sundered suddenly, without explanation. Everybody suffers, and no one says a word.

Instead, the males of the family roamed a ghost town—the replica of an old western outpost at Knott's Berry Farm, the second-best amusement park in Anaheim. We did what a dad and his sons do on vacation in California. Through the bars of the town jail, we gazed at Joe, the life-size carved wooden figure of an inmate, forlorn in his cramped cell, ankles shackled, cigarette jutting from the corner of his mouth. The trick was: he talked.

"Where y'all from?" Joe asked.

"Seattle," we said together.

"Well," he drawled menacingly, "y'd bitter skedaddle back tuh Seattle."

Instead, we stuck around. We toured the wax museum: we gazed at Elizabeth Taylor, eerily unreal, stilled in mid-gesture. Rudolph Valentino, Shirley Temple, Marilyn Monroe. W. C. Fields, fixed in an expression of irritation.

We drove to Marineland, where, in line for the dolphin show, I stood dressed in my summer costume—the one that, awkward and wary of myself, desperate to seem one of the crowd, I hoped made me look like an undorky teenager: cutoff jeans, sandals, mirrored sunglasses, a yellow fishing hat, and a tank top advertising Heidelberg beer. A stranger ahead of me, maybe a college boy, turned his head and grinned at me scornfully. "O-h-h-h, yeah," he taunted. "Don't *you* look cool." He had found me out, he thought. Maybe he had. I kept my mouth shut, pretending I hadn't heard him, twisting in my fist my souvenir booklet, crimping its cover photo of a killer whale surging up from blue water.

Then we drove our big golden Fury—far bigger than we needed now, with only three of us in it—to Hollywood. We took a sightseeing tour, straining to glimpse, through tree limbs and high fences, the mansions of the stars: Gregory Peck, Judy Garland, Jack Benny, and "an actor known for his blue eyes," the tour guide hinted before naming Paul Newman. We toured Universal Studios, boarding a bus that wheeled us through the parted waters of the Red Sea, although the parting looked more clumsily mechanical than divine. We passed the house in front of which Suzanne Pleshette, in *The Birds*, was pecked to death. We spied—washed by sunlight, looming on its hill—the *Psycho* house.

Finally, with a hundred other tourists, we were ushered into a theater—we would see how a real movie scene was filmed: a bank robbery. Better, we were told, a lucky few of us would perform in the scene. The tour guides needed volunteers. A few people raised their hands—some men and women, a couple of children—and were waved down to the stage. "Come on, folks. We need more. How about you, sir?"

The tour guide was looking directly at us. My father pointed at his chest questioningly. "Yes, you, sir. Don't be shy. Come on down." My father rose slowly from his seat, stepped into the aisle, and walked down to the stage. He joined the other volunteers as they huddled around the director for instructions. We didn't hear what they were saying. Our father's role turned out to be minor; as the heist unfolded at center stage, he stood to the side, holding the receiver of a prop pay phone. The other bank customers, including a woman and her children, stood with their hands in the air, while he bent his head furtively toward the receiver. "Help, help. We need help," he whispered repeatedly into his cord connected to nothing.

Afterward, we took to the interstate and headed toward home. We would not be driving along the leisurely coast road this time. Within a day, we were in Medford, Oregon, at a Travelodge. It had been four days since our mother and sisters had left us. Our father sat at the edge of the motel bed, the phone in his lap. Then he called his wife.

Kevin and I, preparing for bed, watched him from the corners of our eyes; we heard snatches of conversation, but not everything. As he spoke to our mother, our father sounded calm. He must be apologizing, I thought, although I knew not for what. Our parents, from what I could hear, were being reasonable with each other. He told her we'd be back in two days. We'd be home, and maybe all would be forgiven. Maybe all would be forgotten.

By the next day, we had made it to Portland, where we stopped for one final night—a movie night, our father said. At a downtown theater, we saw *The MacKintosh Man*, about a British agent pretending to be a jewel thief who sounds like an American even though he is trying to feign an Australian accent. As I watched, I just kept thinking he was Paul Newman: I knew those blue eyes, and I'd just seen his house.

The next day, after three hours of driving, our dad pulled the Fury, still stubbornly leaning to one side, into our carport.

After that, my mother remembers, the house was peaceful for a while—my parents got along, and my father was attentive, in his way, to her and to us. Neither of my parents explained to us what had happened at Disneyland, and we didn't ask.

For decades afterward, we children, grown up, with our memories becoming murkier and murkier, occasionally spoke of that sudden sad moment in the hotel. What had happened? It says something—about our pathological discretion or politeness or cowardice—that we talked only among ourselves, speculating, without broaching the subject with our mother. Had our father said something to her, something so hurtful that she had no choice but to pack her bag and leave? Dana remembered him, throughout the trip, singing snatches of a song: "She walks, she talks, she moves like a cannibal." What song was that? At least based on my own efforts, it is to this day unsearchable on the Internet. Did our father make it up? Who was like a cannibal? Our mother? Every time he broke into song, was he speaking of her, letting her have it? That was Dana's guess: maybe our mother had finally had enough of that damn song.

Finally, forty years after the fact, I asked my mother what had happened.

"He hit me," she said. "I don't know why. It started and was over in a second."

They were in the hotel room, standing near the closet, talking—my mother doesn't remember about what—and he slapped her. He had never hit her before, and he never did again. For an unforgivable moment, he became someone else, or maybe he became himself at last, some angry part of himself that he had become expert at hiding.

Why had she demanded that our sisters return home with her but left my brother and me behind with our father? Kevin and I, over the years, had considered whether she needed us to keep an eye on him. Maybe she didn't trust him to be alone so far from home. No, she said, she just didn't want to rob us of the rest of our vacation, and she thought we were old enough to stay. She didn't fear that our father would prove an untrustworthy chaperone; he had been a responsible father up to that point.

And the phone call from the motel room in Medford? That was when he apologized, right? No. He did not apologize then, she said. And he didn't later. He just came home. *Neither of them ever said a word about it.*

As for Kevin's project of documenting the sounds of our vacation, he tried to keep it going. The day after our mother and sisters flew home, he started recording again, but we were ready by then for the whole thing to be over. It's there on the tape, in its final seconds. "Okay, Chris," Kevin said, "where are we?" It was as if he were returning to a narrative—some logical, coherent one—that had been briefly interrupted.

"What?"

"Where are we?"

"Chris," our father said, "I think we're going to have to get a red light for Kevin's nose."

"Why?"

"So it will go on when he pushes the *play* button."

He didn't have to worry. Kevin didn't push the button again.

40

Nixon is not a crook. Agnew is a disgrace; he resigns and pleads no contest to charges of tax evasion and money laundering. OPEC imposes an oil embargo, and, at gas stations, prices rise and lines lengthen. Still, there is cause for hope and joy: the World Trade Center has risen to its full height and is open at last; the comet of the century, Kohoutek, is hurtling through space and will soon blaze across our skies—we are preparing to be astonished by it; and O. J. Simpson is slashing his way heroically toward a record two thousand yards for a season. My hair is like a black curtain around my head: long, straight, and thick. In my school picture, I wear a cream-colored T-shirt adorned with the logo of Coors beer, which, like every other form of alcohol, I have never tasted. A small oasis of sanity is my English class; my teacher, Mr. Cygan, wavy-haired and sideburned, wears wire-rimmed glasses and a continual expression of intelligent bemusement. Unlike my other teachers, he looks like a scholar. He relishes linguistic nuance and points out that the way we choose to pronounce *textile*—as *TEX-TYLE* or *TEX-tull*—betrays our class aspirations. I am trying to decide whether my favorite song is "My Old School" by Steely Dan or "Goodbye Yellow Brick Road" by Elton John. The choice is important: I always have a favorite song. Without one, I feel inexact. I am unequivocal, however, in my continued longing for Cherie and in my mourning for Jim Croce, whose music I love the most, gone because his plane failed to lift off fully and hit a tree, a sudden dumb death.

And my dad is getting a little weird and scary. He has a small wound on the bridge of his nose that will not heal—a consequence, perhaps, of his diabetes; he insistently, unself-consciously picks at it with the nail of his middle finger, even one afternoon when he is pressed into service to drive me and a couple of my friends somewhere. I sit in the front seat and pray they don't notice. He sings to himself. Some mornings he walks into the kitchen in nothing but a pair of white underwear. When he is fully clothed, he wears a camel-colored coat: somehow that embarrasses me, too—I add it to my unspoken litany of complaints against him.

His job is to find a new job. He invests in a collection of cassette tapes: an audio version of Dale Carnegie's *How to Win Friends and Influence People*. Sympathetic acquaintances set up interviews for him with accounting firms, but either he is insufficiently impressive in the interviews or he doesn't show up at all. Little by little, he retreats, sleeping late until he is alone in the house and it is safe for him to rise and slip out, then returning after everyone else has gone to bed. Sometimes, arriving home from teaching in the afternoon, my mother passes him, dressed in a suit and tie and heading out the door, with no explanation of where he is going or with a muttered mention of an interview. He returns home at four or five in the morning and repeats the routine the next day. He is merely a spirit in the house; we hardly see him. It is as though he has lost the ability to play the role of himself—and who was that self, anyway? I spot him sometimes in the hall or on the stairs, shuffling past me in his underwear and a T-shirt. "Hi, son." "Hi, Dad." Arriving home from school, I see him in front of the house, in a business suit, stepping into his Dodge Dart. On his way to a job interview? Maybe. But there is no new job. Occasionally, in the middle of the day, I walk into the living room and he surprises me: he is a body on the couch, sleeping. I leave, then return. He's gone.

Once, when he is on the couch, my mother enters the room, sits in a chair near him, and, as he is waking up, begins to speak to him. Maybe she is asking him about his progress in the job search. He looks at her and says, "Everything always comes up roses for you, doesn't it?"

A few times, Kevin arrives home from school in the afternoon, walks down the hall to his bedroom, and finds our father there, lying in Kevin's bed or, in haste, rising and pushing his way out the door past my brother, mumbling something like, "How're you doing, son?" On other days, Kevin doesn't see our father but notices signs that he's been there: rumpled sheets, with the scent of aftershave in them; some well-thumbed supermarket paperback, filled with steamy erotic passages, on the floor near the bed. If our father is lounging in the house all day, why doesn't he do it in his own bedroom? Maybe he needs a safe place to hide: from our mother or from the fact that he has nowhere to go, no purpose that might inspire him to rise from his own bed instead of staying there all day, maybe staying there forever.

He is getting through the day, whatever day it is—he sometimes forgets—then getting through the next one, then the next, doing so by avoiding us, avoiding his wife, avoiding real talk. Talk: maybe that will help him. He should see a psychiatrist. But it's 1973, and he's my dad. A door with a loose hinge, a faucet with a leak, he can fix. But problems within himself he solves by ignoring or hoping they go away, or he never fully grasps them in the first place. He's only three generations removed from old world Ireland, from the tradition of a man working hard and, if he has troubles, drinking or singing or wisecracking them away. He's only one generation removed from his own father, who dealt with his problems, whatever they were, by walking out the door and disappearing for good. Unlike his father, my dad hasn't left the house, but he is abandoning his family—abandoning himself, too.

Once or twice during this time, he visits Terry at her apartment on Seattle's Capitol Hill. When a friend of his gives him a present of Alaskan moose meat, he passes the gift on to her. She cooks it and makes coffee, and they talk, but the conversation feels strained to her, slightly unreal. There is no room for honest discussion about the family or about his condition. Sometimes Terry returns home to visit him—she understands that he is sick, and she wants to check on him—and the conversations then are even more difficult for her. He is morose, complaining about the hard life he has had, the hard life he is having: too many people are dependent upon him. In some moments, as he tells a story that has no clear context, Terry wonders if he is hallucinating. Is he describing something he has experienced recently? Or is he musing about something he plans to do?

One day it occurs to my father that the problem is his wife: she's not on his side—she's keeping secrets from him. In a rage, with my terrified mother watching, he stalks through the house, yanking closets open, pulling boxes and blankets down onto the floor, shouting, "Where did you hide my gun? Where is it?"

"I don't know what you mean, Ed," my mother says. "What gun? I don't have your gun."

"You're lying to me. I gave you a gun."

"No, you didn't."

"I sent it from Hawaii. Where are you hiding it?" My father storms out of the house.

He does not own a gun, as far as my mother knows. Why is he so desperate to lay his hands on one? Does he have it in his mind to shoot himself? Or to shoot her and their children? Both possibilities occur to her.

I do not know of this rampage; I hear about it only years later. Perhaps too much like my father, I can sense trouble but cannot confront it squarely. I certainly do not talk about it. I do not ask my mother,

"What's wrong with Dad? Do you think he needs help?" Instead, I keep my head down. As my father avoids the rest of us, I avoid him. But I cannot fend off the images that flash unbidden into my mind: visions of corpses or, more often, of living people who look as though they belong in the grave. For weeks, through November and December, I look at someone—a smiling grocery store cashier, a baby in a stroller, my science teacher at the blackboard, lifting before us a beaker of blue liquid—and see that person's skin as ash-gray, falling off in flakes and chunks. I do not intend this; the vision simply appears to me, unanticipated, unasked for.

I understand what it means: soon either I or my father will die.

I do not tell anyone—what would I say? I am sensing a truth that is to be accepted, not acted upon; it is a shadow cast back upon me from a fixed future. I do not know how I know it or why the knowledge has come to me in the way it has. I just understand that it is true.

The fact is in the house already.

Friday, December 21. Nixon has a plan to present his side of the Watergate story to Congress, but his aides announce that "Operation Candor" will be delayed. The reclusive Howard Hughes has checked into a hotel in the Bahamas under the name of Mr. Ludwig. Bobby Darin, the man at the top of the charts when I was born, has died young of an "imperfect heart." In the Skylab space station, astronauts create, out of food cans, a makeshift Christmas tree. On this date thirteen years ago my father signed the mortgage for our home. In ten days, his severance package will expire; he will no longer be on salary. He will need to find a job soon. He will need to find one now. In three days, our extended family will gather for its traditional Christmas Eve celebration. I have bought a gift for everyone except my father. What might I purchase for a few dollars that he would value? What do dads want? Socks? Shaving cream? I'll figure it out this weekend. It is the winter solstice—Robert Frost's "darkest evening of the year." I mark the occasion in the way I mark every Friday, sitting in the rec room all night, staring at the television. Even after the late news, I am not tired enough to go to bed—or, rather, I am tired but want to stay up past midnight to see all of *Don Kirshner's Rock Concert*. Argent plays "Hold Your Head Up" and "I Don't Believe in Miracles," and then, through the silent house, bleary-eyed, I trudge off to bed. In the morning, I will think about my father's gift.

41

I'm surfacing from sleep. Voices—far-off bursts of talk—are drawing me out. A bustling. Fast footsteps. I'm curled on my right side; now I give in, roll onto my back, open my eyes. Eight-twelve. Saturday morning. A dead time, usually. My brother speaks frantically; my sister responds. They're upstairs, Kevin and Dana.

Something is happening. Something has happened.

I slide from bed, stand up, open the door, and walk upstairs.

"It's Dad." Kevin and Dana, standing in the dining room, have seen me. Nearby, in the living room, the front door is open. The house inhales cold air. He's outside, they say, down in the carport, and Mom is with him.

"He might be dead, he might be dead. We called 911. We don't know."

A heart attack? Dads have heart attacks.

At some point later, after the EMTs have arrived and then stayed too long, lingering in the carport, standing and muttering, their ambulance idling purposelessly in the driveway, and after Kim and Erica have stood puzzled in their pajamas, staring through the front door, then been hurried off along with a distracting toy or two to the neighbors' house, Kevin, Dana, and I understand. Our dad is dead.

We are not a family given to hugging, but we stand by the dining room table in a little circle of three and hold one another. It is over. For six months, our father has lived with us as a ghost, an awkward, furtive presence. Perhaps without knowing it, we have been waiting for something to happen. A question has been stifling the household for months—for years, really—making breathing difficult, and at last the question has been answered. Grief will come, but first we feel something surprising: relief.

We let go of each other. I walk into the living room, where the big tinseled Christmas tree glitters, wrapped presents beneath it, carefully arranged there by our mother. To the left of the tree is the open door. I know that my father is out there, lying on the concrete at the bottom of the steps. I know that I can look at him if I choose to and that, if I do, whatever my eyes take in I will never forget. Do I want to see what has become of him? I must make this decision.

I turn toward my father.

He is lying on his back in the carport. From where I stand, I can see only his head and torso; his gray hair is swept wildly back from his face, which is bright red.

It was our mother who discovered him. Waking and finding herself alone in bed, she rose, as she often has done, to look through the second-floor window and see whether his Dodge was in the carport. It was there, running. Wherever he had gone the night before, he had come home. Was he in the car? Wrapped in her robe, she walked outside into the December chill. She peered in: he was lying on the front seat. She turned back, ran to Kevin's ground-floor bedroom window, and knocked hard. "Call 911!" she yelled. "Call 911!" In the next room, Dana, already awake, was sitting on her bed, playing with her Spirograph, fitting one plastic gear within another and drawing perfect circles. She heard the scampering in the gravel outside her window and then our mother's frantic voice.

She and Kevin hurried upstairs, and my brother made the call,

Dana looking through the front door and down to the carport, relaying information to him. She saw our mother pull our father from the car, then lean with him against a wooden post and cradle his head. Later, our mother would remember that she was saying to him, "You didn't have to do this. You didn't have to do this." What he had done was run a garden hose from the exhaust pipe to the driver's window, turn the ignition, and lie on the seat.

There is no reason for Kevin and Dana and me to stay in this house. We leave through the back door and join our little sisters at our neighbors'. We sit in their upstairs living room, looking through the picture window down toward our carport. The ambulance is there still, idling. The EMTs are speaking with my mother. They are standing near our father's body. They are pulling a sheet over his face.

Across the street, a few doors down, in a neighboring family's upstairs window, two faces appear. A mother and her teenage daughter have pulled aside the curtain and are peering toward our house. The mother raises binoculars to her eyes; then she passes them to her daughter.

We are outraged. We are being invaded—our experience, in the midst of our having it, is being gawked at. We are an interesting thing that is happening on the block.

"We ought to call them," Dana says.

"You think so?" Kevin says. "Should I do it?"

"Do it."

"Yeah," I say, "make the call."

Kevin thumbs through the phone directory, then picks up the receiver. He dials. We wait. "Mind your own business," he says bluntly, then hangs up. In the window down the street, the curtain closes.

A couple of hours later, back in our house, my mother is sitting on the living room couch, near the tree and presents, surrounded by friends and family who have come bearing sandwiches and casseroles.

The room, I understand, is for her alone. I linger nearby in the dining room and hear Grandma Esther saying to her, "That poor tortured man." Is this true? Yes, it is: my father was tortured. He must have suffered much. But it has not crossed my mind that my grandmother has known this. Has everyone known? Have my father's troubles been common knowledge?

Father Lane, the pastor of our church, appears in black shirt and white collar. He stands, of all places, in the narrow downstairs hallway, near the doorways to three bedrooms: Kevin's, Dana's, and mine. He looks preposterous there, like a character from a storybook who has come to life and stepped off the page. He is the man who, in our sudden drama, will be playing the role of the priest. Briefly, gently, he tells me something comforting that I will not remember; instead, I will remember his sour breath—I will remember thinking that he is a person, a normal person, just a man who hasn't had time to brush his teeth.

One of my mother's twin sisters has arrived. She crooks her finger, motioning me over. "Chris," she says, "I have a job for you. It is possible that your father wrote a note. He could have mailed it to your mother. For the next few days, I want you to be the first to the mailbox. Don't let your mother get the mail. If you find an envelope that looks as though it's from your father, bring it to me." That day, and the next few days, I do as she asks. I find no message from my father. I am relieved. And disappointed.

Sunday, the day after my father's death, the viewing is scheduled at the funeral home. The viewing: we are going to look at him. He wanted out, but we won't let him go so quickly, not before we take a last look.

He lies in the casket, his face no longer red. But his hair is wrong: it is combed straight back from his face, without a part, in a way he never wore it. Maybe it's not even my dad in the casket. Is it too late for this whole thing to have been a mistake, a misunderstanding? No, it's him: a bountiful amount of makeup has been slathered onto the bridge of his nose, where his wound still is.

Sitting in a row with my family, the casket before us, I am silent. We are all silent. I look at the room: the muted wallpaper, the dim lights. I look at the casket, then at my shoes, and feel my breath catch. I sob, my shoulders slumped, my chest trembling. Grandpa Lee, sitting beside me, hooks his arm around my shoulders, squeezes, and keeps his arm there. I think: *That's right—until now, I haven't cried.* I think: *This is me feeling the reality of it. He is really dead: that must be what the tears mean.*

The funeral is at noon the next day, Christmas Eve. Terry has given me a Bible and marked a few New Testament chapters. "Choose a passage from these—a short passage, anything," she says. I will read it at the funeral. I select a few verses that most closely reflect my own feelings; their tone seems entirely bitter, discouraged, and without hope. I don't know the context of the verses or their ultimate significance to the chapter. I just pick the language that sounds the most bereft. I also must choose clothes to wear, and I realize, to my embarrassment, that I own nothing appropriate: no black slacks, no simple black shoes, no white shirt. I am unprepared for a funeral. I do what I can with what I have: I wear my moss-green corduroys and, lacking any other shoes but sneakers, my glam rock–inspired two-tone platform shoes, gold and brown. In the church, reciting my sad verses at the lectern where my father stood a few months before, I feel miserable and clownish. In the far back row, I see the members of my basketball team, the entire eighth-grade junior varsity squad, sitting with the coach. He has required them to attend. Although it's Christmas Eve and drizzly, and notice has been short, turnout is good. My dad had friends. Neighbors are there, and fellow parishioners, old colleagues from the company that cut him loose, and even some Forhans: aunts and uncles and cousins. No Nat, of course. My father's father long ago disappeared for good. And no Jim: my father's brother, trained by fate—as my father was—to rely on himself, has long since drifted off into his own life and hasn't spoken to my father in twenty years. In the funeral memory book, set out for mourners to sign, dozens and dozens of people inscribe their names. Erica, my five-year-old sister, has been practicing writing her name, so she signs three times, inserting herself even among the list of pallbearers.

On the front of the funeral card, presented to each mourner, is a quote from Saint Augustine: "In thee is rest, which forgetteth all toil."

After the funeral, it is still Christmas Eve. The whole family—grandparents, aunts and uncles, cousins—gathers at our house, and we engage in the standard rituals: the praying, the feasting, the nibbling on nuts and gingerbread, the unwrapping of gifts. I get what I've asked for: Ringo's new album. (*Now you're expecting me to live without you . . .*) For all of us Forhan children: a Ping-Pong table set up in the rec room. Afterward, when the table is not in use, Kim and Erica will drape it with blankets, transforming it into a fort that, side by side, they can hide in. Otherwise, for weeks of round-robin tournaments, we fix ourselves at either end of it, in a single place of mindless distraction, our eyes focused only on what is before us, only on the ricocheting ball, the wooden paddle sweaty in our grip. *Serve. Return. Serve. Return. Return. Return. Return. Return.*

– Part IV –

A Voice in the Air

42

Kevin

In those last weeks, I was the first to return home in the afternoon, and he would leave the house then. The last time I saw him, I had come home and poured myself a big bowl of cereal. He comes out, and I say, "Hi, Dad." We're having a light conversation, and he says, "Son?"

I say, "Yeah?"

He says, "I'm scared."

"Well, good luck," I say, and he goes downstairs and leaves. And I never see him again.

After all this time? You completely failed to prepare me to be any use to you, and now you're telling me you're scared? You've never told me anything like that in your life. It came out of the blue. Nothing led up to it. It was basically throwing out one last line, and I did him no good. It's not something I blame myself for. It wasn't my job. It would have been easy just to say, "What are you scared of?" That would have been a good answer, but I was essentially trained to avoid meaningful conversation with my parents.

Dana

On a night not long before Dad died, he and Kim and Erica and I were playing Life, the board game. I remember, with Life, you spin a wheel and move your piece—a little plastic car—along a road a certain number of

spaces, and along the way you get married or have children or become a doc-
tor or buy life insurance, whatever. I spun and landed on the green Revenge
Square, which gave me the power to pick any player and take money from
him or move his piece backward. I picked up Dad's car and moved it back
ten spaces. He said, "Why would you do that?" I said, "Because I hate you."

I wasn't saying "I hate you!" as a brat. I just said it, and there must have
been some sort of true emotion in it. I don't have a memory of his reaction.
After he died, I didn't think, What I said is the reason why. *But I sure*
felt bad about it.

Peggy

When Dad died, I was twenty-one and living in an apartment. I returned
there from work at maybe three-thirty in the afternoon, and there was a mes-
sage on the answering machine to call home, which was unusual. I called, and
our aunt Janice said, "Honey, honey, your dad passed away this morning."

When I got home, I walked into the living room, and Mom put a blan-
ket around me and led me to the couch. We sat down, and she just hugged
me for a long time, maybe a half hour. There were voices in the background,
busy noises around me, and I was just sitting there. Then Mom had to get
up to take care of something, and I sat there. Even when the shock wore off,
I thought, I don't want to get up off this couch, *because I'd have to face*
everybody and have to start talking about it.

Terry

When I look at Dad's life, from his early marriage to his death, to me it's
a story of the tragedy of mental health in our society in that time period.
He knew he was ill. Everybody around him knew he was ill. There was
no way to get family therapy. There was no one being honest with Mom
about what kind of care he was getting. I don't think counselors were giving
good help; they didn't understand the real impact of abandonment he had
early in his life and let him deal with that. He was probably being given

very conventional therapy—nothing very creative and nothing holistic—and, meanwhile, when someone is ill, as he goes through his day, the people around him could be a support system or could help destroy him, but if they don't do the whole thing together, he's not really going to get well, or, even while he's getting well, other people are getting ill from having to deal with this sick individual.

When I got the call and was told that he had died, I asked, "Did he take his own life?"

"Yes, he did."

I said, "Okay." I think Dad was having conversations with me about how he should just end it, but I felt powerless. You want to say, "Oh, no, you don't want to do that. Life's good." I remember saying that. But by the time he did it, I understood. There was no way out for Dad. It was actually a heroic act—because it takes a lot of energy when you have none; it takes a lot of planning when all you want to do is sleep; and it's a proactive stance, when for years you've been passive and just let life run you over. He was getting no other help, so he had to help himself.

He had such a tough life and didn't have any way to sort it through, and it just got worse, and he got ill—he had diabetes, and then he drank a little too much, and he had psychological problems that impacted his marriage, and then he did avoidance: I think there's a story there. But how his kids live with that and then continue their own life—what they learn from it, what impacts are in their life: that's a huge story, too.

Kim

I remember talking about Dad to my friends after he died, so that was when I started to tell the story, but I was telling it as a seven-year-old. Even then I had very few memories of him. Only as an adult did I figure out that he hadn't even been in the house half of my life.

This is what I remember of him. He was always sleeping behind a closed bedroom door, or I assumed he was sleeping. We weren't allowed to go in. He was always tired or sick, or he needed quiet time, so we weren't supposed to disturb him.

The other memory I have is sitting in the front seat of the white Dodge. We were driving by Calvary Cemetery, and he told me, "My mother and brother are buried in that cemetery." He told me the story of his mom and Skippy. As I got older, I thought, What an interesting thing that I remember that, and why was he telling me that?—*because now I think he probably had his own death in his head. That could have been very close to the time he died. What he said could have been prompted just by our driving by the cemetery; it could have been like any other normal conversation. But then, when he died, that's what I remembered about him, and that's the story I started clinging to in my head. It was probably the only significant conversation I had with him—driving in that car, with him telling me about his family.*

Erica

A weird thing happens to me when I write the word dad. *I simply do not have and have not had occasion to actually write the word in any context relative to me. I've said the word often enough. Saying it allows it to disappear into history, into thin air. Writing the word is different: it requires far more commitment and immediate recognition as it lies there on the page and stares back at me. It feels like when there's a stranger in the room looking at me.*

I don't see my dad as not being around. My "experience" of his death continues. It's with me every day, and it's part of who I am. It's not so much an event in my life as a characteristic of me and my personality. So, while to me he's never been around, he's always around.

For most of my life it seems that no one talked about him or what happened, at least not in the open and not to me, so there is a lot I did not and do not know. But I knew our family didn't talk about it, and I had no skills or invitation to bring up the subject to anyone. I could feel that his presence and then his absence affected the family and me. So while I grew up without a father, he had a tremendous influence on me.

I was only five when he died. I remember, on that day, standing on the porch while Mom was screaming and his head rolled out of the car into her hands. I remember being shuffled off to the neighbors' house and peering out their window. I remember seeing Father Lane in his stole, making the sign of the cross, and the ambulance in the driveway.

I remember, when I returned to school, the incredible shame I was supposed to feel because suicide was such a sin, and we were taught to be polite about the whole thing. I remember being told that if anyone asked I should say he died of a heart attack. Of course, at five years old, it's hard to know what the truth is. I carried this story and other misconceptions with me until my teen years, when I heard Kim talking to friends about it, and I was shocked to hear the truth.

Not knowing provides the benefit of not even having to deal with bigger questions. Still, I do wish that once I had reached an age of comprehension, I had a fuller understanding of the situation, who he was, and why he might have been how he was.

Our mother

I can honestly say that the thought of him taking his own life never entered my mind, but I knew something would happen. I thought that he would go into a coma, maybe, and not come out of it. Or he would just take off and leave. I did know something would happen, because you can't live like that forever.

On the day before he died, he got up late and left the house. It was the day that school let out for Christmas vacation, and I was in the kitchen. It was about four o'clock. I'd just gotten home about an hour before. He came out all dressed in his suit, and, as he usually didn't do, he stopped on the stairs going down, and he said, "Goodbye." And I said, "Goodbye."

He normally would go out when I wasn't in the room seeing him. He was in the habit of doing that. I didn't know specifically where he was going. I just thought it was the usual thing. Actually, since he was dressed— I remember how nicely he was dressed—I probably thought he had an appointment for a job, because theoretically that's what he was doing.

In retrospect, I think he knew what he was going to do. I do think that. Otherwise, he wouldn't have said goodbye.

43

He never asked to be here. He did the best he could.

It was his father's fault. His mother's. His brother's. All those dead, disowned, and unaccounted for who would not stop walking around intemperately within him.

As a boy, he was mortally wounded. It took him four decades to hit the ground.

But he chose to marry, chose to have children. What about us? He owed us something.

He owed us nothing. He yearned to be without obligation or pain—who can blame him.

I blame him, the coward. He turned away from us, away from life, tried to wiggle his way out of the deals he'd made.

He was brave. Unable to function in this world, he nonetheless roused his will and took a step toward death, that inevitable thing. He welcomed it, whatever it might prove to be.

He planned the act, for months, for years. He instructed himself and obeyed those instructions.

It was a moment's impulse, an unfortunate choice. If only he had returned home earlier that night—if only he had walked in while I was sitting on the couch in the flickering glow of the television, he would have stayed. He would have seen his son. He would have thought twice, and stayed.

He did it at home to make it easy on my mother. There would be no mystery, no investigation, no search.

He did it at home to torture my mother. He knew that she would miss him in bed and look for him. She would be the one to find him that way.

It never happened. That was not him—it was an impostor in the carport, another person's body. My dad is elsewhere and may yet return.

It's what parents do: they leave and don't say goodbye. His mother had done it. His father, too.

Like his immigrant forebears, he began with little and had to improvise a life, create it on the fly, and the life he made—of hard work, duty, crude charm, and silence—became impossible to live in.

He was Buddy as a boy, then Eddie, then Ed. Which was most real to him? Which one did he kill?

The 1950s did him in: the stifling culture of smiling ambition.

He was Irish, an orphan, a diabetic, a perfectionist, a burier of feelings: he didn't stand a chance.

A series of little secrets killed him.

He dreamed up a life and disguised himself in it. When the mask dropped, no one was behind it anymore.

He was bipolar: he must have been. The disorder, it turns out, is rampant in the family. He could stay up for days at a time, working manically, then sleep through a weekend. Toward the end, he mumbled of his worthlessness and helplessness. Did his psychiatrist diagnose him as manic-depressive? What was that medication he was given, the one he stopped taking? Of course, of course, that's it: he was bipolar. He finally sank so low he wanted out.

And what does that explain? Not enough.

He was born too early. He lived and died before we started *sharing*, before we started *talking things out*.

His children were to blame; we were too many.

Our mother: she drove him to it.

No, she saved his life for years. She saved him from himself.

He died of natural causes.

He died of silence. His. Ours.

His life was not his to take.

His life was not his.

He was sick. He did not know what he was doing.

He knew what he was doing. He knew that he was sick.

I forgive him. I do not forgive him. It is not for me to forgive.

He left no note to haunt us.

To haunt us, he left no note. Maybe he couldn't begin to explain. Maybe a note of explanation wasn't necessary.

But it was. Here I am, trying to write it for him.

His life was a gradual vanishing, a slow unnoticeable erasure of the self he might have been. By the end, he was not himself; he was the husk his self had left behind. There was little left for him to kill.

He killed my dad, asshole.

Bastard.

Poor tortured man.

44

We kept the car. The white Dodge stayed in the carport, where our father had parked it, where he'd lain down and died in it. We kids took turns driving the Dart—first Peggy; then Kevin; then, when I turned sixteen, me; then Dana. Each of us got behind the wheel, sat where our father had last sat, started it up, just as he had, and drove to work or to a friend's house or—

We kept the car. How were we able to do this? And why? Did anybody suggest we might sell it, even give it away? But it was useful, it ran well, and it was paid for. It was only a car. It didn't have to be a symbol or even a reminder. After enough time, a year or two, I came to think of it as just the Dart, not the place where he'd *done it*.

Still, something was wrong with it: the shelf between the backseat and rear window, constructed of stiff red cardboard, began to blister. It bubbled, blackened, peeled. Was this normal—just the consequence of years of exposure to sunlight—or was it a late and continuing effect of the fumes with which our father had filled the car?

What were we thinking? *We kept the car.*

We kept it until we could keep it no longer, until keeping it was a burden, until years later, when I was hundreds of miles away at college, and it had taken on the habit of sputtering suddenly to a stop, and then something essential within it broke for the last time, and it would not budge, and Kevin threw up his hands and took twenty dollars from the driver of a tow truck, and the guy hauled the damned thing away for good.

45

A month after the funeral, my mother received a letter from a man whose name she did not recognize. He enclosed a check for a hundred and fifty dollars, explaining that he owed the money to her husband. It was a gambling debt.

The letter was one small clue, a reminder, of the life my father inhabited outside of the family. He had a life at work, a life in Alaska, where he traveled continually throughout his career, a life with people we did not know. What was that life like? And what was he like when he was in it, when he was far from us?

Almost forty years after my father's death, hunting for answers, I tracked down a former professional colleague of his—maybe the last one still living. Kirk, also an accountant, traveled with my father several times a year to the pulp mill in Alaska to audit the Alaska Lumber and Pulp Company's financial reports.

He remembered my father well. Kirk had been impressed by his amiability and intelligence and professional integrity. Beyond that, he wasn't sure he had any information that could help me. "Well," I said, "tell me about those trips to Alaska. What were they like?"

Kirk and my father would fly to Sitka, the remote town along the water, and check in to a hotel. In the morning, they would drive to the company's offices at the pulp mill, ten miles out of town, and go over the books. My father, being in charge of the Japanese company's financial activities in the U.S., had a difficult job, Kirk said. AL&P was continually in financial trouble. The pulp industry was unstable, the cost of doing business in Alaska was steep, and the company "played games with where the money went."

"Your father's main job," Kirk said, "was to prevent the company from foreclosing." But he did his work well: "The records were always clean."

After a day's work at the office, Kirk and my father would head back into town for dinner—a big one. "We'd be gobbling up twenty-ounce steaks." Who knows what my mother, who weighed my diabetic father's portions by the gram, would have thought of those meals. During one dinner, my dad excused himself to go to the bathroom. Kirk waited for him to return. Then he started worrying and went to check on him. In the bathroom, he found my father, confused, "out of it": having a diabetic reaction. Later, Kirk asked him, "What should I do if that happens again?"

"Feed me chocolate," my father told him.

After dinner, Kirk would return to the hotel, but, for my father, the evening was just beginning: he went to the Elks lodge to meet with his regular poker group. One of the members was a priest. According to Kirk, my father would stay up all night—he might go two or three days without sleeping. "He was not disciplined about his health." Sometimes, when the two of them had to travel two hundred miles to the lumber mill in Wrangell, they played cards with the company's Japanese employees.

Even in Seattle, Kirk told me, my dad was in the habit of playing cards for an hour or two after work. I thought about all those evenings, through all those years, when our mother had set a place at the table for him and he arrived late—an hour or two, sometimes, after he had promised to.

"Why wasn't he going home to his family instead?"

"Well," Kirk answered, "he was a gambling addict. You know that, of course."

A gambling addict. No. I didn't know that.

"Oh, he was a dedicated gambler—but he didn't win much. He owed a lot of money. I had assumed the gambling contributed to his death."

My dad might have killed himself to escape his debts?

What about drinking?

"He wasn't much of a drinker. I don't recall ever seeing him drink, really." If he was up till all hours playing cards, Kirk said, he would likely "have a beer or two," but that didn't mean he had a drinking problem.

So maybe that explains it: all those late arrivals home, all those long nights away. Early in their marriage, hadn't he sat my mother down and tried to teach her how to play poker, tried to excite in her an interest that matched his? Maybe he hadn't been vanishing into some dim bar; maybe he hadn't been escaping into some stranger's bed. Even during his last months, when he had put on a suit and pretended to be heading to a job interview, maybe he'd been heading for the gambling table, where he would lay his money down—lay our money down. What was the seduction? I imagine him trying one more hand, then another, getting swept up in the thrill of it, the drama, the chase, taking solace in the safety of it: at this table, in this circle of poker buddies, he could feel neither depressed nor helpless; it was only numbers he was dealing with, and he knew about numbers—they were his trade. His job was to make numbers balance, make them come out even, be unassailable, while he remained invisible; but here, with luck, with patience, with skill, he might make numbers work for him. He might win just by sitting and thinking, counting, calculating his chances, saying little, revealing nothing with his eyes, making not a single gesture to give himself away. And if he lost? No harm: it was only play, and there was the next hand with which to win it all back, or the hand after that. There was always time—or, rather, time was not a condition of this realm. While he sat studying his cards, he was happily alone in his life, in this floating, enclosed fragment of it; there was only this silence to inhabit, this silence of numbers and chance doing their work, this abstracted, projected space, this closed circle, this knowable world of controlled risk.

My mother knew that he gambled in the last year or two of his life—the check from the stranger after my father's death confirmed that. But she had had no idea of what Kirk told me: that he had gambled for at least a decade before that, and all the time. How much did he lose? Only he could know: he controlled the books. Beyond the monthly allowance he issued my mother for household expenses, the money, however much it was, was his. He always paid the bills on time—the mortgage, the utilities, the insurance—but he must have been setting aside money for gambling. Kirk said the stakes were low in those poker games, but one of my sisters remembers a day when Dad reassured Mom, "Well, I didn't lose the house." Had he really gambled the mortgage, or was he being teasingly, or cruelly, hyperbolic? And wouldn't that conversation mean our mother knew about his poker playing? But she says she didn't realize what he'd been doing until after his death. Still, one of us children remembers our parents arguing about his gambling. One of us remembers, fuzzily, a story being told long ago—by whom?—about Dad getting lucky and winning a color television and then, maybe, a car. Wasn't there a time when we had one too many cars? Who knows? Where do such stories come from, and how can we know if they're true? Each of us recalls only fragments, and what we knew was too little to begin with.

Before I ended my conversation with Kirk, I had one last question for him. I wondered what my father felt about us: his wife and children. Through all of those business trips the two of them took, during their long plane flights, their full days working together, and those daily dinners, what did my father say about his family? Nothing, Kirk said. He never said a word about such things.

46

Days after my father died, I rejoined my church basketball team. After practice one afternoon, the twilight descending, I lingered outside the gym to wait for my ride home. One of my teammates, Perry, a lumbering, quiet, kind boy, walked past me, then turned around. "Chris, I should tell you something."

"What?"

"That last night, the night before your dad died, my dad was with him. They had a drink together at the Wedgwood Tavern."

"Really?"

"Yes. I thought you'd appreciate knowing."

I did appreciate it. It was information. But what could I do with it? What might it explain? Did my father spend the evening in the tavern because he needed to eat up time while waiting for us all to go to sleep? Was he steeling his nerves with drink? What did he talk about with Perry's father? What does a person talk about over a drink when he intends, the next morning, to be dead?

I had told my best friend, Al, about my father. Otherwise, as I returned to school after the Christmas break, I intended to tell no one. The city had two daily newspapers, and the *Times* had not reported the suicide. The *Post-Intelligencer*, though, had published a small paragraph about it. I could take comfort, at least, in the thought that most junior high students didn't read the paper, let alone the tiny items in the back pages.

On my first day back in school, at the end of science class, I was gathering my books. Nanette, who I had heard might have a crush on me, slipped me a folded note and, without a word, walked out of the room. I opened it: "Chris, is it true that your father committed suide?"

Suide. No, my father did not commit that.

I did not respond to Nanette. But word had gotten out. It was junior high: the manner of my father's death was a weapon that could be used against me. For days, in civics class, Tony, sitting in the back of the room, whispered, "Forhan. Hey, Forhan." When I turned, he began miming, patiently, the act of getting into a car and turning the ignition key. Grinning, he pretended to inhale deeply the fumes coming through the open car window. Then he slumped in his seat, eyes closed, tongue hanging slack from his mouth. Other students giggled or covered their eyes with their hands. I did nothing. Preferring not to be there, I acted as though I weren't.

I might as well not have been there—in that school, in my own life: I felt blurry and indeterminate, or I was sensing more intensely the blur that I had always been. For a couple of months, I had exulted in being a basketball player on the JV team: our coach, a parish dad, was relaxed and rumpled and funny, and I was a star. Even with my limited shooting repertoire—I depended almost wholly on a quick burst to the hoop from the right and a layup—I was the leading scorer, at fourteen points a game. I was flashy enough to draw the attention of the varsity coach, a square-jawed marine with a blond buzz cut. He needed me on his squad, he told me. His boys were creating something special in the top league— with my help, they might have that perfect season they were dreaming of. I made the switch. At the first team meeting I attended, the coach introduced me by saying, "Is everyone getting a good look at Forhan's hair? Kind of long, don't you think? I guess the new guy doesn't care about rules." It was then that I learned about a team rule the coach had established before the season started: no hair so long that it went past the top of the ear or reached the collar. "Well," the coach announced, "he's a late addition to the family. I suppose we have to let it slide." Whether it was my aversion to barbers or my one-dimensional game or my inability to meld with a group that had forged its own identity months earlier, I found myself transformed from a high-scoring court wizard into a grumpy longhair riding the pine. In practices and games, the coach rarely looked at me. Only late in a blowout win would he wave me in. I finished my truncated varsity season with a scoring average of one fifth of a point per game. Maybe I wasn't who I thought I was.

And my dad was dead. My dad was dead. And the geography unit I had begun to study when he was alive I was still being tested on, and the sun still rose, and people stood in winter jackets on sidewalks waiting for buses, their breath a cloud in the air before them, and Karen Carpenter sang gleefully about being on top of the world, and I tied my shoes every morning and ate and drank, and my skin sometimes itched, my body still existed, and it was important to trim my nails and comb my hair and get to sleep on time so I would have enough energy for the next day, and it was important to wear my retainer faithfully so my teeth would stay straight, and it was important to be confirmed, it was the next thing to do—it was important to be initiated as a full-fledged, willing member of the Catholic Church. I was fourteen: old enough, I was told, to make my own choice about whether to accept Christ as my Lord, as my father had done thirty years before, and as his parents had done and their parents before them. I had, indeed, made my choice: I had rejected Christ—at least the story I had been told about him, the one in which he was the one and only god who had died for my sins and been resurrected, the one who promised he would return for me one day, who promised there was, without question, a world for us beyond this one. My father was in the ground in the Catholic cemetery, and he was floating in the murk of my memory, in fragments, but he was, most important, elsewhere, basking in the glow of God's love—at least if he had been forgiven his final crime. Everyone around me seemed to take such ideas seriously, but they struck me as being, at best, unsubstantiated. Still, I did the safe thing: I prepared to confirm my faith publicly. This involved joining dozens of other eighth-graders in the school gym for a series of meetings during which we nibbled on cookies and listened to songs from the cast album of *Jesus Christ Superstar* and then discussed them in small groups.

To celebrate the end of our formal preparation for confirmation, we organized a big potluck spaghetti dinner. Each boy or girl would bring from home a contribution to the meal, something we could share as we partook in the elation of claiming a personal stake in the Catholic faith. I had not chosen this faith; it had been sprinkled upon my forehead when I was an infant, and I had been asked week by week, year by year, before I had developed my reasoning abilities, to recite the prayers and participate in the rituals taught to me. I was old enough to feel whether I was a true believer, but I was not old enough to have the nerve to profess what I really thought. I held my tongue. I was beginning to sense that existence is terrifyingly and beautifully bewildering, but, instead of being encouraged to experience that bewilderment on my own and pursue my hunches about it, I was expected to accept someone else's metaphysical construct. About that which is the most essential thing in life—the ultimate mysterious ground of existence, the inexplicableness of our simply being here, of our being alive on this particular planet in the first place—I was being asked to adopt the beliefs of others. Could I, for a lifetime, perceive every moment through the filter of that fixed idea, merely because it was the local custom? And would this not, I was already beginning to feel, be the worst kind of lie because it was a lie I would have to tell myself?

To the celebratory dinner, I brought garlic bread and paper napkins.

47

In school, when given a choice, I sat in the back row of any classroom, where I could lower my head and whisper to my neighbor or pretend I wasn't there. Until now, I had cared about school—or, in school, I had performed with care. I knew that I was supposed to. I still knew it, but I had trouble summoning the effort. I had usually earned A's, occasionally a B. Now my grades were plummeting: I earned a C in English and a D in algebra.

As my performance in the classroom wavered; as I felt my attention detach, splinter, and flit off toward a thick mist at the edge of my thoughts; as I felt a yearning for sense—for an explanation of the world that would account for my being here in this strange, changing body and for my father having achieved his wish to be only a buried, decaying one; and as I hadn't yet the mind that could have defined my discomfort so clearly, I engaged in a manic, blind descent into school activities.

The student variety show was approaching; anyone who had an idea for a performance could sign up. Al and I had one: we would join with two other friends and be a hillbilly band playing old-time music. We'd dress in overalls and straw hats and stand on the stage barefoot, playing a washtub bass, guitar, jug, and washboard. If we were serious about this, we knew, we would need to practice, even if our instruments were primitive, and we would need the guidance of a professional—

that meant the band director, Mr. Holbrook, the same Mr. Holbrook who, two years before, leading my elementary school band, had tried to persuade me to take the clarinet seriously.

One day after school, we four friends gathered in the music room with our instruments. I was on washboard. Mr. Holbrook stood before us. Baton in hand, he announced, "Okay, I'll count you off. Let's start on the downbeat. One—*No!* The downbeat. Start on the downbeat. Try again. One—*No!* The DOWNbeat!"

I didn't know what the downbeat was, and I didn't feel like asking. None of us did. Aw, we decided, let's just lip-synch to records.

The hillbillies were out. Inspired by *American Graffiti* and the 1950s nostalgia that was heavy in the air, we came up with a new plan: a rock-and-roll revue. I would be the front man, the master of ceremonies. I didn't care; I wasn't shy—or, rather, this would be a way to circumvent my shyness: I would ignore myself, act as though I didn't exist. I would be Bick Bark, with a name based on Dick Clark's and a gravelly voice based on Wolfman Jack's. I hid behind round mirrored sunglasses and wore white jeans and a sky-blue sweatshirt on which, with a thick black felt-tip pen, I had drawn stars and squiggled wavy lines and written, in large block letters, BICK BARK. With every student in the school in the auditorium—with Cherie there, and Debbie, and Nanette, and Tony—I stood at the lip of the stage behind a microphone stand and spoke in the voice of a stranger, introducing the songs that my friends—in jeans with rolled-up cuffs and grubby white T-shirts, their hair greased into DAs—pretended to sing: "Teenager in Love," "Rock Around the Clock," "At the Hop."

We were a smash. The audience clapped and even sang along, and we earned a raucous ovation. After the show, I remained Bick Bark. I kept his clothes on. This came in handy at the after-school dance when a pretty girl who had previously kept an oblivious distance from me sidled over and whispered, "Are you really Bick Bark? Will you dance this slow dance with me?" Would I ever. I settled my hands on her waist, she wrapped her arms around my shoulders, and we rocked gently back and forth, her head on my chest, the apple scent of her shampoo in my nose. She was the age my mother had been when she first danced with my father, when they did the slide together, when they sensed that they already somehow knew each other and should stay together. At the end of the song, the girl smiled, slipped her hands from my shoulders, then stared—aghast, repulsed—at her palms. They were black with ink; I had come off on her hands.

Even if I was in hiding, distracted, and playing the role of the mediocre student, one of my teachers took notice of me: one day, as the rest of the class headed out the door toward lunch, she waved me over to her desk. She had a proposal. I had leadership ability. I should run for school president. I should at least think about it.

Later that day, at home, I decided, yes, of course: I should be president. It was a thing to be, another role to play, a predefined identity to slip into, a safe place to put myself. Whichever eighth-grader won the election in the spring would spend the next year as leader of the student government. I wasn't thinking much, though, about next year. I was thinking about the campaign, about how it was something in which I could lose myself, in which I could invest my time and art supplies. For the next week, my bedroom became campaign headquarters. I sat on the floor, cutting badge-size circles out of orange and blue construction paper, writing meticulously on them and on large posters my slogans: "Bick's the Best," "I'm for Bick," "Bick Clicks." Bick had been working for me: he would be the candidate.

My two competitors were Laurie, a quiet, thoughtful flutist, and Joe, a serious, bookish, true school citizen who ran on a platform of more openness and fruitful interaction between administration and students. My platform was that I was Bick Bark and I had cool buttons and posters. Secretly, too, I coveted the honorary dark polished wood presidential gavel that I would receive if I won, and I hoped that walking past my posters on the school walls for two weeks would make Cherie realize that she was blind and misguided and had actually loved me from the start.

Bick won by a landslide. The year's final edition of the school newspaper recounted the election, the front-page article saying, "Chris, not being sure of his status as Chris Forhan, put on the gimmick of being Bick Bark." Side by side with that article was another, reporting the victory of the student who had run for Girls' Club president: "Angie is planning new activities for the school and will try to make seventh graders feel welcome. The interesting fact is that, when she won the election, she didn't have any posters up in the halls." A campaign of ideas. I hadn't thought of that.

On the next page of the paper was this article, written by my friend Al:

Rumor Spreads Quickly

If some students heard a rumor going around about three weeks ago regarding Chris Forhan, next year's president, getting suspended, it's not true. This rumor was started by a person who thought it was funny. He told a couple of people that Chris sneaked into the balcony and turned the spotlight on Mr. Richardson at the choir concert May 22. Before a person starts spreading stories, he should know the facts.

The inventor of the rumor was probably Al himself; his article had the tone of an act of forced penance. It was someone else, though, who spread the rumor that I had been spied naked, streaking across the football field.

I was Bick Bark. I had stepped into an invented character's clothes and, in full view of the school, stepped onto the stage. Bick was popular. Bick was president. Bick was the subject of wild rumor and conjecture. The boy I'd been, the kid whose dad had done himself in, had disappeared, happily so.

48

We wanted beer, my friends and I, and we'd heard where we could get some. Word had spread around my high school that a convenience store in central Seattle, the black district, sold alcohol to teenagers, no questions asked. Could it be true? Four of us were willing to find out.

I'd never had a beer. It was time I tried one.

I was a month away from turning sixteen—still too young to drive. John, a year older, would take his family's old sedan, and Al and Scott and I would come along. Scott lived across the street from Al and was a central member of the group I had begun to hang around with. One of Scott's favorite rituals, as we were cruising nowhere in particular, was to roll down his window and, as we passed a man tugging at his ear, yell authoritatively, "No ear tugging after four o'clock!" To a pair of girls in the crosswalk wearing knit caps, "No knit caps after six!" To a dog: "No barking on Fridays!" Scott had come into possession of a fire extinguisher and begun filling it with water and bringing it along on our travels. He would pull up beside someone walking along the street and call out, "Excuse me—can you tell us how to get to the Space Needle?" When the kind stranger put his fingers to his chin and said, "Let's see—" Scott would lift the extinguisher, blast him in the face, then hit the accelerator. Through all of this, I hunkered down in the backseat, cringing, mortified—too much a good boy to enjoy Scott's shenanigans, too much a coward to demand that he stop.

On the excursion to buy the beer, I was not a coward. I believed in this mission. It did not seem to me reprehensible for a teenage boy to desire to try alcohol, but I also did not doubt that if my mother knew what I was doing, she would make me pay. To take this drive, to make this purchase, to pop the cap from a bottle and take a swig, I would have to become—I would have to liberate—a boy I never was at home, in her presence: a boy who followed his whims, even if that meant ignoring the rules. I imagined if my mother were to discover what I was up to, her conception of me would be altered forever: she would understand at last my depravity and weakness, my general unseemliness. I was a teenager, biologically programmed to feel constrained by the values of my parents. Still, this sense of my mother as a strict moral arbiter—had my father felt it, too? Maybe he'd kept part of himself secret because of it. I was beginning to live a life outside of my home, a life that I wouldn't give up. If I could live that life only by hiding it, I would.

The store was there, just where we'd been told it was: a small, nondescript place on the corner of a busy street. We strolled in. It was empty except for the cashier. He eyed us impassively when we entered, then looked away. We must have looked like what we were: four furtive white boys from the suburbs. He must have known why we were there.

We had decided we would try to buy a six-pack or two. But which of us would do it? We huddled briefly in the aisle next to the chips and peanuts and whispered haltingly. "Sorry," Al said. He had no money. "I have a dollar, that's all," Scott apologized. John had two dollars, enough for a six-pack. So did I. We would do the buying. If John succeeded, I would try, too.

John sauntered over to the refrigerator case, then eased the door open and snatched a six-pack of bottles. Rainier: we'd heard that was good. The rest of us watched silently as he carried the beer to the register. Looking unsurprised and a little tired, the cashier took John's money, handed him some coins back, and slipped the beer into a paper sack. John headed out the door. Al, Scott, and I glanced at each other. This was easy.

It was my turn. I repeated what John did. By the time I was taking the heavy sack from the cashier, Al and Scott were out the door and headed to the car, which was parked at the curb. I left the store, the glass door swinging shut behind me, and hopped into the backseat, setting the bag on the floor next to John's purchase. Then we were off, laughing. As we drove up the hill, a car pulled alongside us to the right, an arm extended out of its open window. In the hand was a badge, glittering silver in the late-afternoon light. There were two men in the front seat, waving us back over to the curb.

"Fuckfuckfuck," Scott said.

John parked, and we stepped out. The two men approached us. "You boys have something in the car you want to show us?" one of them said.

"No," John said. "What?"

"Did you buy some beer just now?"

"Son," the second man said, "would you mind opening the doors of your car?"

John did as he was asked, opening the front and back doors on the curb side of the car.

"May I have those bags, please?" The man pointed to the floor near the backseat.

John leaned down, grabbed them, and handed them over.

"Any of you boys twenty-one?"

None of us spoke. The man opened the back door of his car and set the six-packs on the seat.

"Don't tell my mother," I said. I looked one man in the eyes, then the other. "Don't tell my mother." My secret life—the one that had brought me to this moment—and my life at home were at risk of colliding. I was pacing on the sidewalk, back and forth, pleading. "Don't tell my mother. Are you going to tell my mother? I don't care that you caught us. Just don't tell my mother. She'll kill me. My mother can't know about this. Please. Don't tell her."

"There's no need to worry," one of them said, "as long as it wasn't you who bought the beer. Did you buy the beer?"

I hated myself for having had two dollars in my wallet.

About my mother, they made no promises. I would just have to wait and see, they told me. It depended on how the case panned out. It was the cashier they were after, not us. They'd been sitting in their car for hours, surveilling the place. Whoever they caught would be a prime witness against the cashier.

"Okay, okay," I said. "Just don't tell my mother."

When I returned home, I spilled the whole story to Dana. I had to tell someone. "Are you going to tell Mom?" she asked.

No, I wouldn't tell her.

"I think you should tell Mom."

I couldn't. I'd sweat it out. I'd bury the problem and, if I got lucky, never be required to speak of it.

I waited: I waited all the next day, then the next one, for a phone call. I prayed not to get one, prayed that the episode would fade away, be forgotten.

And then, one late afternoon, the call came. Two detectives, I was told, needed to speak with me in person, and they were on their way over.

With only minutes left before the doorbell would ring, I trudged upstairs and announced to my mother that I had something to tell her, something important. She looked at me quizzically. "Okay," she said. I walked into the living room and sat in a chair. She followed and sat on the couch a few feet away.

My mother knew me as a good boy. I had mainly stayed out of trouble, and it hadn't been difficult. But now I had broken the law, then covered up the transgression.

My throat dry, heart pounding, I explained to my mother what I had done. She did not move from her seat. She stared at me. "I'll never trust you again," she said.

It wasn't the buying of the beer that bothered her, she explained, although she didn't approve of it. My crime had been my silence: my assumption that part of my life should be kept a secret. My crime—as I think of it only now—had been my father's crime.

The detectives didn't stay long. They asked me to narrate the series of events surrounding the purchase of the beer. Had the cashier asked my age? Had he asked for identification? Then they told me that I would be expected to testify in court. The cashier had a long history of selling alcohol to minors, and it had finally caught up with him. Throughout the interview, neither of them cracked a grin. After our door closed behind them, as they were descending our porch steps, maybe one of them muttered, "Poor dumb sucker of a kid."

In court, I answered the lawyers' questions as accurately as I could. Yes, I had willingly purchased the beer; it was my idea. No, the cashier did not ask me to produce identification. No, he did not remind me that there was a minimum age for purchasing alcoholic beverages. No, I could not say for sure that the man sitting in the courtroom was the one in the store that day. His face had faded away as soon as I had turned toward the door.

My punishment was not finished. If I hoped to have the citation for buying alcohol expunged from my record, I was required to attend alcohol school; one afternoon a week for two months, I would join a dozen other teenagers for group counseling. Mainly out of a sense of duty as a friend, but maybe also out of a sense of guilt—he hadn't had to tell his parents or testify or enroll in alcohol school—Al accompanied me, every week, on the four-mile walk to the counseling center. He waited outside while I joined my troubled peers, a tough bunch—leather-clad, straggle-haired, callous, and sad. None, it appeared, had recently completed a year as junior high school president. Week after week, I listened to lectures about drinking and depression, about drinking and skipping school, about drinking and dying behind the wheel. I filled in the bubbles and blanks on surveys designed to elicit in me recognition of my reckless relationship with alcohol and the ways in which it was deadening me to my family, my friends, and myself. Meeting after meeting, I was polite and silent; I did my time; I spoke briefly and only when spoken to.

One afternoon, though, I was required to stand before the entire group and make a speech—we all were. We sat in a circle and, one by one, rose and testified about what it felt like to be drunk and why we liked it so much. The others spoke in rich detail, with fondness, of wild sensations of joy and fearlessness, of drunken urges to fight, to weep, to scream at their tormentors—the bullying vice principal, the disloyal sister, the feckless father who had abandoned them—or to declaim freely, without shame, their tender love for their true friends, the few who understood and accepted them. Then it was my turn. I stood, hesitated, then made an embarrassed admission: I had never been drunk. I had never tasted alcohol. I had only wanted to try a beer. Was that such a big deal? I was almost sixteen, after all; I was curious—but, before I could so much as pop the top off, I had been caught, and now here I was, and, believe me, I wished I could explain what it felt like to be drunk, I wished I knew what it was like, and if I was lucky, I would find out one day, and that day would come soon.

After my eight weeks of meetings, during my exit interview, the counselor sat behind her desk and looked at me sympathetically. "Sorry about that," she said. "I know you didn't belong here."

My record was expunged. For my trouble attending the trial as a witness, the state mailed me a seven-dollar check. I was too ashamed to cash it. To do so might be to confess my crime all over again. My aunt was a teller at my bank: there was a chance that I would end up standing before her and she would say, "A check from the state? What have you been up to, Chris?" I slipped the check inside a book in my bedroom and forgot it, or tried to imagine that I had. Months later, the state sent me a letter asking what had happened. It needed to balance its books for the fiscal year. Had the check not reached me? Did I need another one? No, what I needed was to have the whole torturous, embarrassing episode expunged from the record of my life.

I plucked up the courage and cashed the check. I was lucky—it was my aunt's day off.

Not long afterward, I got my wish: I got drunk. The parents of a friend of a friend of my friend were out of town, so their house was available for a party. I had no idea how to drink; I was unaware that between the moment one sips alcohol and the moment its effects kick in, there is a delay. I was handed something simple, maybe a rum and Coke. It tasted sweet—not bad at all. But there wasn't much alcohol in it: I wasn't feeling anything. I drank another. Meanwhile, one of our group, Randy, was being more careful. He had not drunk much, that evening or ever, but, wanting to look as though he knew what he was doing—wanting to align his behavior with the deepening general stupidity being displayed by the partiers—he hesitated in the stairwell, tilted his head, gazed at a potted plant, and delicately lifted one of its leaves to his parted lips, pretending to eat it. Is that the kind of thing one does under the influence of alcohol? I didn't think so. I was sitting on the stairs, considering Randy, then considering a row of knick-knacks lined on a narrow shelf on the wall: small porcelain puppies and a figurine of the Virgin Mary, arms extended toward me. She seemed to be moving, seemed to be about to speak. Why was I sitting on the stairs? Hadn't I just a moment before been walking down the stairs, intending to go somewhere? Mary was looking at me. *My dad's dead,* I thought. *My dad's dead.* He hadn't been on my mind, but suddenly he was. Then I said it aloud: "My *dad's dead,* my *dad's dead.*" I said it louder, and then I wailed it. "My dad's *dead!*" Tears welled in my eyes. I pounded my knees with my fists. "My dad's *dead!* He's *dead!*"

Al was suddenly sitting next to me, putting his arm around my shoulders. "I know, Chris," he said. "I know. We all know now."

I ended the night outside, on my back, faceup in the flower garden, no desire to rise.

49

A couple of years before this, while still living at home, Kevin had summoned the nerve to make an announcement to our mother: he would no longer attend Mass. He could not, he told her, profess what he did not believe. None of us children had said such a thing before. I, certainly, was too craven to do so. My habit on Sunday mornings was to tell my mother I would be attending a later Mass than she; instead of driving to church, I would drive to the record store and browse the bins for an hour. When I had been forced to make a difficult admission to my mother, it was because two detectives were minutes away from ringing our doorbell. When Kevin was forced to make a difficult admission, it was because his conscience would not have it otherwise.

Our father's kind of courage—and he did have courage—was in charting a plan for his life, a plan of education and professional mastery and advancement, when he had few models for doing so, and then applying himself to that plan, remaining dutiful to it. A consequence, though, of such diligence and single-mindedness might have been that he ignored complicated, troubling, ragged aspects of himself. As he adopted acceptable modes of being, acceptable identities—soldier, husband, father, career man, churchgoer—I suspect that griefs and yearnings he had long harbored were silenced. Maybe this is merely—merely!—the human condition. But what if a man defines himself by his competence in the workplace and then that competence fails him? What if he conceives of himself as surviving on pluck and will and then that will slackens?

What if he gets sick? What self does he have left then? Can he recognize it?

My mother accepted Kevin's proclamation that he would not belong to her church, no matter how his announcement pained her—no matter how it meant the failure of her efforts, from his birth, to instill in him the faith that had given her life such purpose and moral clarity. What alternative did she have?

Kevin had chosen honest perplexity over false piety, and, at the same time, he was choosing poetry. It makes sense: a poem is a place to discover what we know—and a place to map the limits of our knowing. Soon he began sharing his poems with our mother, and, however questioning they might have been of the faith that sustained her, she was proud. At twenty, he wrote a poem called "Grace Before a Meal," in which the traditional consolations of religion are absent. One evening—irony and paradox I can't untangle—our mother, when we sat down to dinner, asked Kevin to read the poem aloud as we bowed our heads. For a moment, our household's ritual honoring of God for His gifts was replaced by an honoring of the chilling and exhilarating silence that abides beneath all our chatter and guesswork about Him.

An element of hollowness is present in the stew
The upright glasses and laid-out spoons have nothing to say
The seated guests have nothing to say
Between the scraping of chairs and the lifting of spoons,
The candles hold their tongues forever & ever Amen.

50

At sixteen, I was hired for my first real job—in a nursing home, the kind of place where Grandma Carey, my father's grandmother, spent her last years. Her mind mostly gone, she passed away two years after my father did, without ever having been told that her favorite grandson had killed himself—passed away, probably, with no memory that he had existed.

In a white button-down shirt and paper cap, I worked in the kitchen, washing dishes, mopping floors, and setting up the racks of food trays—the silverware and napkins, the salt and pepper packets, the skim milk, the hot water for tea or Sanka—that were delivered to the patients three times a day in their rooms. The door between the kitchen and public hallway was open during the day, and the sounds of a jaunty piano and hesitant, stiff singing reached me from the communal room: "Daisy, Daisy, give me your answer, do. . . ." "And we won't come back till it's over over there." I glimpsed the old people shuffling past the door in slippers or rolling by in wheelchairs, gripping the black rubber railing on the wall for help making turns. Marie, nearly hairless, skeletal, in a thin, tattered robe, minced along with the delicate steps of a geisha, murmuring, "Yes. Yes. Yes." Mr. Walker sped along in his wheelchair, the stump of his amputated leg pointing forward, as if accusingly, at whoever was in his path. Answering and re-answering a question that no one else heard, he insisted, through sneering lips, "No. No. No. No."

Thankfully, in the evening, after the patients had eaten dinner and the racks of trays had been wheeled back into the kitchen, I was allowed to close the door. I felt contentedly alone then, singing to myself, dipping the mop into the bucket of steaming bleached water and slapping it onto the linoleum floor, pouring juices for the next morning's breakfast—thirty-six orange, twelve apple, five cranberry, four prune—in small plastic cups on a wide tray and sliding it into the refrigerator. My first and largest task before turning out the lights was to wash all the pots and plates and cups and silverware. I stood at the stainless-steel sink, snug in my corner, as if in a cockpit, long counter to my left where the dirty dishes were set, immense dishwasher to my right, a handle to slide its door up and then slam it sat-isfyingly down, like a garage door, before I pressed the red button to begin the wash cycle. One night, humming, in the midst of my familiar, simple, repetitive work, my mind elsewhere, anywhere but there, I grabbed a plate with my left hand, plucked the knife and fork off it with my right, and tossed them into a plastic basket, used a spatula to scrape off the excess food, then grabbed another plate, then another, then another—and then I stopped. I stared at the plate I was holding. No. Could it be? I looked closer. Yes. Gleaming, sticky, nearly black, next to a lump of untouched mashed potatoes and a brownish-pink square of country-fried steak, was a tidy pile of human excrement. A mute, potent protest: the act, perhaps, of someone who felt he'd outlived his usefulness yet was being made to suffer the indignity of remaining alive, someone whose purpose had van-ished but who still had a mind, some kind of mind.

Was it a protest against me? Or, more generally, against my kind?: those who delivered from the kitchen, daily, and would deliver until this person's death, congealed oatmeal, cold white toast, bland canned peas, a pear wedge fished from a ten-pound tub. Maybe it was a protest against everything. Or nothing. Whoever sent the message to me, I saw his point.

51

Entering high school, I had left my junior high heart behind me. My ardor for Cherie had cooled, then vanished. This puzzled me; my pure, earnest desire for her had felt so unwaveringly true, so much an axiom of my existence on earth, that I had presumed it would remain a lodestar until my death, a fixed fact by which my happiness would forever be measured. But now I was suddenly, seemingly permanently, ecstatically unhappy about someone else: Sue, a cute, thoughtful, quiet girl in my typing class, an impassioned Catholic who had room in her heart only for Christ, then later for a muscled lunk named Tim, but I was counting on my guileless charm and devotion and tenacity to lure her away from both of them and into my arms. How little it takes to believe the unlikely, to let desire do reason's work. Sue knew I liked her—I told her; everyone told her. She kind of liked me, too, enough to flash me a bashful smile when we passed in the halls; enough to let me walk with her the half mile to her home from school, after which I retraced my steps to begin the walk to my home; enough, even, to go out with me a couple of times: to a baseball game, to a movie. But she didn't like me enough, finally. She could not be my girlfriend, she explained to me. Instead, she would always be my good friend. And isn't that, she mused, more to be valued, really? *No,* I thought. *No, it isn't. It is not to be valued.*

Thwarted, with nowhere outside me to go, my desires were chan-
neled back inward, into poetry, into song. In memory, my junior and
senior years in high school are a long, dim, drizzly winter afternoon. I
sit alone in my room, drafting and redrafting lines of poetry in which
my unimpeachable feelings for Sue, cruelly spurned, refuse to die; they
make a clamorous sound but a coded one—they are expressed in references only she would recognize. Sue alone would be able to construe
my meaning should she ever—*Please, Lord*—ask to read one of those
poems I keep reminding her that I write, or should she ever discover
a piece of paper lying conspicuously on my desk in typing class, as
if, oops, I've accidentally left it there, and should she, curious, pick it
up, and study it, and bite her lip, and place her fingers gently against
her chest, then read it again, slowly, then again, until she knows it
by heart and understands me at last and regrets her foolishness and
admits to herself that she wants me for her own. It's my last, best hope.
When not writing a poem, I am gazing at Sue's photo tacked to my
wall while I sing along with my records. Every song is about her. This
is easy to imagine when I'm listening to Electric Light Orchestra's
"Can't Get It Out of My Head" or Tom Petty and the Heartbreakers'
"The Wild One, Forever." It is harder when the song is Blue Öyster
Cult's "7 Screaming Diz-Busters."

I wasn't listening much to the Beatles anymore—certainly not to
Paul McCartney's solo work. With "Silly Love Songs" riding high on
the charts, he and his new band were coming to town, but I wasn't
going. All that cloying gooeyness: I was disdainful of it. McCartney
was irrelevant, I thought, a goofy tunesmith, a candy salesman. He
was okay. He'd done some things in the 1960s. But he was no Supertramp.

When I told Al that I wouldn't be going to the concert, he looked
at me straight: "Don't be a dumb shit. It's Paul McCartney. It's a Beatle. He comes to town, you see him."

We saw him. Trusting me again even after the beer fiasco, my mother agreed to let me drive the Dodge to the show. In the seat where my father had lain his head for the last time, I rattled down the freeway with Al and a couple of other friends, and soon, in the dark, under the concrete dome of Seattle's new functional gray hunk of a sports stadium, I was standing among sixty-seven thousand people, and there he was: Paul, a football field away but there nonetheless, an actual Beatle, visiting from my past, visiting from another world, from his world, wherever that was—Paul, in glimmering black satin pants and jacket, Paul leaning forward at the black piano, belting out a song of amazement about his love for his wife, whom he couldn't stand to be without, whom he would never dream of leaving, who even now stood just feet away from him, crooning along with his song, which was her song.

A few months later, he released a recording from that concert tour, and I played some of the songs on the school radio station: fifteen hundred watts of solid power, 89.5 on your FM dial. Though the signal reached throughout Seattle, we never sensed that we had many listeners. The station was operated by students—amateur broadcasters who might yearn to be accomplished professionals one day but whose main job now was to avoid sounding too nervous and bumbling and creaky-voiced. I found a home at the station, an identity: I was one of the radio guys. I liked the idea of being on the air; it confirmed me, even if that me wasn't *me*, exactly. Two years earlier, I had hidden in the clothes, and behind the grizzled voice, of Bick Bark. Now I would hide behind my own voice. With the live microphone inches from my lips, I was unavoidably present, appearing in a stranger's home or car—if only by accident, while he was searching on the dial for another station; at the same time, I was alone, safe in the studio, almost anonymous, a name without a face. My obligation was to speak not my heartfelt thoughts but a disc jockey's practiced, impersonal patter.

We played the hits and oldies and album tracks and, on Saturdays, jazz. Sundays were silent. The students had the run of the station, mainly. We chose the music to be played, although the one among us who was program director was required to listen to each track on every new album, keeping an ear out for vulgarities. If he heard a profanity or a reference to genitalia, he marked the track as unplayable. One day we discovered that even irony could be taboo. One of us played, on the air, Randy Newman's new single, in which he sang, "Short people have no reason to live." We thought the song screamingly funny, an over-the-top, unsubtle comic attack on mindless prejudice. We got it—it was difficult not to—but Mr. Adams, our faculty adviser, was not amused. The song demeaned short people, he said; it would not be played again on his station. Mr. Adams himself was decidedly short. The satirical nature of the song was lost on him. It went right over his head.

Satire, sarcasm, irony: these were the stock-in-trade for my friends and me—safe modes in which to express ourselves without fully expressing ourselves, we who were made of need and nervous glances, who were generally embarrassed, inept, and monosyllabic when it came to sincere, serious talk. It was a mode of discourse familiar to me from my home. When our father had fallen into the habit of inserting into conversations the statement "Well, it's relative," we had responded each time, in unison, "Relative to *what*?"—ignoring the substance of his thought and instead poking fun at his fussy inexactitude. When I entered the kitchen one afternoon and caught my little sister rapidly stashing an unpermitted bowl of ice cream in a cabinet, I flew into mock fury, raising my fists toward the ceiling and screaming, "How dare you!" I took comfort in pretending that something mattered when it didn't, in mocking those who cared passionately about the irrelevant. All the while I was unmindful of how this habit could be a means of self-protection: a way of not speaking aloud, and unironically, of the things that do matter.

MAD magazine and *National Lampoon* and *Monty Python's Flying Circus*: these were the master practitioners of the humor my friends and I prized. The jokes we told felt accurate as expressions of the jokes we felt ourselves to be; they arose from our hunch that existence is absurd and unfathomable—that the mere fact of being was worth making fun of. At its best, such humor was evidence of our humble refusal to presume: evidence of our attentiveness to the existentially unknowable, of our distrust of the falseness of convention, and of our wide-eyed appreciation of people's common humanity. At its worst, it was evidence of our cruelty and stupidity.

Al, his brother Kurt, and Scott had started a punk band—the Cheaters—and devoted much of their time, when not practicing or inventing absurd and comical logos for the group, to haunting radio station lobbies and record stores and downtown clubs and theaters where they might cross paths with musicians. They met Graham Parker and Cheap Trick. Teaming with an amateur photographer acquaintance, they stalked the members of KISS at their downtown hotel and took pictures of them without makeup; the band's manager grabbed the camera and stripped the film from it. When the Ramones came to town, my friends and I lingered outside the theater after the concert, keeping our eyes out for a Ramone, any Ramone. At last, Dee Dee, in his mop of black hair, leather jacket, and torn jeans, strolled out the side door and down the sidewalk. We followed at an indiscreet distance, waiting for whatever might come next, waiting to decide why we were trailing him. Then Scott yelled, "Dee Dee! Get out your knife! I've got mine! Ramone! It's a rumble, just you and me." Dee Dee turned around, sneered, chuckled, and kept walking. Scott had no knife. He had no interest in fighting a Ramone. His interest was in pretending to be the sort of person who was interested in fighting a Ramone.

I think of myself in such moments—and they were continual throughout high school—as being almost invisible, a peripheral figure, a voice on the radio but not a real person willing to show his face, a watcher, not a member of the band, just a hanger-on, a junior high friend of the bass player with nothing to do but go where he and his friends went. The world they were becoming citizens of was a real world, an identifiable one, with distinctive rituals and knowledge whose shape and significance remained always just beyond me. The Cheaters cut a single and landed a couple of gigs as an opening act at the Bird, a punk club that hosted shows of local bands and others driving up from Los Angeles or San Francisco. As we entered the club one night, we overheard an exuberant spiky-haired guy who was pointing to a button on his shirt. It said DEVO. I had no idea what the word referred to. "Devo is *it* now," he pronounced rhapsodically, evangelically. "Mark my words: there's no other band. Devo is all that's going to matter from now on." Inside the club, the audience, meager but crazed, in slashed T-shirts and frayed Army jackets, hunks of metal dangling from their ears and noses, squeezed toward the lip of the stage and pogoed or taunted the musicians, tossing popcorn at them, and the bands retaliated by spitting back. In my JCPenney clothes—flared jeans, plaid button-down shirt, and down jacket—I kept my distance, leaning against a far wall that was squiggly with graffiti. Occasionally, amid the music's sloppy thrash and drone, its frantic motion, I heard something that entered me and stayed put. "Jesus Christ is a monkey on your back!" railed the singer of one band. The song was "Boss on the Cross." It was audacious and funny and true and, while it lasted, made me forget my suburban shopping-mall clothes.

At home, the music I listened to was often something new that I had smuggled out of the radio station. In the fall of my senior year, I had begun playing on the air a song by a new artist with a comical name: Elvis Costello. "Alison" was gorgeous and tender and bitter and sad—I decided I should take this guy's album home. On the cover of the record, called *My Aim Is True*, the singer looked nothing like the swaggering, glamorous, shampooed stars in satin pants whom I was used to seeing on album covers. He was skinny, gawky, splay-legged, and pigeon-toed, and he wore nerdy black-rimmed glasses, but he was grinning deviously and throttling the neck of his electric guitar as if he could kill me with it. Elvis Presley had died three months earlier, and on the cover of this new Elvis's record was printed, top to bottom, over and over, brooking no dissent, "Elvis is king." Who was this guy? I put the needle in the groove, and then I kept it there: day after day, after walking home from school, I put the album on, listened to it all the way through, and listened to the whole thing again, then again. The more I listened, the more I understood who this guy was: he was me.

The songs trembled with desire, vitriol, disillusionment, and guilt. They were witty and enraged and self-implicating, their pithy images boiling over with intelligence and pain. Elvis sang to someone of loving her more than everything in the world but not expecting that to last. He sang of a woman who, as detectives drag the lake for a corpse, coolly files her fingernails. He sang of feeling like a juggler with too few hands. I hadn't realized a person could say these things, or say them in this way; I hadn't known for certain that what I felt, others felt. The album was a stone tablet carved with eternal verities, a gift of permission handed down to me from a cloud. Elvis was all that was going to matter from now on.

Kevin had moved out of the house by then, into a tiny furnished studio apartment over his landlord's garage. One afternoon he was back home visiting, and I brought the record upstairs and told him that he had to hear it. I pulled the disc from its sleeve, slipped it onto the turntable of the family stereo, and played my two or three favorite songs. "Hmm," he said. "Pretty good. There's a little reggae beat there."

A few months later, walking through north Seattle, miles from home, I saw, blocks away and strolling toward me, my brother, of all people, even farther from his own apartment. I hadn't seen him in weeks, but here we were, sharing the same unexpected route. We stopped to greet each other, amused by the coincidence. "Hey," I said. "What are you doing?"

"Singing the entire album of *My Aim Is True* to myself."

"Me, too," I replied.

When Elvis came to town, I made sure to see him. Even after moving across the state to college the next year, I took a Greyhound back to Seattle in the middle of the week to see Elvis's show with Al. He and his band played for a furious forty minutes, speeding up the tempo of each song, hurtling through it as if they couldn't wait to get offstage. Between numbers, Elvis said hardly a word. Then he stomped off.

Was he done? Was this it already? We cheered and cheered— we kept our side of the bargain—but we could not persuade him to return for an encore. Instead, probably at the direction of Elvis, in order to clear the room, someone sent an ear-piercing, unrelenting squeal of feedback through the speakers. Beside me, Al dropped into his seat. He began to shiver, his face expressionless, his eyes wide. I shook his shoulders. "Al!" I said. "Al! Are you okay? Speak to me!" He was pretending to be catatonic; I was pretending not to know that he was pretending. It was a thing we did: letting a moment of reality become suddenly, easily, the backdrop of a fiction we were enacting. It came naturally to us—a way of living slightly to the side of life, of watching it while watching ourselves watching it. "Let me help," a stranger next to us yelled through the noise. "Let's find a doctor for your friend." The jig was up. Al stopped trembling, stood up, and followed me and the rest of the crowd streaming out the doors and onto the sidewalk.

We had slipped into such playacting at an earlier concert, too. In the Coliseum, the big arena downtown where the Sonics played their games, Al and Kurt and Scott and I stood on the main floor, shoulder to shoulder among thousands of fans listening to an opening act of little interest to us. It might have been Ted Nugent. We had come for the main act—Cheap Trick? Blue Öyster Cult? I don't remember. What I remember is that Al and I—simultaneously realizing that, standing there, we could be mistaken for numbskull teens grooving to numbskull music—decided to entertain ourselves by pretending to be numbskulls, the sort of humorless louts who often mystified us. Al pushed me. "Hey, man!" I yelled. I threw myself at him and wrapped my arms around his head. He slipped out and took a wild fictional swing at me, and I swung back. We were giddy, distracting ourselves from the dumb, unironic music by acting dumb and unironic. And then someone's arms were encircling my chest and squeezing hard—a security guard's—and then another guard was joining him, and they were lifting me off the ground, and Al was disappearing into the crowd, and they were hauling me away, pointing me toward the exit door, yelling, "Out! You fight, you're gone!" and the door was slamming shut behind me, and I was outside, alone, in the dark and cold and silence.

I had nothing to do, nowhere to go. My friends were my ride home. I hoisted myself onto a low concrete wall. I sat and waited. After a few minutes, chilled from sitting still, I slipped down off the wall, paced up and down on the sidewalk for a while, then sat on the wall again.

Two hours later, waves of concertgoers surged out of the arena. Al,

Kurt, and Scott found me waiting. They enjoyed the requisite laugh at my expense, and we drove home.

While being carried off the arena floor, I had complained, desperately, bitterly, to the guards, "But we were kidding! It was a joke!" It did not matter: they saw what they saw. It would not have helped my case if I had argued, "Don't you understand? *Nothing means anything.*"

52

At the radio station, I had worked my way up to being the morning disc jockey. Five days a week, I arrived early to school, warmed up the transmitter, and, at seven o'clock, began the broadcast day. For ninety minutes, playing songs by Neil Young, James Taylor, and Joni Mitchell, I was a voice in the air. While introducing the names of records and bands, while announcing the weather forecast, while encouraging listeners to call with requests, while extemporizing—I hoped—with a delightfully dry wit, practicing my enunciation and my seeming naturalness, acting as though I were every listener's mellow friend, I was only a small part of myself: a part I could control and perfect, in the dark.

By the time of Kurt's late-afternoon shift, the music on the air got harsher, louder, more electric and strange: the New York Dolls, Roxy Music, Frank Zappa, the Tubes. Al worked at the station, too—and Paul, who had little interest in music but who had a golden voice and a holy devotion to broadcasting and ended up making a lifetime career of it. Anthony, happy and angular, all bones and hair like a picked-at Brillo pad, worked behind the scenes as an engineer alongside Dan, an occasional DJ and tireless prankster.

Dan's dad was a vampire. Every weekend, he rose from the dead. I'd seen him: the Count, the host of Channel Seven's *Nightmare Theater*. Late each Friday night, to the sound of distant howling, the camera panned toward a coffin, whose lid creaked open to reveal a skeleton in repose. Slowly the bones took on flesh and movement, and then, black-caped, fanged, and pallid, Dan's dad sat up, cackled, and, through thin, bloodred lips, introduced *The Bride of Frankenstein* or *The Creature with the Blue Hand*.

One morning during my show, Dan called me. "Uh, yes," he said, "I'd like to make a request." He didn't identify himself, but it was self-evidently Dan: the voice was unnaturally low and fake. This was another of Dan's practical jokes, and a clumsy one. I called his bluff. "You want to make a request, huh?"

"Yes. Yes, I do."

"Forget it. We don't need any stupid fucking listeners calling with their goddamn idiotic requests. No fucking way am I—"

At the other end of the line, there was a tiny, muffled gasp. Then a click. Dan had hung up.

No. A listener who'd called to make a request had hung up.

I set down the receiver and stared at the phone. The song I had been playing was beginning to fade out. I was trembling. I turned toward the microphone. What could I say? I could tell the truth; I could be myself. I could say, "To the listener who just called, I apologize. You won't believe the misunderstanding that led me to say what I did. I'm sorry. Please forgive me. Please. Maybe even call back. I'll explain."

Instead I said, "It's twelve minutes in front of eight o'clock. Mild temperatures in store for us today, and a brisk wind. . . ."

The next day, after classes had ended, I was at the station and was told I had a phone call. I picked up the receiver. "Hello?"

"Is this Chris Forhan?"

"Yes."

"Fuck you, asshole."

I couldn't argue with that.

53

Glib, oblivious, scared, practiced at fending off glumness with wise-cracks and sneers, I was offered for an hour each day, in the class of Frances Myers, a glimpse of another way of being, a glimpse of a way out, of a way to use language to reveal—and wonder about—unsettling truths, not to deflect attention from them.

Mrs. Myers was a genuine teacher, a life-altering one. She had been Kevin's English teacher three years before and, already past seventy by the time I was sitting in her classroom, might have been the oldest teacher in the school. She was among that generation of highly intelligent women who came of age in the 1920s and, with few other options for a way to use their minds in a career, went into teaching. She had a round, kind face and wore large glasses with black plastic rims. She was of modest height—shorter than most of her students—and was slightly plump; hers was the body, I imagined, of a woman who had devoted her life to sitting in comfy armchairs, turning the pages of fat eighteenth-century novels, sipping occasionally from a snifter of sherry. Her wardrobe was unassuming: flat-soled black shoes and simple dresses or skirt-and-vest ensembles—homemade?—in solid autumnal colors, usually some shade of russet. She brushed her gray hair flat on both sides and tied it in the back in a small bun. Everything about her appearance signaled that appearance is important only insofar as it does not suggest you lack dignity and seriousness. And everything that she said, always in a firm but calm and measured way, signaled that literature is worth being serious about, which means that our own lives are worth being serious about, the ones we ourselves are in the midst of experiencing and therefore being bewildered and terrified and delighted by, even if we are only eighteen—or maybe especially so.

Nonetheless, at that age, we were still kids, which meant that our preferred method of showing respect for someone was to make her the butt of a joke. During class one day, it was necessary for Mrs. Myers to slip out of the room for a moment, perhaps to collect a stack of fresh mimeographed handouts about Hemingway or Conrad. After the door closed behind her, I proposed a plan to my classmates: when she returned, each of us would be staring at the ceiling, feigning interest in something peculiar up there. She would be bound to look up, too. We would have her! Without a word, we would have made her follow our lead; she would show herself to be merely human—perhaps in the same bumbly way that we were. For a moment, all of us, including our dear teacher, would be in on something together, something we students had created, something that we all, even she, might end up chuckling about.

When Mrs. Myers returned to the room, every student in the class was peering upward at the perforated white ceiling tiles. She looked up, too. Then she lowered her gaze. "No, people," she said flatly. Her eyes were narrow. "No."

There were no more jokes after that—just books. Good books. Great books. In my previous English classes, I had been assigned stories and poems and plays chosen not for their literary merit but for the ease with which an adolescent might comprehend them. Their syntax was simple, their plots broadly drawn, their symbols few or clumsily overt. Their subjects were phantom hitchhikers, friendly dragons, and plucky squads of Little Leaguers with can-do attitudes. Now I was being asked to read Kafka, Ibsen, Eliot, Chekhov, and Shakespeare. Mrs. Myers was traditional enough to require that we choose a passage from *Hamlet* and memorize it; four decades later, I still have a pretty good handle on the Dane's droll, aggrieved graveyard musings about how our bones cost no more the breeding but to play at loggets with them.

It was *Crime and Punishment* that hit me hardest. What a thoughtful, tortured soul Raskolnikov was, and how like him I was! I had never encountered someone so desirous and doubtful, so dream-haunted and wounded, so eager to experience what was genuine and so ill-equipped to do so, someone whose work, as he explained it, was "thinking." Just like me! The fact that he murdered two people in cold blood was no impediment to considering him my twin. And why? It was a matter of point of view; from the first page, Dostoevsky asked me to see the world through Raskolnikov's eyes, to contemplate it with his mind, so a lack of identification with him was impossible. It was a literary device, a mere trick of language, but one that made me feel deeply and strangely alive—or that reminded me how deeply strange it is to be alive. I couldn't get over it.

This feeling, in my most satisfying experiences of reading, of being overwhelmed by an essential truth and therefore of completely identifying with a work of literature, of losing myself in it and, paradoxically, of finding myself: this was my sole understanding, at that point, of what makes literature matter. The idea was crude and circumscribed, but it was not false. In Mrs. Myers' class, I fell in love again and again, and I began, in earnest, clumsy fashion, to try to articulate that love.

When we read A. E. Housman's collection of poems *A Shropshire Lad*, I fell hard, willingly, happily, for its mournful, bitter, and witty pondering of youthful love and death. Assigned to write an analytical paper, I chose as my subject the poem that begins "Look not in my eyes, for fear / They mirror true the sight I see"—a poem about a young man lost in love. Just like me!

At a desk in my bedroom at night, in the small glow of my reading light, I went at the poem with diligence and patience and a detective's squinting, avid eye. In my essay, I mentioned the poem's use of iambic tetrameter—I had that much of the technician in me—although I probably didn't say much about why the meter matters; I did not note how, in the statement "But why should you as well as I / Perish? gaze not in my eyes," much of the emotional power can be attributed to the way the line ends in mid-thought and, when the next line picks up the thought again, it does so with a trochee, letting the word *perish* break in like the blow of a sledgehammer. Though I felt that sledgehammer, I did not know how to talk about it.

Concerning Housman's use of the term *star-defeated,* I was on solid ground, having encountered "star-crossed lovers" in *Romeo and Juliet.* But the poet spends the second half of the poem talking about a "Grecian lad" who turns into a jonquil. I guessed that a jonquil is a flower. To confirm this, I opened the dictionary, and I read that a jonquil is otherwise known as narcissus. Supposing that I'd better look that up, too, I discovered the Greek myth that explains the reference to the "Grecian lad," and I heard the click of connection. I felt like a dogged scholar, an unearther of meaning, a discerner of subterranean connections. Something else about the poem intrigued me, something oddly askew about the speaker's plea. He is overcome with love and therefore, if he were anything like me, must desire to be loved in return, yet the desire he expresses to his beloved is that she turn away from him, that she not look in his eyes. (I blithely assumed that the poem addresses a she. The author was a man, wasn't he? I knew nothing of the homoerotic nature of much of Housman's writing, and it wouldn't have crossed my mind to wonder why the beloved is implicitly compared with a young, pretty Greek boy.) This passionate desire not to be desired is, as Mrs. Myers would have reminded me, a paradox; it might be how a certain kind of pain—the sweet pain of unrequited love—can be enacted, and there is an interesting hint of aggression in it, too, or of passive-aggressiveness. The lover expresses his own pain through the pretense of protecting the object of his love from a similar pain. He is not entirely ingenuous. "See what you have done to me, however unwittingly?" he might be saying. "My suffering will not end. You clearly are uninterested in loving me, but at least I can warn you against loving yourself too much." All of this is there—the yearning, the tenderness, the helplessness, the petulance. And it's only words, only words. I was wildly in love myself, with a girl who would not have me, and her disregard served as further fuel for my love, so finally it was perhaps only the love I was in love with. I ended my literary analysis with a single-sentence flourish: "About this poem, all I can say is, 'I wish I'd written that.'" Mrs. Myers forgave me the dopiness and awarded me an A.

When a visiting poet came to the school for a day, Mrs. Myers selected four or five of us—the high achievers in the class—to spend a class period with him in a conference room in the library. This was a real poet, and a living one. So such a thing existed! From looking at him, you wouldn't know he was a poet; with his jeans and sneakers and cursorily combed hair, he did not seem so unlike us. We sat with him around a Formica-topped table. After reminding us that poetry communicates through metaphor, he asked us to come up with a single image that might serve as a metaphor for ourselves. I thought for a minute, jotting down a few possibilities. When my turn came, I announced that I was a windmill, flailing my arms while being unable to budge. It struck me as pretty good, a single emblem of multiple contradictory feelings: a yearning for freedom and a simultaneous sense of obligation to that which prevented me from being free—to that, in fact, which might define my essential identity in the first place. One of the other students, Margaret, whom I admired for her emotional steadiness and her supple intellect and her bold decision to enroll, the next fall, in an experimental, arty hippie college without traditional majors, stifled a laugh and declared that it might be the dumbest thing she'd ever heard.

Mrs. Myers, however, was not so dismissive of my poetic potential. She chose me to represent the school in a nationwide poetry competition sponsored by the National Council of Teachers of English. I composed a cryptic poem whose references were almost entirely private and whose few understandable lines were mawkishly sentimental. It was a loose collage of thoughts about darkness and mournful solitude and futile love, requisite topics for my writing at the time. The poem's meter and mood were inspired by a doleful Supertramp song about a man's shadow speaking difficult truths to him. On my way out of class one day, I stopped at Mrs. Myers' desk and presented her with my handwritten manuscript.

She studied it for a moment, lips pursed. "This is what you'd like to enter in the contest? This is the poem you've chosen?"

"Yes."

She paused, then slid the paper into a manila folder. "Okay," she said, and looked up. "Fine. Thank you, Chris."

Months later I received a form letter, an impersonally worded announcement that the poem had been read by the judges and would not be receiving recognition.

I would not be deterred, though—not by that rejection notice nor by the hundreds I received as the decades slid by. I could not, would not, stop writing poems.

A year after graduation, I returned to my old school for a visit, in search of Mrs. Myers, especially. I was coming back in glory, was I not? I was in college and still writing poems, going at it like gangbusters. I wanted to thank Mrs. Myers but mainly to surprise and delight her with my return—one of her favorite students, one of her truly gifted writers, swaggering back to chat about old times.

The final bell of the school day had rung a half hour earlier. The halls, nearly empty, echoed with my footsteps and with a locker clanging shut far away, around a corner. Mrs. Myers' classroom door was open. I stepped inside. She was sitting at her desk, a paper in her hand. "Mrs. Myers?" I said. She turned her head toward me. "It's Chris."

She squinted.

"Chris Forhan. I was in your class last year."

She smiled. "*Ye-e-e-s*. Kevin's brother. How *is* he? Is he still writing?"

Part V

Silence and Song

54

Yes, Kevin was writing. It was all that mattered to him, it seemed. Was there something about our being the sons of a father who killed himself that caused us both to turn to poetry? The relationship between the two things is covert, but it exists. For millennia, a father's job has been to show his sons how to live; our father neglected that job—or he unintentionally took on the opposite task, teaching us that the value of life is questionable. If life had value, if life was worth living, that value and worth were surely present in our own lives, present within us. Poetry, we were discovering, was a way to let those things have their say.

At the top of a narrow, creaky back staircase, in his cramped apartment above a garage, Kevin was staying up through the night, sipping cheap booze, smoking, thumbing through books of poems, and clacking away at his typewriter. Like Keats, like Rimbaud, he breathed poetry, or bled it. This was not a pose; he was not pretending. He was young and in love with what language could do. He was reading Shakespeare, Donne, Blake, Whitman, Stein, Stevens. He was giving himself over to impossible projects—devoting months and months, for instance, to the composing of nine-line stanzas in which each line contained exactly nine syllables. He was getting a music into his mind and into his muscles. He was trusting a hunch: if he followed poetry into the dark, followed it as far as it could take him, it might illuminate that darkness—providing a temporary light, perhaps, but a true one. Fiddling with syllables until they sang, turning a line just right to make a sentence's rhythm and sense dance, causing a word to knock softly, like a billiard ball, against another it had never encountered: these might be the means of an alchemy by which he could create something new in language, something that breathed a pure breath, something that could sustain his life or deepen it.

And he was only nineteen, only twenty, twenty-one, and he was my brother, he was good, he was on to something, and the feelings in his poems were ones that I felt, too, and the thoughts were those that, dimly lit, flitted within my own skull but that I could not articulate. He wrote a poem that began "I'm head bent dreaming on the keys / Of any way I might approach you." Who was that "you," that someone "scraping a thick grudge" off his walls? That sounded familiar. And that house with "an ambulance parked outside," someone "sleeping locked in his car," the glass "all fogged up inside"—I knew that house. I knew the person in that car.

Before my eyes, my brother was making poetry out of life, out of his life, out of mine, making a life that mattered by making poetry— by trying to get at the truth, however murky, and put it into words. It didn't seem such an odd and lonely thing for me to try to do the same.

Perhaps, had our father grown old, he would have spoken to his adult sons of his doubts about God and about himself. Perhaps he would have shared with us his sense of uncertainty and unease about the choices he had made, and about the choices he was making. Perhaps there was some poetry in him. But the father we knew, if he had such feelings, kept them to himself. Outwardly, he remained a man who followed a path of unwavering certainty—of duty and hard work, of belief that such things bring the rewards of material comfort and social acceptance, and maybe belief that duty and hard work are their own reward: that they are, in themselves, an unquestioned good.

Following such a path, however, can distract a man from himself, from desires and fears and misgivings that, ignored too long, might destroy him. Kevin was taking the opposite path: one of loyalty to his own ambivalence and uncertainty and to his suspicion that the tentative truths he stumbled upon through his own experience had more merit than the rigid ones he had been instructed to believe. He would not follow custom out of fear or courtesy, as our father might have done; he would try to let his own intellect and curiosity guide him, even if they guided him into difficulty and mysteries. He cherished wonder and possibility, and he understood that they are nearer cousins to skepticism than to faith. As I was beginning to do, he was finding in poetry the satisfactions that were not present for him in religion. If poetry and religious faith are similar in attempting to comprehend—or at least frame or point toward—eternal mysteries, poetry could be of use in a way that religion isn't: it is fluid, shifting; its images and forms change; its instinct is to move in order to hit a moving target.

Like my brother, I was addicted to the intoxication that came—occasionally, unexpectedly—in the writing of a poem: the feeling of being outside of time, of floating amid scatterings and fragments of thought that, if I was sufficiently patient and self-forgetful, might suddenly cohere into a shape that surprised and delighted me with its rightness. Sometimes, in a few lines, I felt that I had pinned existence to the mat and it had given up its secrets. The feeling was fleeting, but it did not seem untrue for being so. Maybe it was true because it was fleeting, the quick glimpse of a fact that would blind me if I stared at it too long. What mattered most to me about the poems I was reading—and, I hoped, those I was writing—was a sense of the strangeness and mystery and beauty of our being here in the first place, of this place itself being here.

Nowhere else in my life—save, perhaps, in late-night conversations I was having with Kevin—did I feel that this splendid bemusement, this sacred astonishment, was honored. Only in poetry, only in poetry. Of course, the poems I was writing were horrible: inadvertent hodgepodges of the styles of whichever poets I had fallen for lately, with so many disparate, wispy ideas swirling about and sinking within them that they were muddles—incomprehensible to anyone but myself. But I was not aware of their faults. I was an initiate, blind with enthusiasm.

I was also incapable of being as wholly loyal as my brother was to this path. Without being entirely aware of it, I was beginning to forge my own way between my brother's and my father's, maybe a way that would prove impossible. I was writing poetry, but I was not making the activity central to my life. Like my father, I would go to college, then immediately enter a conventional career, the kind that had nothing to do with poetry, the kind that, in years to come, I might mention with breezy assuredness to strangers, and they would nod agreeably, with genuine interest, and not knit their brow and purse their lips anxiously.

What career would I enter? What would I be? I thought of these as identical questions. I decided I would be a television newsman. I had always liked watching the news and thinking about it—not just the stories but the way they were presented. I had spent an August evening four years before pointing a microphone at the television, recording the coverage of Nixon's resignation on a cassette tape. I had joined the staff of my junior high newspaper, writing up the exploits of the basketball team and the hiking club. Thinking it would be cool to be on the radio, I had turned high school into a three-year broadcasting apprenticeship. Without planning to, I had been preparing for a career in broadcast journalism. A TV newsman: that was an authentic, respectable thing to be, wasn't it—a fixed identity in which to cloak myself? Poetry felt essential to me, but it was private; it came alive in the off hours, in the dark, and, because its rewards were altogether internal and its pleasures unmitigated, it felt a little wicked. I would keep it to myself.

I decided to attend Washington State University, an easy choice. The school was far enough from home—three hundred miles away, on the other side of the Cascade Mountains, surrounded by the rolling wheat fields of the Palouse—that I would feel truly on my own there, as I yearned to do, and WSU had a good broadcast communications program. Also, I could afford it. I didn't have money to attend a private university or an out-of-state school; at WSU, I would pay in-state tuition, and I'd have a little extra money every month from scholarships. I would also receive an accidental gift from my father: because he was dead, the Veterans and Social Security administrations would send me a small check every month.

Beyond that, though, I needed a little more cash. I needed a part-time job. As soon as I arrived on campus, I auditioned to join the staff of KWSU, the university's National Public Radio station. I was hired. Within a couple of years, I would be back working the shift I knew from high school: I would be the early-morning announcer, hosting the local segments of the national *Morning Edition* program.

As a communications major, I learned to write crisp, clear news copy; I learned to edit audio- and videotape; I learned about the Fairness Doctrine and landmark Supreme Court free-speech cases. With my cassette recorder in tow, I interviewed professors of veterinary medicine and geology for the radio station. When an eccentric local postal employee and his accordion were hoisted by crane one hundred feet in the air, where he played a polka while hanging by his ankles, I recorded the reactions of pleasantly baffled bystanders. For the student cable television channel, I yanked on my big boots and slogged through the snow with a cameraman to interview a pig farmer; I knotted a necktie, pulled on a sweater and jacket, and co-anchored the weekly newscast, becoming practiced at reading from a teleprompter and sitting without slouching.

But two buildings away, I was taking English classes—more of

those, finally, than communications courses. The summer after my
freshman year, I stayed in town and signed up for an early-morning
class in British Romantic poetry. It was taught by a young, silver-
tongued Welshman who arrived every day bleary-eyed, stray locks of
dark, unwashed hair plastered on his forehead, wrinkled black vest
askew on his shoulders, thermos of steaming coffee gripped tightly in
his hand. How long had he stayed up the night before? What had he
been up to, and what had it to do with the words he recited to us so
gravely, nearly in a whisper?

Huge and mighty forms . . . were a trouble to my dreams.

What the hand dare seize the fire?

For he on honey-dew hath fed,
And drunk the milk of Paradise.

Late at night, hunched over my desk, studying a page illuminated
by a tiny downturned cup of lamplight, I felt romantic, too. *Here I am,*
alone but not lonely, reading poetry, the poetry of the great dead, poetry
ready to reveal to me the big secret, if I can only find it. With a ruler and
a fine-tipped red pen, I underlined slowly, deliberately, the lines I felt
I would need to return to. *A sense sublime / Of something far more deeply*
interfused. Where but to think is to be full of sorrow.

On my own, browsing the shelves of the university bookstore, I
stumbled upon Charles Bukowski and began writing skinny little
poems about flies and grimy undershirts. I found Sylvia Plath, and my
poems became outlandish, compact, and explosive; they borrowed her
energy but none of her control. The "secret heaven-zoo" I mentioned
in one addled rant of a poem—what was that? I know that I was
thinking of a girl back home whom, just before leaving for college,
I had befriended and ineptly kissed. What I imagined she had to do

with secrets and heavens and zoos, I haven't a clue. In another poem, I knew whom I was thinking of when I wrote, "It's you face down in a / saltwater marsh, / your barrel smoking," but I let Plath do the talking: "God, Daddy, it's you."

Were my poems really poems? Were they good? I sent some to my mother, and she wrote back, "I like your poems. They are so somber, though. Do all poets have to be sad or philosophical?" Kevin was encouraging about my writing, but he loved me; he was obliged to be nice. There had to be a poetry professor somewhere on campus. I decided to track him down.

Alex had arrived at WSU only a year before I did. He was quiet and serious and young, still in his thirties, with one book of poems out from a small press. He had studied at the most prestigious MFA program in the country, the Iowa Writers' Workshop, but he was ambivalent about the notion that the writing of poetry could be taught. One day, in the poetry-writing course I had enrolled in, halfway through class he paused. He leaned back in his chair. "Look," he said, "I can't do this anymore. I don't believe in this kind of class. It's over. No more workshop." In the silence that followed, we all looked at one another. Was he kidding? He wasn't. Alex proposed that, class being over, we should repair to a nearby pub for drinks and sandwiches, so we did.

Poetry, he was reminding us, is too important, too wild and weird, to be institutionalized and commodified. Its origins are secret, its powers inscrutable. How could one teach such things? This, I thought, was the teacher for me. He was confirming what I had already begun to feel: that poetry is a delicate and deadly serious matter, a gift that vanishes in the hands of any who would trivialize it. It is not just a subject of study; it is a way of perceiving, a way of understanding, a way of being alive in the world—or being alive *to* the world. I hadn't enrolled in Alex's class in order to prepare for a career. I had enrolled because I couldn't help myself, because I felt that I might choke on the backed-up sludge of my own being if I didn't. I needed to be with people who understood my odd urge to write poems, people who would give me permission to keep doing so.

The next week, we students showed up in the classroom at the appointed hour, and Alex was there. He made no mention of the previous week's announcement. Maybe he had changed his mind; maybe the dean had changed his mind for him. I was relieved. I wanted to continue meeting with these people; I wanted, every week, to hand Alex the latest poem I had labored over; I wanted to walk to the English Department office the next day and pick up the ditto—the typed copy of the students' poems that the department secretary had made. I loved seeing all of our poems collected together in blurry purple ink, our names below them. The ditto was a little weekly anthology, a publication. Its readership was small—just us—and the poems were imperfect: that was the point. But we were treating them as poems, as acts of language worthy of being shared and contemplated. For those of us who had until now kept our writing private, this was no small thing.

In the poetry class, I was a different person from the one I was in the Communications Building, where my peers were people who called each other *bunghole* and disco-danced at frat parties and looked blank or vaguely panicky if I told them I wrote poetry. We fledgling poets were a ragtag band of misfits who'd found a temporary home together: Ruth, brainy and amiable, a women's studies major; Carl, of the trim dark mustache, sardonic and provocative, who devoted his first semester to composing a winking misogynistic lyric sequence entitled "Women as Automobiles"; Patrick, who parodied him with "Woman as Bathtub," in which an intimate relationship with either one involves "a ring afterward"; Michael, a graduate student, older and taller and wider than the rest of us, with patchy whiskers and thick-rimmed glasses, who favored Ginsbergian odes to inner-city bus stations; Yvonne, dark-eyed and serious, who wrote in the sorrowful shade of the other poet in her family, her dead older sister; and Jed, bearded and gentle, probably the best poet among us. "Out of which lilac": which of us wrote that line? I remember only that the rest of us agreed it was one of the best of the semester.

It was not I who wrote it. After all, as Alex pulled me aside one day to say, my poems lacked music. "Have you read Wallace Stevens?" he asked. "You should read Stevens."

In the campus bookstore, I bought a paperback copy of Stevens' selected poems. Thumbing through it, I could see—I could hear— what Alex meant: the language was sumptuously insistent with music. I understood maybe half of what Stevens was saying. No, one quarter. But it didn't matter; the vowels and consonants lured me in—the sound of the whole voice, the whole mind, of the poems. The lines seemed piercingly funny and sonorously oracular, sometimes simultaneously. Traveling home to Seattle for Thanksgiving break, crossing the state on a Greyhound bus, I kept Stevens' poems open on my lap. The meandering ride would take nine hours: I had nowhere else to be, nothing else to do. The hours passed, the bus wheezing into one small town, then another, then another. The autumn sunlight dimmed and disappeared. I clicked on the overhead light. I was deep into the long poem "The Comedian as the Letter C." The title had seduced me first, and then the first sentence: *Nota: man is the intelligence of his soil, / The sovereign ghost.* I would need to read that again. Then again. This poet was philosophical; I would have to use my head to keep up with him, but I was game for the challenge. I kept at the poem, through *imperative haw / of hum*, through *The book of moonlight is not written yet*, through *exit lex, / Rex and principium, exit the whole / Shebang*, through *Mere blusteriness that gewgaws jollified*. In my seat at the back of the bus, blackness encircling the narrow column of light in which I read, the muffled groan of the engine the only sound, I felt extravagantly alone: filled with the sounds of the poem, filled with its thoughts—as far as I could follow them. And I was following them, mainly. Probably. Maybe.

When, at last, I stepped off the bus, weary and invigorated, I felt like a different person. Or I felt, for the first time, fully myself. I felt that the world within me, my private mess of gladness and grief and tentative, intense impressions of truths to trust, had been confirmed by another, by a stranger, by a dead man, in a language of lush uncertainty. I felt that what a poem communicates might not be meaning, exactly, but something larger, something more like a sense of absolute authority—a sense of openness, of receptive attention to a life that enchants and baffles.

Around this time, in a class on modern poetry, I sat among a group of students puzzling over Stevens' "The Emperor of Ice-Cream." Here was an exceedingly odd poem that seemed subversive and wacky and chilling and true, even though I couldn't quite put my finger on what that truth was. With the professor guiding us, line by line, through the poem, we stalled on the lines *Take from the dresser of deal, / Lacking the three glass knobs. . . .* Why were these knobs missing, and why were there three of them? "Stevens makes the point," the professor said, "of saying that there are three missing knobs. Now, of what else might the number three remind us?"

I raised my hand tentatively. "The holy trinity?"

"Yes, yes, interesting," said the professor, after hearing the answer she had led me to by the nose, but what intrigued me more was the rumbling, giddy noise the poem was making: *Call the roller of big cigars, / The muscular one, and bid him whip / In kitchen cups concupiscent curds.* Why was that voice so appealing and right? And how could one begin talking about it? Maybe one didn't need to. Maybe one only had to say the lines aloud, over and over again.

With Stevens in my ear, my own poems began to sing a little. I wrote one about an unidentified "you" who I imagined was some version of my father, floating among *l*s and *o*s:

A moon zooms northward
through the boiling blue.

You, in the pool, refuse
to move . . .

On my visits home to Seattle, I checked in with my brother, nervously reciting my recent poems to him. Were they poems? Did they
have potential? Yes, Kevin kindly said, forgiving their trespasses.
Kevin, who had been busy finding his own poets to love, read me
Ashbery's "The Instruction Manual." I loved it because he did, and
because the poem seemed so delighted to exist, so delighted in existence—an extended act of imaginative liberty, with hints of something
sadder in it (*What more is there to do, except stay? And that we cannot do*).
Kevin read me a few of the riddling, jagged, heartrending *Dream Songs*
of John Berryman—Berryman, who was eleven when his father, one
early Saturday morning, put a gun to his chest and fired.

That mad drive wiped out my childhood.

———

I'd like to . . . ax the casket open ha to see
just how he's taking it, which he sought so hard.

———

Also I love him: me he's done no wrong
for going on forty years—forgiveness time.

55

Was it the fact of being the son of my father—son of a dead man, son of a man who, alive, I remember touching my mother with affection exactly once—that made me, in matters regarding the opposite sex, generally bungling and bashful? Thankfully, my timidity didn't matter to Lauren, a dimpled, auburn-haired, petite and brainy broadcasting major who decided she liked me. From the beginning, I could sense, even amid her high spirits, something worldly-wise and weary about her. At first we knew each other merely as pals within a group of pals. Then, one day, sensing that we were becoming friendly in a different kind of way, Lauren said, "Sit down. I have something I want to show you."

She unbuttoned her left sleeve and rolled it up, then lifted her wrist toward me. Around it, like a fat pink rubber band, was a scar. "A couple of years ago," she said, "I was working in a cannery. My arm got stuck in the machine, and it cut off my hand. The doctors were able to reattach it. But I can't move all of my fingers, and there's a lot of numbness."

I am not proud to say this: I was heartsick on Lauren's behalf, but the ghastly and veiled nature of her injury made her more interesting to me. It seemed a badge of seriousness, a sign of her authenticity as a feeling, suffering person, and I was flattered that she considered me serious enough to share it with. For the next two years, we were a couple.

Lauren had recently returned from a year in Germany, where she'd had a German boyfriend. She had liked Dieter, she said, but their union was imperfect: his penis was bent. Debilitatingly so. His self-consciousness about it was the worst thing, she said; his dysfunctional member made him feel unworthy of her.

A few months into our relationship, Lauren warned me that Dieter had called her: he had flown all the way from Germany. "He wants me back," she said. "Don't worry. You're my boyfriend. That won't change. But I feel bad—he's come halfway around the world to try to win me back. He wants to talk with you."

"With me?"

"He's being gallant. He thinks the honorable thing to do is ask that you step aside."

"I don't even know him. Do I really have to talk to him?"

"Well, no, not if you don't want to. But he's traveled a long way. Would it hurt you that much?"

Dieter, as threatened, tracked me down. He knocked on my apartment door; I invited him in and offered him a seat.

"Yes," he said, leaning forward, pressing his palms together. "I have come to tell you and to tell Lauren that my penis is straight now. I am okay. I have had the surgery. I am ready to be Lauren's boyfriend again. I am asking you to give her up."

"Um, I'd rather not," I said. "But it's not up to me. You'll have to speak with Lauren. It's her choice, her life."

Dieter returned to Germany, disappointed. With him, I had held my own. But with Lauren's family, whom I met when we traveled through her hometown, I felt flummoxed and insubstantial. Sitting on a high stool at the kitchen counter, I heard Lauren, her parents, and her older brother speak freely and openly, launching into passionate, friendly debates, breaking into peals of laughter at old shared jokes. Where were the tense moments of wordlessness, of silent judgment? Where was the satirical, self-protective teasing? These people did not seem to be speaking in code or censoring themselves; they seemed to feel safe saying what they thought, as if there were no risk in it. In such a household, in such a conversation, I could find no footing. I hadn't the training.

That evening, as we drove away from her childhood home, Lauren said, "My parents think you're polite."

"I'm glad."

"And my brother thinks you're stupid."

"Why?"

"You don't talk."

It's true. I didn't talk. My tongue was bent, debilitatingly so.

I felt most at ease with language when the communication was one-way and scripted: when I was reading an announcement into the microphone during my morning radio shift or, in the privacy of my notebook, tinkering with syllables, with the rhythms and whispery implications of them. Only a part of me was speaking then, a part I felt comfortable with, and no one talked back.

So timorous in conversations with strangers, so used to stewing in my private juices, I began to sense that broadcast journalism was an imperfect career choice. At the heart of reporting is a genuine curiosity about other people and a relentless desire to learn the truth about them, especially uncomfortable truths, the ones they would prefer to conceal. Me? I didn't like to use the phone. At the grocery store, if the shortest line led to a noticeably chatty cashier, I chose the longer one. Before leaving my apartment, I peeked through the curtain to confirm that I would encounter no neighbor or postal worker with whom I might be required to converse.

A journalist is required to converse. In my junior year, I was selected to have a very difficult conversation. Two disgruntled members of the WSU basketball team had revealed to a friend of mine, another apprentice TV reporter, that a few star players were receiving special treatment from the head coach, and that treatment might be illegal. If not, they claimed, it was at least unethical. Players' academic transcripts might have been altered. Poor performers in the classroom were being reinstated and playing again, maybe without first meeting the university's criteria for improving their grades.

Four of us journalism students were put on the story. We would investigate and then, on our weekly cable TV news program, share what we had discovered. My duty was to confront the coach, a burly, gregarious, charismatic man who, I suspected, could squish me between his fingernails as if I were a flea. I would go to his office. I would ask him to respond to the charges against him.

Our faculty adviser, wanting us to catch the coach off guard, recommended that we not call him first. Instead, with a cameraman, I walked into the basketball office in the athletic building and asked to see the coach.

"Do you have an appointment?" asked his secretary.

"No," I said. "We're with *Cable 8 News*—it's a student TV program—and we have some important questions for him. He really should talk with us."

"Now?"

"Yes, please, if possible."

The secretary left her desk. A minute later, she returned. "He'll give you five minutes. But no camera."

Alone, I entered the coach's office. Surrounded by cabinets filled with golden trophies and plaques and signed basketballs, he sat, glowering, steely-eyed, behind a desk. "What's so goddamn important?" he said. He did not ask me to sit.

I explained the charges that his players had made against him. I told him that we planned to air a story about them. Did he have a response? For twenty minutes, glaring at me, he fumed, sputtered, and yelled, claiming that the complaining players were bush leaguers. They were crybabies, fueled by envy. In taking them seriously, I was proving myself a fool. He'd recruited them and given them a chance to succeed, but they had underperformed, and now they were inventing stories to excuse their own failings. He wouldn't get into a "pissing match" with them. As for me, I should be ashamed of myself. Had I no self-respect? What kind of journalism were they teaching in the Communications Building, anyway?

Pretending that I wasn't trembling—having pretended so since I entered his office—I muttered my thanks, spun around, and left. I was Mike Wallace: I had ambushed him. But I wasn't sure I liked it. The next day, as I was walking across campus to class, the coach crossed my path twenty steps ahead. He spied me, pivoted, and strode straight toward me. "Hey!" he screamed, jutting his arm out, pointing at me, jabbing his finger at the air repeatedly, as if shooting off rounds. "Did you ever take a course in logic? Do you know what logic is? You need to learn about it!" Then he turned and stomped off.

I had done a journalist's duty. I had nettled a public figure. I had asked the hard questions. I had parted a curtain in service of the truth.

But I was beginning to feel that such curtains might be better parted by others. I wasn't up to it. I was a coward, probably. Nonetheless, after graduation, I would seek a job in broadcasting. This, too, was an act of cowardice, though I preferred to think of it as practicality. I had made a career decision years before; why change now and watch the work I had done come to nothing? Years before, Kevin had tried college—his most gratifying moments had been in poetry courses—but he had dropped out, unable to stomach the idea of all those classes he would have to take because they were required of him, not because he had a genuine interest in them. He was working on a Seattle pier now, driving a fish delivery truck by day, writing poems by night. I, though, like my father, had stuck it out, through the physical education and geology and sociology classes, through the exams and term papers and oral presentations, and earned a degree—earned my ticket into a professional world waiting patiently with its fixed structures and meanings that I could take on as my own.

Still, I had begun to sense that a life in television might be a kind of betrayal, a silencing of the self I had coaxed into the light and encouraged to start talking. The truths I was interested in uncovering were of a kind not heard about on TV: they were permanent and unspeakable and incompletely knowable but present in poetry, behind the words, like ghosts. When I reported the news, the words I used were just words, delivering information only, erasing themselves in the moment they were spoken. How much good could they be on mornings such as that December one when I arrived at the radio station, as usual, at five-thirty, the sun not yet up, to prepare for my shift? Dave, the news anchor, was already there, the normally jovial, nimble-witted Dave, but he looked stricken.

"Morning?" I said.

"They got Lennon."

He bit the words as he said them. He didn't have to say more. Somehow I understood immediately what he meant.

For the next three hours, I sat in front of the control board, microphone propped in the air before me, feeling inadequate to the task of talking. I merely played Beatles records and, when I spoke, said mainly that there was little to say. I was no broadcaster. I was someone who wished he were home, alone, who wished he hadn't woken up yet.

And what words did I say on the air that week in May, the one that began when I rose Sunday morning to an eerie gloom, a dimness not right for that time of day? Stepping outside, I saw, in the west, a wall of black cloud advancing steadily toward me; in the east, the sky was a lucid blue. By the time the cloud had swallowed the sun entirely and a dark snow had begun to fall, I had heard that Mount St. Helens, three hundred miles to the west, had erupted. This was not snow; it was ash—a cadaverous gray descending upon everything, an inch of fine, dead powder shrouding the town. What words I spoke on the radio afterward, who knows? I remember only that morning: sitting by my window, silent, watching ash sift from the sky and gather on the branches and roofs and cars and roads, the world becoming blank and mute as the moon, and as implausible.

56

The town of Great Falls, Montana, hugs a bend of the fretfully meandering Missouri River. The falls themselves are famous for stunning
Lewis and Clark with their unruly beauty, then setting them back
weeks in their transcontinental journey, forcing them to lift their dripping boats and supplies from the water and portage for miles through
untamed terrain. When I moved to Great Falls after college, lured
by an offer to be an actual professional television reporter for eight
hundred dollars a month, the area seemed hardly less wild and remote
to me. The town was at the southern edge of a glacial plain of wheat
fields and ranches and archaeological digs and tiny unincorporated
outposts with one blinking stoplight and two taverns. Winter began
in October and ended in late spring; in the midst of it, with the town
ice-bound, with mountains of plowed snow shoved to the edges of
parking lots and the sides of streets, the little hairs in my nose and ears
froze as soon as I stepped outdoors. I hadn't known they could do that.
Until my car's ignition clicked and clicked and refused to turn over in
the morning, I hadn't known that I should attach a portable heater to
the engine at night to keep it warm while I slept. My first apartment
was across the street from an air force base, close enough to its radar
system that, every twenty-three seconds, my television and stereo and
clock radio beeped wanly. Other than being a home to flyboys, Great

Falls was a town of cowboy painters and cattle auctions and pick-
ups with gun racks and Reagan stickers and Patsy Cline on the radio
wringing my heart and Merle Haggard singing outlandishly of the
good old days "when a girl could still cook and still would," his throaty,
taut-jawed baritone making him sound almost persuasive. In the local
movie theaters, the feature film was abruptly halted midway through
and the lights flicked on to give moviegoers a chance to buy popcorn
and Goobers. The town's major landmark, looming darkly and conspicuously on the north side of the river, was a giant smokestack—
once the world's tallest—sticking up like an extinguished cigarette.
The stack had been left there by the Anaconda Copper Company,
which had closed its smelter and refinery and abandoned the town a
couple of years before I arrived. One of the first stories I reported for
KRTV was about the demolition of the stack, to great fanfare, before
a crowd of tens of thousands.

Shortly after I arrived in Montana, my mother wrote to me. She
was thriving, having settled into a career as an elementary school principal and gotten married again—to Russ, whom, as chance would have
it, she had known thirty years earlier, in high school. He, too, had had
a long first marriage and several children. As a teenager, Russ had
been sweet on my mother; to his everlasting joy, they once shared a
kiss, chaste though my mother may have meant it to be. It was eight
years now since my father had died; in those years, my mother had not
spoken much to me about him. However, as I began my TV career, he
was on her mind:

> Chris, I have no doubt that you will reach all your goals, even if they
> change along the way. You've got what it takes: ambition, persever-
> ance, youth, and talent. My one concern is that you have a lot of
> the qualities that your dad had, the ones that helped him reach his
> career goals, but they also prevented him from taking side trips and

relaxing once in a while. He was very hard on himself and could never quite reach the perfection he expected of himself.

Was I a perfectionist? Did I work too hard? Was I setting myself up for failure? I was surprised by my mother's warning; I thought I was doing merely what I was supposed to do. I hadn't considered that there was an alternative.

At KRTV, I was assigned to anchor the weekend evening newscasts. On weekdays, I would be an all-purpose reporter, my particular beat being the county courthouse: the affairs of the county commission and the local criminal justice system. But I had an idea of something else I might do. Two months after I began working at the station, I approached Ed, the news director, with an earnest but unusual proposal: what did he think about a cameraman and me driving down to Missoula, three hours away, and spending a day with Richard Hugo, who taught at the university there? We could make a thirty-minute documentary out of it.

Ed looked at me blankly. "Who's Richard Hugo?"

"He's a poet. An important one. And he lives in Montana—we're lucky about that. He even writes about the state, about its rivers and little towns and taverns. I'd love to interview him and get a sense of his daily life."

"Poetry? I'm not sure I see the purpose in this. Let me think about it. I'll get back to you."

I waited and waited, imagining in the meantime how I might approach the project: maybe Hugo would let me sit in on a class or two; maybe he'd take me fishing or drinking. Spending a whole day with me, he might loosen up, let his guard down, reveal something of the inner life of a poet, let slip a few secrets about the art.

Weeks passed. I heard nothing from Ed about my idea. Finally, grudgingly, he agreed.

The next morning, Ed poked his head out of his office door. "Forhan!" he yelled, and motioned for me to come into his office. He was holding a fragment of wire copy that he had ripped from the Teletype. He gave it to me, then sat back on the edge of his desk, his hands behind his head. "Your poet's dead," he said.

Was he grinning a little?

For the next few weeks, Ed teased me relentlessly about the Forhan jinx. Poets and I were a fatal mix. "I heard that Richard Brautigan came through town yesterday," he'd say, "and he started to feel *really sick*."

A few weeks later, Kevin wrote to me. He was responding to a letter in which I had praised his poetry unreservedly. "The pride is brotherly," I had written. "The awe is not." I had reminded him how important his writing was to me, how important it was that he keep writing.

Chris, you remember that letter you wrote? I've read it twice, once two months ago, and once again just now. I didn't want anything to do with it in the meantime, and I believe you understand why, and that you'll forgive the wait. It meant a great deal to me, more perhaps than it should have, and it came at a perfect time. The next day I made a deliberate decision about my writing, one I'd been on the verge of making for months, one I seem to have to make all over again every year or so—a choice, if you will, between cowardice and uncertainty. I always choose the latter, but it came a little early this year—thank you.

A short while before your letter arrived I heard Richard Hugo read, he was in town. Everyone commented about his sad state, his weight, his limp, his wheeze—a couple of weeks later he was dead. The last poem he recited was a new one, about trees and grass and elfin spirits and lovers, and he read it magnificently. It was one of those poems that remind you of what's possible.

What's possible: I wanted to achieve that in poetry. But I was a TV newsman. Had I chosen cowardice over uncertainty? Had I chosen the safety of a stable, respectable career over a more meaningful life, an unpredictable but vital one devoted to art and imagination? I had chosen steady health benefits and the possibility of professional advancement—I was thinking of the future. My brother, meanwhile, was summoning up, and summing up, a past that was waiting patiently to be reckoned with:

> *Stranded shrub root.*
> *Brick, ash, boot. Brick cool.*
> *Shadow cool, palm to the fire.*
> *Toes on the hearth. Mother,*
> *Father. Oak twisps. Twist of smoke.*

Those lines were in a poem called "Adding Up Home." It was my home; those were my parents; the twist of smoke was mine, too—my ungraspable childhood, its ungraspable implications. And the words were my brother's.

If my mother was right, I was following my father's path of professional ambition and perfectionism and duty. I might be turning toward the world and away from myself. I might be living my father's life over again. My brother was trying to make a different kind of life, in poetry—and he was trying to make sense in it of what our father was, of what our father did.

A Strange Farewell

> *I wish my father had grown old,*
> *troubled with wisdom, a bit daft, frayed*
> *at the edge, but of use, like a patch quilt.*

My father was a crazy coward,
and I won't live that life over again

but it's a strange farewell to want to live
by strength of will, and die by accident.
We all beg wisdom of the dead,
but in secret: perhaps an ambitious weakness
for saying the unsayable

is the babbling of drunks, fools, and poets.
It seems that among the living
wisdom is essentially incidental,
silence in the presence of a child,
baseball talk at a funeral,

a loving nod in that odd moment of weakness.
But I wish my father had grown old,
not perhaps fully recovered, always wearing
the same tie, occasionally ill at ease,
and babbling away.

I had been reading, still, mainly Stevens and Ashbery, and—although I would not have said so then—my own poems were intellect-driven, abstract, emotionally restrained, and generally impenetrable. I was so intent on manipulating language to make it inhabit an elaborate, projected poetic realm that I was often blind to what the language was really doing. Dana came north to visit once, and I showed her some of my poems. She had recently moved to Yuma, Arizona, her own remote small town, after marrying a marine stationed there. Like our marine father, he was smart, articulate, distant, and unyielding—Dana was only a few years away from leaving him. As she lay on my living room carpet, scanning a new, long, allusive poem I was proud of, I awaited, in silence, her verdict. The poem was spoken by a persona, some indeterminate actor; it was called "The Last Time I Played Hamlet." Would my sister understand the concepts the poem was contemplating, the particular rocky philosophical path the language was traveling down?

After a few minutes, she looked up. "It's true," she said, "what you write about Dad. I've felt that way, too."

No, no, I told her. The poem is about Hamlet, about an invented character playing Hamlet. Was she familiar with the play? The situation, I said, is all set up in the poem's first few lines:

The last time I played Hamlet
releasing the fiction of my own madness
was not enough. The ghost of my father
would not appear, no matter my rage,
and I praised my uncle's best intentions.

"The ghost of my father / would not appear." Dana was right. The poem was not about Hamlet.

57

I felt alien in Montana and increasingly alien to broadcasting as a career, but I wasn't thinking of a way out. After all, I had enlisted. Perhaps too much like my father, I was sticking with it, buckling down, doing the work I'd signed on for, ignoring the self within me that was capable of real joy, forcing it to lie sleeping throughout the day, then coaxing it awake late at night, feeding it crumbs as I hunched over my notebook and worried out a few lines of poetry.

A year after I began working at KRTV, the other TV station in Great Falls tried to woo me away. Though I was only twenty-three and felt like an apprentice, the station manager of KFBB asked if I wouldn't like to take the next step in my career. How would I feel about being his news director? I would produce and anchor the week-day evening newscast and manage the small news department: four reporters, a weatherman, and a cameraman. The new position would come with a hefty raise: I would earn fourteen thousand dollars a year. What choice did I have? I said I was thrilled to be asked and grateful for the opportunity.

I still liked writing for television, working to craft clear—maybe even elegant—sentences that said much in few words. I liked editing stories, inventing ways for images and words and sounds to interact and make meaning. In my new job, I liked putting reports on the air that another news director—one keener to broadcast actual news—might not have. On one slow news day, I sent a reporter out to proofread the town; he came back with pictures of ungrammatical or misspelled billboards and an interview with the county sheriff about why, on the sign outside his building, the word *sheriff* appeared in quotation marks. ("Is this an actual quote? Or are you only a hypothetical sheriff?") I liked appearing on the air, attempting to sound genuine and to speak substantively, attempting, in my chats on the set with the sports guy or the weather reporter, to sound as if I were engaged in a real conversation. *As if:* that was the problem. I was still Bick Bark. I was pretending. With television, everything seemed a simulation, a packaging of reality, and therefore always a step removed from it. I felt myself growing loyal solely to that secondary, circumscribed reality: the newsworthy one. If a report came over the police radio of a major pile-up on the interstate, I prayed for fatalities. That would be a story we could lead with. I wanted pictures, dramatic pictures: the murder suspect, shackled, being led away to jail; flames feeding on a family's home and shooting into the night sky; a zoom-in to the widow's tearstained face. Reality on its own was not enough: what mattered was its potential as fodder for a newscast. What mattered was what I could do with it, what it could do for me. I was nurturing my glibness and cynicism, surrendering myself to a smallness of vision. If I had a soul, I was suffocating it.

Week after week, an advertisement appeared in the regional inner pages of *TV Guide*: a photo of me in my sharpest jacket and tie, posing at the anchor desk, smiling broadly, proclaiming my profound and abiding commitment to bringing the news to the people of north-central Montana.

But that guy in the tie with the pancake makeup and the fixed, sprayed hair felt more and more like someone else, someone I didn't trust. The person I trusted was the one who was already out of there, the one who, back home in Seattle for a visit, at a party, made wistful by wine, tried to harmonize with Kevin and Dana a rendition of the Roches' song "Runs in the Family"—*One by one we left home. / We went so far out there. . . .* The person I trusted was the one who was writing poetry—or trying to write it. I sent my attempts to Kevin, mainly so the famished half of my divided self could be nourished by the words of someone who understood, of someone who *knew*—words such as these that my brother sent me just when I needed them:

> You clearly are a good, great enough poet to pursue the craft for your own reasons and be understood/excused by a good one out of every three thousand people, no matter what the results are. You're already (or have always been, without my realizing it) as inventive and resourceful as I am, without being as obsessively weird, which bodes well for your future as a published poet. It's inspiring to find someone close to me with a subterranean psyche. Isn't that one way of saying it? I know what the workaday world does, subverting and weakening the notion that a man's idea of what's real in the world is flexible, adaptable, liable to constant scrutiny until he becomes less himself than a part of what is already established, a cog, and if this notion of resistance has become in itself a triviality, recognized and described until it has become in itself mundane, I still believe in the power of this kind of resistance, sitting in a crowd of friends or co-workers I still feel it, nothing I've experienced can match it, and a poem can show it! That's the secret of why I've done what I've done for the last several years; my failures, at least, are my own.
>
> We are not permitted to say these things. It's a shock to realize that our greatest thrill and accomplishment, to ourselves the most important achievement, is in this revelation of ourselves by degrees.
>
> I see nothing but mystery everywhere. I refer to my failures

because I'm not up to my own standards. Intuition has led me to feign weakness to escape triviality. And yet triviality is real; triviality is the Devil. The Devil wins in the end. Today I went to the airport to send some seafood, air freight, to California. It's my job. And, Chris, they were mailing a body out, somewhere, on the airplane! They weighed this cardboard coffin on the scale, while I watched, to determine the shipping charges. I sneaked a peek at the airbill: the human remains, it said, of Charles H. Smith, one hundred and ninety pounds, with the cardboard. And all of us, the man from Republic Airlines who laid the body to the scale with a forklift, the funeral parlor worker who stood and whistled—I swear to you, whistled!—as the work was done, and I, waiting with my thousand pounds of freshly killed seafood for my turn at the scale, were reduced in my mind, with the picture of the fresh corpse, in the posture of sleep, impossibly vivid in my imagination, to the status of dumbfounded pallbearers, with everything held dear to ourselves in our lives made pointless and stupid by the hopelessly awkward presence of the dead man. Triviality; mystery! I must not allow the overwhelming stupidity of persons and places and things to make me insensible to that moment when everything I believe can be called into question. None of my questions has been answered.

None of my questions were being answered, either. Except. Except: I met Rebecca—an artist. An artist! A painter. *She* knew; she was aware of the enduring, unsettling, glorious mystery one could sense if only one were silent long enough to listen. When witnessing some drunken lout acting stupidly—trying to climb a telephone pole, beer can in hand, or shouting provocative inanities at a pretty woman—Rebecca had a habit of remarking sourly, "Doesn't he know he's going to die?"

She had recently earned an MFA and was making a living by teaching in the Great Falls artists-in-the-schools program. Meanwhile, alone in the studio, she was devoting her life to her work; combining pastel drawings and glued pieces of tissue paper, she was making image after image after image of human torsos, the mindless and unmoving part of us, all inscrutable throbbing feeling. It was the fact of her being an artist, certainly, that drew me to Rebecca—and her kindness, and her beauty, which she had the habit of obscuring beneath sweatshirts and army pants. I met her first at the local arts center, where I was reporting on a story—the kind of artsy feature I preferred. I overheard her speaking seriously, unironically, to another woman about astrology. Under my breath, I said something sardonic, and Rebecca pounced. "And what's your sign?" she asked. Hearing that I was a Scorpio, she said, "I'm not surprised." A half-serious, half-teasing debate about the merits of astrology ensued. Astrology, I proposed, is superstition. Its premise contradicts the laws of physics. And it's reductive; it pretends that life is not as bewildering as it is. No, she argued: astrology works. It has worked for thousands of years. It's mysterious but nonetheless has an internal logic—it can be a trusted guide to those who want to understand this strange, anguish-filled life.

That first conversation hinted at what was to come: a powerful and long relationship, a marriage, eventually, that lasted fifteen years but ended mainly because, regarding what mattered to us most—our sense of ultimate reality, our metaphysics—we could not converse freely and sympathetically without frustration and defensiveness and injured feelings. As our marriage progressed, instead of figuring out another, more tender and generous way to talk about it, I fell into the habit, like my father, and like myself as a child, of staying silent when I might have spoken, of trading a confrontation with a difficult truth for the relief of keeping my feelings concealed—for the relief, I told myself again and again, of keeping the peace. As the years went by, and Rebecca and I stayed together, we nurtured the artist in each other but felt an essential gap between us. We each grew lonely.

And there was this: Rebecca was not instinctively enamored of existence. She had suffered and seen suffering and was not fully persuaded that life was worth the pain. She sometimes complained that life on this planet was too cruel, too difficult. "Compared to what?" I would ask. "It's cruel, yes, but it's joyful and beautifully strange, too. Anyway, it's all we have. Shouldn't we embrace it? There's nothing else to embrace." I was being glib, perhaps—speaking in platitudes. But I believed them. Some of the distance between Rebecca and me, I realized, was that she was drawn to death. It made a kind of sense to her as a relief from suffering. Not long after our marriage ended, I heard a poet friend and teacher of mine, Gregory Orr, speak of the trauma at the center of his own childhood: when he was twelve, on a morning hunting expedition, he shot and killed his eight-year-old brother. It was an accident. Certain that the chamber in his .22 was empty, he casually waved the rifle backward over his shoulder and fired, not seeing that the barrel was pointing at his brother. Out of the horror, guilt, self-hatred, and meaninglessness that rushed into his being, he discovered the consolation of poetry. He also discovered a fact about his father: when he was a boy, while skeet shooting, he, too, had accidentally shot and killed someone—his best friend. Although a pulled trigger scorched his life and his memory, he later, as a grown man and father, filled his house with guns and taught his own young boys to hunt. He did not speak to his children about his accidental boyhood crime, but he re-created its circumstances; he built a life in which a rifle could easily find itself in the hands of an impulsive, reckless boy. It is a common thing, probably more common than not: we never shake the essential emotional experiences of our childhood; in fact, we create a life in which we oblige ourselves to revisit them. I had always assumed that my relationships with women were somehow shadow versions of my relationship with my mother. When I heard Gregory speak, it did not seem to me that his family being traumatized by two accidental shooting deaths was a coincidence. Instead, it struck me that his father had, perversely and unconsciously, found a way to re-create his childhood trauma, as if it were so essential to his being that he could not put it completely behind him. And another thing struck me: I had not married a version of my mother. I had married my father. I had created a circumstance in which my job was to try to persuade a person I loved that life was worth living.

But two decades before that recognition, as Rebecca and I were starting—in a series of small moves, a series of little risks—to merge our two lives together, a new way of conceiving of my life seemed possible. Unambivalently loyal to her desire to be an artist, Rebecca had gone to graduate school. Why couldn't I do the same? It was evident by now that if I were to be happy, if I were to be true to myself and not subsumed by a life I did not completely believe in, I would have to put poetry at the center of my attentions, not at their periphery. I had been letting my consciousness be shaped by television, by the tidy packagings of reality, the continual partial lies, that it required. I felt most exhilaratingly alive in the midst of writing a poem that felt true. My work in TV news could not provide such sensations. It was their enemy.

I would apply to graduate schools. I would quit my job, quit my career. Rebecca and I would marry, and, since her contract with the school district was expiring, we would move wherever I was accepted. After that, who knew where we would live or what we would do. For now, it didn't matter. What mattered was that I would devote myself solely to poetry; I would go where it led me.

58

Like my parents, Rebecca and I were married in Seattle. Unlike them, we asked a judge, not a priest, to preside. Like my parents, we had a two-day honeymoon in Victoria. Unlike my father, I was awake for most of it.

Back in Great Falls, we packed up a U-Haul, then drove across the country to the University of New Hampshire, where I would study with Charles Simic. I had seen his poems in anthologies, and they seemed wholly unlike any others: they were deeply strange, imaginatively free. He wrote about going inside a stone, about building a "strange church" with his shoes as the altar, about looking at a fork as if for the first time and imagining that it "must have crept / Right out of hell." His were the kind of poems one might write in a dream or scrawl on a cave wall to be discovered by happenstance centuries later and understood.

I assumed that I knew nothing about poetry and gladly gave myself over to Charlie's influence. When he helped me improve my poems, he didn't do so by telling me that he could not understand them; he did so by telling me that they were not interesting enough. He taught me to put pressure on my language, to ask of every line, of every image, that it delight or enchant or meaningfully mystify. The first week of class, he put it this way: "You want to write poems that will break people's hearts, make them jump off roofs, join monastic orders."

I had come to the right place.

One of the first poems I wrote in New Hampshire was an account of a dream I'd had in which my father returned from the grave and, to my frustration, avoided speaking about the fact of his death. Instead, he told me that he had witnessed an interesting incident—the demise of someone else: a little boy who plunged off an overlook into a deep canyon. The child had walked too close to the edge. In the poem, as in the dream, I was befuddled and angry. Why could my father not speak to me for once, directly, candidly, and emotionally, about himself? Was I merely a stranger to him, someone who might only accidentally catch his eye, as if I were the poor nameless boy who had tumbled to his death? I accused my father of making superficial pronouncements, of not taking his own suicide as seriously as I did—"as if you thought / you could / still change your mind," I told him, "as if you'd the right / to talk to me / about dying."

Too late, I was pleading with him to speak with honesty and fullness, pleading with him to reveal what he truly felt, to admit that his death was real. And his life.

EPILOGUE

Silence is the sound of inwardness, of a solitude essential for the making of the self, or the discovery of it. Silence is a cave, a comfort: it is safe. And it is dangerous: the sound of he who would make himself known by speaking, and create himself in the world by doing so, but who hasn't the courage—or, not having been instructed in candor, hasn't the skill. His silence is a white screen onto which others project their shadows. Silence signals unspoken questioning or signals unquestioning assent—a surrendering to notions of who to be, and how to be, that are aswirl in the culture's chatter or inherited from long-dead faceless ancestors tilling some hillock in the old country. Silence is the sound of someone preparing to speak in his own time, when he is ready, or it is the sound of he who, whatever he has of import to reveal, has long since forgotten what it is.

I choose not to be silent. This book is the consequence of that. I have learned—I am still learning—how easy it is, out of fear or out of habit, not to speak directly and honestly, how easy it is to evade conflict by addressing it sideways or not at all, to slide by on bleak and easy humor, as my father did. In poetry, especially, I have found a way to let what would otherwise remain hidden speak. Decades after his death, long after my few graduate school efforts to write about him, my father would not leave me alone; he began again to appear in my poems. I worried about how my mother would react to these excavations of my memories of him and of my childhood home. Would she think of the poems as indiscretions, a reckless publicizing of the family's sadness? Would she think of them as needlessly reopening a wound? I was concerned about a poem that referred directly to the morning of my father's suicide—but my mother wrote to me that I need not worry: "It is all true and I recall those feelings myself."

When the poems weren't enough—when I knew that my investigation into my father would deepen and expand, taking the form of this book—I went to my mother for help. I wanted to know everything. Would she tell me her story? Would she trust me with it? A writer's selecting and shaping of memory, his searching for something true in it, is a dangerous, maybe partially futile business, particularly when the memory is someone else's. He risks glibness, a cheapening of feeling: the simplifying, and thus falsifying, of a life because that life's evanescence and intricacy cannot be rendered adequately on the page. But my mother agreed to speak with me. She sat for hours, answering candidly and thoughtfully every question I put to her, even if the answers brought her to tears, even if she knew her words could end up in a book.

Once, when I was sharing with her an early draft of this manuscript, the whole project suddenly struck me as outlandish and impudent. She had wondered whether I might delete from the book a certain questionable theory about her father, and she had quibbled about the exact phrasing of something she'd said in a quarrel with my father over forty years before. "I can imagine," I wrote to her, "most people by this point saying, 'Can't you just take me entirely out of your silly book? That was my dad, my marriage, my argument. I'd like to keep them to myself.'"

My mother is not wholly pleased with the contents of these pages;

she regrets that I do not remember my childhood with more pleasure. But she does not regret her gift to me: she talked to me; she told me the truth. She, too, has had her fill of silence.

I still dream about my father, although the dreams come less frequently than they once did. Almost always he is, astonishingly, alive—and ready, at last, to talk. He has returned, sheepish, apologetic, from the realm of the dead, or he never died in the first place. It was a horrible misunderstanding, he explains: he was kidnapped and kept under guard in a small room for years, away from any phone. Or he was an undercover government agent obliged to fake his own death; he might have revealed this to us from the start, but the mission would have been compromised.

In one dream, he is a dapper, tuxedoed figure who appears at a table next to mine in an outdoor café. "Dad," I say, "you're dead. What are you doing here?"

He looks at me, nearly expressionless, only halfway back in the world. "Woman," he replies. "I never said thank you." I understand: he is referring to my mother—the girl he married when she was only seventeen, the girl who could not nudge him awake on their honeymoon, the woman who bore him eight children, who remained loyal to him, entwined with him in marriage, even while he was slowly, silently unraveling. It pains him that he left so abruptly without telling her what she deserved to hear.

In another dream, almost forty years after his death, I receive a letter from him. It is signed "Dad" in his familiar, elegant script and is written in a breezy, informal way, as if the letter is just the latest installment in a continuing conversation. He tells me that he hasn't been traveling around the country in search of a new house after all, so he won't be making plans to see me. Sorry: he knows it has been a long time.

Is this letter really from my father? Is it possible? I think back to him lying outside his car; I remember his body in the casket; I remember the funeral and the subsequent decades of silence. In the letter, he makes no mention of the death I have lived with for forty years—as if it never happened, as if he merely still exists, as any number of fathers do, and he is sorry that we have not been in touch for so long and sorry we won't be seeing each other again soon. How can I confirm that the message is truly from him? I need to be sure. If I can do that, I will respond to him. I will write, "I'll come meet you anywhere. Just tell me where you are."

Fifteen years after my father's death, I was living in a little town amid the North Carolina tobacco fields. Only an hour's drive away, in Jacksonville, lived the uncle I had never met: Jim, my father's older brother. He was a retired marine, living with his second wife. Of my father's family, he was all that was left—save perhaps Nat, his father, who had disappeared decades before, and who knew if he was dead or alive? When my mother and Russ, her new husband, visited me from Seattle, my sister Dana drove down from Virginia, and we all decided to pay Jim a visit. My mother had not seen him since the earliest years of her first marriage, four decades before. As far as she could recall, that was the last time my father, too, had seen or spoken to his brother. There had been no bitter estrangement; they just lived different lives, in different states, maybe different worlds. Jim, though only sixty, had suffered a debilitating stroke. We sat for an hour in his living room, and he hardly spoke; his wife did most of the talking. She was pleasant and engaging, chatting easily and exhaustively about their children and their life in Jacksonville, but, the entire time, I was thinking about my father. I was looking for him. I wanted something of him back—whatever my sitting in the same room with his brother might offer. Did we ask Jim about his past, about my father's past? Whatever we asked, he stuttered and mumbled incomprehensibly in reply, and his wife swiftly interrupted, steering the talk toward another topic. I stared at Jim's face. I stared into his eyes. I was searching for my father, searching for something that wasn't there.

Skippy, my father's drowned brother, lies in a cemetery a little over two miles from the house where I grew up. When we were young, we Forhan children drove by it hundreds of times, glancing at the passing headstones through the chain-link fence. We never entered the gates. Seventy-five years after Skippy's death, Dana, Erica, and I decided to visit him. Knowing his plot number, we walked across the grass toward the corner section called Guardian Angel, the one reserved for children. Where was he? We paced methodically, peering at the ground, searching foot by foot, in widening circles, for his stone. At last we sought help in the cemetery office. The director opened his big book. "Your uncle's there, trust me. It says here, though, that he was never given a stone." My father's mother, Bernadine, is buried in the same cemetery. We decided to search for her. We found her plot, but, again, there was only grass upon it, no stone. These people—our grandmother, our uncle—whom my father kept buried in his memory and would not speak of, were conspiring with him in death, lying hidden, unremarkable, unmarked, as if they had never been.

And Nat Forhan, Fred Forhan, Fred Grant—my father's father? He died in 1994. Maybe. Probably. After not hearing from him in years, one of his sisters, Pauline, received a call from a nursing home in Portland, Oregon: someone had died there, and he was probably her brother. His name was Fred Grant, but in his papers were references to Nat and to her—and his birthday was listed as December 29, Nat's birthday. True, the dead man had identified his year of birth as 1917, eleven years later than Nat's, but that didn't surprise Pauline: her brother was vain enough to be capable of lying about his age.

However, there is this one problem, this mystery: there was an actual person, an actual Fred Grant, born in Oregon on December 29, 1917. He and his family—the Grants—are in the federal census records for decades. And this man is the only Fred Grant identified in Oregon death records for the 1990s. Is it possible that Nat stole, or borrowed, the identity of this real Fred Grant? Yes, except what are the odds of Nat—who, because of his middle name, Frederick, had long referred to himself as Fred—stealing the identity of someone else with that name? More confounding than that, what are the odds that the real Fred Grant shared his birthday?

Beyond the intriguing puzzle of it, maybe it does not matter. Nat is the grandfather who was never my grandfather, the man who was never my father's father, except biologically. He is the father my father was content to see once, then never again, whatever name or city he might vanish into. He is the man who remains what he seems to have devoted his life to becoming: a nothing, a name in the air.

Forty years after the death of our father, my youngest sister, Erica, like him, is a certified public accountant, a highly accomplished one. She was only five when he killed himself and is therefore haunted by him in a way different from that of her siblings. To her, as his own father must have been to him, he is not the parent who left her so much as he is the parent who never existed; he has always been wholly a ghost—an absence, an idea: the idea of absence. As he did, Erica dons a business suit each morning and drives to downtown Seattle to her office—for a time, it was in the same soaring black box of a building that housed our father's office. And the plaque he received around the time of her birth, the one honoring his work as president of the local chapter of accountants? It hangs in Erica's office in her home.

For two decades before she died, my sister Patty worked in a small factory in the Fremont neighborhood of Seattle, stopping off after work at her favorite local haunt: the Dock Bar and Grill, a modest one-story building at the northern lip of Lake Union, a block from the water. Years after Patty passed away, beginning to piece together the family history, I searched in an old phone directory, hoping to find a listing for Forhan's Tavern, the establishment begun by my father's uncle in the 1930s. Yes: there it was. I jotted down the address and got into the car. I would drive to take a look—maybe the building was still there. It was. And it was unchanged, except for one thing: the tavern was now called the Dock Bar and Grill. On all of those evenings after work, when Patty slid onto a stool at the bar and ordered a beer, she was sitting where, fifty years earlier, her drink would have been poured by her great-uncle, a man she'd never heard of. On all of those evenings, she was surrounded by her own ghosts and did not know it.

Seattle is a palimpsest. Over the years, my siblings and I have made summer-evening visits to Gas Works Park, climbing its big hill to talk and gaze at the lake and the skyline. This is the park built on the grounds of the old gasworks where my great-grandfather worked as foreman; to our left, beyond the rusty generator towers that still stand, was once the small company house where he and his wife raised their eleven children. Behind us are the streets where my father walked with his mother when he was a small boy and where his uncles and aunts and grandparents, the people I never heard about growing up, lived and worked.

How odd, I mention to Kevin one day. For years, my brother has been a brewer, working among the small and fervent group of beer aficionados plying their trade in Seattle. I am visiting him, sitting atop the small boat he calls home, docked at a marina along the Fremont Cut, not far from the old neighborhood where our ancestors lived. He has poured me a beer. How peculiar, I tell him, to learn for the first time about those relatives who preceded us, to think about those people who seem so different from us, who are such strangers, yet who not long ago walked the very sidewalks we do now. My brother the poet, he of the ruminative, mordant wit, replies, "Let's see. I'm an emotionally wounded, metaphysically bewildered man with a vaguely literary bent who is lounging on a boat drinking a beer. I'm not sure I've fallen very far from the tree."

Ten years older now than my father ever was, I am married again, contentedly, permanently, to another poet, a woman of great beauty and vigorous intelligence, wit, and feeling. In Alessandra, I do not see my father, and, with her, I try not to act like him. Sometimes I catch myself, in moments of conflict, in moments of frustrating misunderstanding, protecting myself by going quiet or by relieving the tension with a feeble joke, some easy irony upon which I can safely float. Then I stop myself. What am I feeling? Why? I try to talk about it—and Alessandra listens, with gratitude, with love.

We have two young sons, Milo and Oliver. I have not spoken often with them about my father—their grandfather. One day, though, I find myself chatting about my childhood. "Our daddy," I say, "used to string Christmas lights along the edge of our roof."

"Whose daddy?" says Oliver, who is three.

"Whose daddy? My daddy. He's not alive anymore. But he was my daddy when I was a boy. His name was Ed."

"*Ed*," Oliver muses. "Like *dead*. They rhyme!"

I am sitting in my office at home, squinting at the computer screen, fingers hovering above the keys. I've been at this for hours, adrift in the riddle of my long-dead, distant father, wondering how to decipher him, wondering how to imagine my way into his life through language. "Daddy?" The voice comes from behind me. "Daddy?"

"Just a minute."

"Daddy?" It's Milo, my five-year-old.

I keep my eyes on the screen. "Give me a minute. I'm working."

No, no. I lower my fingers from the keyboard and turn around. Milo's eyes are dark, his brow furrowed.

"Come on up." I reach toward him, hook my hands beneath his arms, and lift him onto my lap. "Sorry, buddy. What's your question? What is it you want to know?"

PHOTOGRAPHS

ACKNOWLEDGMENTS

This project began as a nagging itch, a question I wanted answered. Initially and for a long time afterward, I had little sense of whether I would end up with a book, let alone one that others would care to read. I am indebted to many people for their help in making this a real book. For their assistance in my research, I am grateful especially to my siblings: Erica Forhan, Kim Lambert, Dana Forhan, Kevin Forhan, Peg Forhan, and Theresa Steig; also relatives whose existence I discovered only when I started digging: Jim Stoeber, Mike Forhan, Virginia Forhan, Jeannine Forhan-Bruce, Shirley Nelson, and, particularly, Barbara Delaney; also Perry McIntyre, Paul David Merry, Debbie Davis, Andrew Ritchie, Nicholas Adam, Lisa Fusch Krause, and Kirk Lanterman.

I wish to thank Butler University and the Indianapolis Arts Council for the gift of time and funding that allowed me to write this book.

For their generous, thoughtful reading of early drafts, I am grateful to Carol Reeves, Andy Levy, Allison Lynn, Michael Dahlie, and Susan Neville. For their enthusiasm about the book in its final stages, I am thankful to Laura Kasischke, Larry Watson, Nick Flynn, Colin Harrison, and Nan Graham.

I am indebted deeply to three people who instilled me with confidence about the project and guided me, with patience and a bottomless reserve of keen insights, through multiple revisions: my agent and masterful perceiver of the big picture, Bill Clegg; my editor at Scribner, the gentle and surgically precise John Glynn; and, especially, my wife, Alessandra Lynch, who reminded me in the first place that I did indeed have a story to tell.

To Russ Scott, second father, my appreciation and love.

My most profound gratitude is reserved for my mother, Ange Scott, who trusted me with her story even though its details, in the way I have conveyed them, necessarily have been subsumed into my own; she would not, as she reminds me, tell the tale in the way I have. I am astonished by my mother's generosity and support, which can be understood only as acts of love—as were the daily ways, for decades, she protected, nurtured, and guided her children on their journey into the world.